INSIGHTS

General Editor: Clive Bloom, Senior Lecturer in English, Middlesex Polytechnic

Editorial Board: Clive Bloom, Brian Docherty, Gary Day, Lesley Bloom and Hazel Day

Insights brings to academics, students and general readers the very best contemporary criticism on neglected literary and cultural areas. It consists of anthologies, each containing original contributions by advanced scholars and experts. Each contribution concentrates on a study of a particular work, author or genre in its artistic, historical and cultural context.

Published titles

Clive Bloom (*editor*)
JACOBEAN POETRY AND PROSE: Rhetoric, Representation
  and the Popular Imagination

TWENTIETH-CENTURY SUSPENSE: The Thriller Comes of Age

SPY THRILLERS: From Buchan to le Carré

Clive Bloom, Brian Docherty, Jane Gibb and Keith Shand (*editors*)
NINETEENTH-CENTURY SUSPENSE: From Poe to Conan Doyle

Gary Day (*editor*)
READINGS IN POPULAR CULTURE: Trivial Pursuits?

Gary Day and Clive Bloom (*editors*)
PERSPECTIVES ON PORNOGRAPHY: Sexuality in Film and
  Literature

Brian Docherty (*editor*)
AMERICAN CRIME FICTION: Studies in the Genre
AMERICAN HORROR FICTION: From Brockden Brown to
  Stephen King

Rhys Garnett and R.J. Ellis (*editors*)
SCIENCE FICTION ROOTS AND BRANCHES: Contemporary
  Critical Approaches

Robert Giddings (*editor*)
LITERATURE AND IMPERIALISM

Robert Giddings, Keith Selby and Chris Wensley
SCREENING THE NOVEL: The Theory and Practice of Literary
  Dramatization

Paul Hyland and Neil Sammells (*editors*)
IRISH WRITING: Exile and Subversion

Maxim Jakubowski and Edward James (*editors*)
THE PROFESSION OF SCIENCE FICTION: SF Writers on their
  Craft and Ideas

Mark Lilly (*editor*)
LESBIAN AND GAY WRITING: An Anthology of Critical Essays

Christopher Mulvey and John Simons (*editors*)
NEW YORK: City as Text

Adrian Page (*editor*)
DEATH OF THE PLAYWRIGHT?: Modern British Drama and
  Literary Theory

Jeffrey Walsh and James Aulich (*editors*)
VIETNAM IMAGES: War and Representation

Further titles in preparation

Series Standing Order

If you would like to receive future titles in this series as they are
published, you can make use of our standing order facility. To place a
standing order please contact your bookseller or, in case of difficulty,
write to us at the address below with your name and address and the
name of the series. Please state with which title you wish to begin your
standing order. (If you live outside the United Kingdom we may not
have the rights for your area, in which case we will forward your order
to the publisher concerned.)

Customer Services Department, Macmillan Distribution Ltd
Houndmills, Basingstoke, Hampshire, RG21 2XS, England.

The Profession of Science Fiction

SF Writers on their Craft and Ideas

Edited by

Maxim Jakubowski
and
Edward James

Foreword by
Arthur C. Clarke

M
MACMILLAN

First published 1992 by
THE MACMILLAN PRESS LTD
Houndmills, Basingstoke, Hampshire RG21 2XS
and London
Companies and representatives
throughout the world

Printed in Hong Kong

British Library Cataloguing in Publication Data
The Profession of science fiction: writers on their craft
and ideas. –(Insights)
1. Science fiction
I. Jacubowski, Maxim   II. James, Edward 1947–   III.
Foundation   IV. Series
808.38762

ISBN 0–333–52481–0 (hardcover)
ISBN 0–333–52482–9 (paperback)

74544

Contents

Foreword

It has always seemed passing strange to me that whereas Britain is the spiritual home of science fiction (*vide* Mary Shelley, H.G. Wells) the so-called literary establishment has never taken it seriously. The few exceptions can be counted on the fingers of one hand, e.g. C.S. Lewis, Angus Wilson and Kingsley Amis. (We still owe Kingsley a vote of thanks for his pioneering *New Maps of Hell* – I've just recalled that I first met him when he was working on it at Princeton, in those distant days when he was still a fairly angry young man.)

It's easy to blame the problem on Snow's notorious 'Two Cultures' – but, of course, they don't really exist: people are either cultured or uncultured. Someone who's never read *any* science fiction automatically belongs to the second category. (So, of course, do a great many who have read it. . . . .).

As far as I know, no budding D. Litt on the British side of the Atlantic has tried to match Bruce Franklin's claim in *Future Perfect* that *every* major American writer wrote some science fiction. Yet a surprising number of major English authors have essayed the *genre* at least once, and I'm not thinking merely of such first-class second-raters as Doyle, Haggard, Priestley, Nevil Shute. . . . I'm thinking of the top-rankers – Kipling, Forster, Lewis, and of course, Huxley and Orwell.

It's really time we Brits recovered from the Gernsback Syndrome and stopped being apologetic about what may be one of our most significant contributions to literature. The Science Fiction Foundation is helping towards this goal, through volumes such as this, and its excellent (though occasionally somewhat esoteric) magazine *Foundation: A Review of Science Fiction*. I congratulate its hardworking – and largely unpaid – officers for their enthusiasm and devotion.

And incidentally, I think our local Cold War is over: "sci-fi" is now as acceptable as "sf" – at least when you're talking to the natives.

Arthur C. Clarke
Colombo, Sri Lanka

vii

Notes on the Contributors

J.G. BALLARD was born in Shanghai in 1930 and dramatised his experiences there in *Empire of the Sun*, short-listed for the Booker Prize and since filmed by Steven Spielberg. His science fiction spearheaded the British New Wave in the 1960s. Major titles include *The Drowned World*; *The Atrocity Exhibition*; *The Terminal Beach*; *Crash*; *Hello America*; *High Rise* and *Myths of the Near Future*.

JAMES BLISH (1921–1975) was the creator of the *Cities in Flight* sequence, a milestone in sf as future history. His urban preoccupations are also manifest in the *After Such Knowledge* series. *A Case of Conscience* (1958) was one the first major treatments of religion in an sf context.

DAVID BRIN has a doctorate in astrophysics and is one of a rare breed of sf writers from the world of science. He has won most of the major awards in the field for his strongly extrapolated and speculative novels which include *Startide Rising* and *The Postman*.

ARTHUR C. CLARKE was awarded the CBE in 1989, the first ever British sf author to be thus recognized. One of the masters of the genre with classic novels like *Childhood's End*; *Rendezvous with Rama*; *A Fall of Moondust*; *The City and the Stars* and, of course, the sequence of novels that began with *2001: A Space Odyssey*, Clarke, who lives in Sri Lanka, is also one of the Science Fiction Foundation's patrons. He has also initiated the Arthur C. Clarke Award, one of the field's more prestigious prizes, given every year to the best novel of the year.

D.G. COMPTON is one of Britain's most underrated sf writers. The author of *The Continuous Katherine Mortenhoe*, filmed by French director Bertrand Tavernier, he has also written in the detective genre. Other novels include *Ascendancies*; *The Steel Crocodile* and *Synthajoy*.

MICHAEL CONEY, although British, has long been resident in Canada's British Columbia. He has won the BSFA Award for

Brontomek!. Other novels include *Hello Summer, Goodbye* and the *Song of the Earth* series which includes *The Celestial Steam Locomotive* and *Gods of the Greataway*.

RICHARD COWPER is a pseudonym for Colin Middleton Murry, son of the famous writer John Middleton Murry. His major sf works appeared in the 1960s and 1970s and include *Clone*; *Breakthrough*; *The Twilight of Briareus* and the *Piper at the Gates of Dawn* series, a remarkably bucolic and spiritual post-holocaust-in-Britain sequence.

RICHARD GRANT is one the most promising new voices in sf. An American, his first novel *Saraband of Lost Time* was a runner-up for the Philip K. Dick Award and his second, *Rumors of Spring* was shortlisted for the Arthur C. Clarke Award. He also reviews for the *Washington Post*.

M. JOHN HARRISON is a British writer who first came to prominence in the heyday of British sf's New Wave with novels such as *The Centauri Device* and *A Storm of Wings*. His recent novel about rock-climbing, *Climbers*, was awarded a major literary prize.

MAXIM JAKUBOWSKI has written or edited over twenty books in various fields. A council member of the Science Fiction Foundation and Chairman of the Arthur C. Clarke Award, he is also known for his editing of crime fiction, having created two classic imprints: *Black Box Thrillers* and *Blue Murder*. He owns Murder One, Britain's first crime and mystery bookshop and edits *New Crimes*, a paperback anthology/magazine.

EDWARD JAMES has been the editor of *Foundation* since 1986. He is an early-medieval historian and archatologist at the University of York and has reviewed widely within the science fiction field.

GWYNETH JONES is a relative newcomer to the sf field. A resident of Brighton, she has also written extensively in the field of children's book (often as Ann Hallam). Her sf novels are *Divine Endurance*; *Escape Plans* and *Kairos*.

GARRY KILWORTH won the *Sunday Times* sf short story competition in 1974 and has since become one of Britain's foremost genre authors. A recent novel about foxes, *Hunter's Moon*, reached the bestseller list. His sf includes *In Solitary; Gemini God; A Theatre of Timesmiths* and *Abandonati*.

URSULA K. LE GUIN is one of America's foremost authors, respected both inside and outside the sf genre. She has won most of the awards the field can give for books such as *The Left Hand of Darkness; The Dispossessed* and her *Earthsea* series (recently completed by a fourth volume, *Tehanu*). She is, with Arthur C. Clarke, a patron of the Science Fiction Foundation.

NAOMI MITCHISON was born in 1897, daughter of the biologist J.S. Haldane a sister to scientist and writer J.B.S. Haldane. A highly-regarded historical novelist, she is the author of two sf novels, *Memoirs of a Spacewoman* and *Solution Three*.

PAMELA SARGENT's work began attracting attention in her native America in the 1970s. An important proto-feminist sf author, she has also edited a number of seminal anthologies by women writers. Her novels include *The Alien Upstairs; The Golden Space; Venus of Dream; Venus of Shadows* and *The Shore of Women*.

NORMAN SPINRAD, an American now resident in Paris, is one of sf's great iconoclastic authors, ever controversial and vociferous. *Bug Jack Barron* was attacked in Question Time in the British Parliament, while *The Iron Dream* was banned in Germany. Recent novels include *The Void Captain's Tale; Songs from the Stars; Child of Fortune* and *Little Heroes*.

JACK WILLIAMSON is one of the elder statesmen of sf and his writing now spans almost sixty years. His popularity and talent have never waned, from his *Legion of Space* to his recent collaborations with Frederik Pohl, through classic novels like *Darker than you Think; The Humanoids* and the *Seetee* series.

GENE WOLFE was born in 1931 and, although a technical journalist, came to sf writing late in life. In a short time he has established himself as one of its best writers. His tetralogy *The Book of the New Sun* is already considered a classic, while books such as *The Fifth Head of Cerberus; Soldier in the Mist; There are Doors* and his many story collections, constitute a major corpus of work by any standard.

Introduction

Dictionaries tell us that "profession" means various things: an occupation; the body of people engaged in that occupation; the act of professing, avowing or declaring; and (as in "profession of faith") the declaration of faith in a religion, especially by those who enter a church or a religious order. Most of those who write in these pages would describe their main occupation as being the writing of science fiction. Some would feel themselves part of that close-knit body of people who call themselves science fiction writers, who know each other socially, who meet each other and their readers at science fiction conventions, who belong to writers organisations, and who collaborate, and argue, and feud. And, finally, some would indeed write about their commitment to science fiction as if it were a profession of faith. Writers within the genres of popular fiction with which science fiction has often been compared – westerns, romances, crime fiction – seldom refer to their genre as having a serious didactic, educational, consciousness-raising purpose; science fiction writers often do. And for some, science fiction has been, if not a religion in itself, at least a substitute for it; a profession of faith which not only offers a rational vision of the universe and of the place of homo sapiens within it, but the opportunity for achieving and arousing an emotional and even mystical response to that vision.

The term "science fiction" was not in general use on either side of the Atlantic until after the Second World War, and there has been continuing debate as to how it should be defined, and what its origins were. Those two problems are, of course, inextricably entwined. If we define science fiction as a branch of literature concerned with the imaginative creation of possible worlds and societies beyond those of which we actually have experience, then science fiction goes back at least to the second century AD and to the Greek writer Lucian, whose *True History* told of an imaginary visit to the inhabitants of the Moon. Thomas More's *Utopia*, Bacon's *New Atlantis* and Swift's *Gulliver's Travels* would all be science fiction. If science fiction is "the search for a definition of mankind and his status in the universe which will stand in our advanced but confused state of knowledge (science), and is

1

characteristically cast in the Gothic or post-Gothic mode",[1] then it
is logical to argue that Mary Shelley's *Frankenstein* is the first great
work of science fiction. Other critics have felt nervous about using
a term effectively invented in the late 1920s and applying it to any
work written before then just because it appears to have a similar
subject matter. Certainly before the 1920s or 1930s there was no
idea of a separate genre, and there was no agreed name for what
we call science fiction. Jules Verne wrote "extraordinary voyages";
H.G. Wells and his imitators wrote "scientific romances"; others
talked of "wonder tales". Would it not perhaps be better to seek
the origins of science fiction in the writings of those who first
consciously belonged to the profession of science fiction writer –
the writers in the American science fiction magazines of the late
1920s and 1930s?[2]

Rather than determine origin, however, it might be more helpful
to look briefly at what became accepted, by the second half of the
twentieth century, as the distinctive features of science fiction. It
can be distinguished in a number of ways, some obvious and some
not so obvious, from what those within the science fiction community sometimes call "mainstream" or "mundane" fiction.
"Mainstream" fiction, from the growth of the novel in the eighteenth century and onwards, has largely concerned itself with the
portrayal and investigation of character and of human relationships, within either a contemporary setting or a setting in the
relatively recent past. Literary criticism, in Britain particularly that
school associated with F.R. Leavis, evolved a canon of great novelists, the Great Tradition, whose approaches, methods, style and,
above all, subject matter aspiring novelists needed only imitate.
Science fiction, even by distinguished representatives such as H.G.
Wells, has been excluded from the Tradition, partly because of its
lowly associations (as "mere entertainment"), but more because it
simply does not subscribe to the same aims and aesthetics as the
Great Tradition.

Science fiction has almost never been primarily concerned with
either character or human relationships. It tends not to look at the
idiosyncrasies of individual men and women, but at whole
societies. Its underlying themes – often hidden behind a façade of
action and adventure – tend not to be those of love, jealousy and
the passions, but the future development of human society, the
relationship between society and technology, the possibilities
inherent in scientific and social development. Some of the stock

icons of science fiction, such as the robot or the alien, may stand as metaphors for contemporary issues (automation, race relations), but they may be no more than expressions of the author's interest in future possibilities. Science fiction is often derided as being escapist; it is worth remembering that it is only in science fiction that one finds fictional discussion of the problems of nuclear power, the possibilities of nuclear warfare, and the dangers of environmental catastrophe or of overpopulation. Most fiction is unconcerned with the massive changes that science and technology have brought, and will bring, to our society; science fiction has faced this problem, and dealt with it either directly, in stories set in the near future, or by analogy, in stories distanced from Earth by millennia and by light-years.

Science fiction is not, however, by any means always concerned with science – and when it is, the science is as often sociology as physics. Although the term "science fiction" seems ineradicable, many prefer to use the abbreviation "sf" – not just because it is shorter, but because it can be variously expanded, as, for instance, to "speculative fiction". ("Sci-fi", an abbreviation which many sf writers abhor, does not have that advantage.) Speculation is at the heart of sf: the question "what if . . .?" is a standard opening to new plots. "What if . . .?" does not have to relate to the future, even though a future setting is what separates most sf from "the mainstream". Novels based on historical questions such as "What would life have been like for Neanderthals?", or counter-factual questions such as "What if the Roman Empire had never collapsed?", "What if the Spanish Armada had succeeded?", or "What if Hitler had won the War?" all tend to be treated novelistically by professional sf writers, and marketed as sf.

Sf, like science itself, depends on freewheeling speculation, within the bounds of reason and logic: thus, no dragons or ghosts (unless they have a rational explanation). Its subject is (wo)man; as Brian Aldiss remarked in 1982, no-one will want to read a novel about a race of intelligent molluscs (upon which John Brunner immediately wrote *The Crucible of Time (1984)*). But it is (wo)man in relation to the universe, the infinity of time and space, which interests the sf writer rather more than (wo)men in relation to each other. Mankind is rarely presented, save ironically, as being protected by supernatural beings; mankind is portrayed alone, facing Otherness or the immensity of creation. The "sense of wonder" which is often regarded as that most prized critical reaction to a work of sf is, as the Romanian critic Cornel Robu has recently argued,[3] the modern manifestation of the sublime, an aesthetic principle regarded as distinctly superior in the eighteenth century but curiously absent from literary criticism since. Both Edmund Burke and Immanuel Kant investigated the feeling for the sublime in literature and art, that strange pleasure derived from terror and the contemplation of the infinite and of natural forces beyond human control: "the mere ability even to think the given infinite without contradiction is something that requires the presence in the human mind of a faculty that is in itself supersensible", wrote Kant in 1790. As Robu noted, half-jocularly, the very adjectives used by Burke and Kant were the adjectives chosen for the titles of the first science fiction magazines – amazing, astonishing, astounding. The sense of wonder, the awe, felt in the contemplation of time and the universe – so similar to the feelings of those who profess a purely religious faith – is perhaps the purest and most archetypal of feelings which science fiction can inspire.

The American sf magazine *Astounding*, particularly under its great editor John W. Campbell Jr. (from 1937 to 1971), is where the essential core of sf can perhaps be found. But it was in *Amazing*, founded in 1926 as the first magazine devoted exclusively to what its editor Hugo Gernsback called, first, scientifiction and, later, science fiction, that we find the origins of the modern genre – in those reprints of Verne and Wells, and the stumbling, semi-literate stories from young, enthusiastic Americans. It is there too that we find the origins of the modern profession of science fiction writer. The early American science fiction magazines brought forth dozens of writers who felt themselves to be actively working within, and helping to define, the new genre.

One of the characteristics of the modern genre was also established early on in the history of the American magazines. Their writers were heavily influenced by the strong reader reactions which were published in the letter columns of the magazines; this was the origin of that close relationship between writer and reader which has distinguished science fiction from other branches of modern literature. Science fiction "fans", as they called themselves, wrote to the magazines, published their own magazines ("fanzines"), and, from the late 1930s onwards, organised conventions, where they could meet with other fans and with authors (many of whom had risen from the ranks of fans themselves). This was initially an American phenomenon, although it spread very rapidly to the United Kingdom (indeed, the first sf convention in the world, in 1937, was held in Leeds), and, more recently, to other parts of the world. The domination of American fans, and American writers, remains undiminished, however. If the annual World SF Convention is held outside the United States (as it is every three or four years), then American fans still outnumber the rest; American sf fills the sf shelves in British or Scandinavian bookshops, and translations of American sf dominate the market in France, Spain, or Italy. British writers, to succeed, have to write sf which will sell in the States; French or German writers have often felt that success for them could only come through imitating American trends.

The role of fandom in the history of science fiction, and in the history of the profession of science fiction writer, is one that still needs exploring. It is clear, however, that its effects have been both positive and negative. It has given science fiction writers an extraordinary amount of feedback and support; it has offered them immediate criticism, and also helped to create a theory of what sf was all about; it has contributed to the *esprit de corps* of science fiction writers, and their sense of belonging to a community and a profession; and the amateur publications of fans has been an excellent school and testing ground for scores of young writers. But fandom has also contributed considerably to the ghettoization of science fiction, to its introspective and, in literary terms, conservative nature, and to the consequent disregard of science fiction by the general readership and by literary critics. The sf author and critic Brian Stableford has recently set forth the problems very succinctly:

> There was a time, from the 'Forties to the 'Sixties, when Anglo–American science fiction was largely the preserve of fans who read a great deal of it (and little else). This meant that the sf writers of those days could (and, if they wanted to publish in the leading magazines, must) presume that the hard core of their audience consisted of people who had a rough and ready knowledge of what had already been done within the field, and what passed for conventional attitudes to certain notions. The tacit contract into which writers and readers entered assumed that a certain amount of imaginative spadework had already been done in considering the implications of such ideas as humanoid robots, generation starships, time paradoxes and so on; certain logical problems had been pointed out, certain possibilities

explored, and all of this could be taken as read. New readers were expected to catch up as fast as they could, and relatively little allowance was made for them.[4]

One major consequence of this state of affairs was that those who were not familiar with science fiction and who had not begun reading it from a relatively early age, found it very difficult to penetrate its mysteries, and gnerally left it to one side. Those works which were accessible, sometimes written by professional sf writers but just as often not, could occasionally achieve considerable success; in the 1950s John Wyndham's *The Day of the Triffids* and Nevil Shute's *On the Beach* were good examples. It is a mark of the ghettoization of sf that when a writer from outside the sf community turned his or her hand to sf, as Nevil Shute did, readers and critics within the field often greeted their attempts with derision: those writers were often treating themes, as if they were new, which science fiction writers themselves had refined and explored from every angle. Sf was seen, by its practitioners, as a tradition which had to be known and which had to be added to. Sf writers were, thus, often involved in a dialogue with each other, writing stories which commented on other stories – a dialogue of which the fans were knowledgeable, fascinated and participating observers.

That situation began to change, above all in the 1970s, for several reasons. The amount of sf that published each year had increased considerably from the late 1960s onwards, and familiarity with the whole field became very difficult to acquire. New fans arrived, drawn to sf by *Star Trek* or, later in the 1970s, by *Star Wars*, who wanted an easier entry into the field. By the 1980s sf writers had to compete for readers with the newly-emergent genres of fantasy (post-Tolkien) and horror (post-Stephen King), and some did so by offering an easily accessible fiction, often barely distinguishable in content from that of those other, rival genres.

If the influence of fandom on sf writers is a suitable topic for some future academic tome, so is the impact of changing publishing trends and markets. In the United States, from the 1920s through to the 1950s, most sf was published in cheap magazines, the "pulps". This fiction rarely made it into book form at the time, partly because much of it was short stories, but largely because it was not until after the Second World War that the paperback industry became firmly established. The 1950s saw the rapid development of paperback science fiction in both Britain and the United States, and a flourishing of science fiction magazines. Britain not only published its own sf magazines (notably *New Worlds*) but also produced reprints of several of the more successful American magazines, including *Astounding, Galaxy* and *The Magazine of Fantasy and Science Fiction*. During the 1960s the paperback market gradually reduced the dominance of the sf magazines; paperbacks were extremely significant for the science fiction profession too, because they increased the financial returns, and made it possible for more than a handful of writers to make a living as a full-time science fiction writer. It was the paperback which made the names of those who had begun in the magazines – Arthur C. Clarke, John Wyndham, Isaac Asimov, Robert Heinlein – familiar names even to those who knew very little about science fiction. By the late 1980s, with increasing affluence among science fiction readers (who, according to polls in the States, appear to come from the older age groups), and with the rise of the number of collectors of first editions, the number of books published every year was quite considerable. In the United States, for instance, according to the survey by *Locus*, the sf trade newspaper, there were 279 original sf novels published in 1989, a drop from the figure of 318 for 1988, but still a very considerable rise from the 187 of 1981; there were also a large number of reprints. With some of those original novels earning seven-figure advances (in dollars), it is clear that the science fiction profession has become big business – at least for publishers and booksellers, for only a relatively few authors have achieved bestseller status. It is novels that sell, however – particularly novels in trilogies or in series, since that persuades book distributors to redistribute old titles when new ones come out – and not short fiction; the market for short fiction in Britain or the States is much smaller now than it was in the 1950s or 1960s.

The third and final change to the profession of science fiction writer also came in the 1960s. During the 1940s and 1950s the writers and their fans lived in a small, closed community, which often felt itself superior, in insight, to the great world outside. The atom bomb (predicted years before its realization by sf writers) confirmed them in that belief; so did Sputnik in 1957, which caught all but them unawares. During the space race which started in 1957, culminating twelve years later in the triumphal Moon landing, sf writers suddenly found themselves taken seriously, and read much more widely than before. The literary revolution of the later 1960s, the so-called "New Wave" of sf, in both Britain and America, helped to make not only sf writers rather more respectable, but their books as well. Sales grew; and, with the help of sf in the media, sf imagery and ideas became widely known and accepted within the culture as a whole.

Alongside this development came the rapid emergence of sf as a topic of academic discourse. The harbinger was the founding of the academic journal *Extrapolation*, back in 1959, but the late 1960s and early 1970s saw a huge growth in the number of sf courses, above all in universities in the United States. Some of these courses were perhaps born more of the pressure to lay on courses which students would find attractive than of a committed belief in the importance of sf as an academic subject, and some of the early academic criticism was below the standards one could find in amateur fanzines. However, enough committed and informed academics were created in this process to ensure the survival and development of sf in numerous university English departments throughout North America. The injection of Marxist theory and structuralism into the system by the third major academic journal in the field, *Science-Fiction Studies*, helped give the criticism a firmer methodological foundation, and keep it up-to-date as far as critical theory was concerned. *Science-Fiction Studies* was founded in 1973, and at first was edited jointly from Indiana State University and McGill University in Montreal; later in the 1970s the base shifted firmly to Canada, where it now remains. Nowadays, *Extrapolation* and *Science-Fiction Studies* flourish, and are the two journals which come to all those, academics or not, who subscribe to the Science Fiction Research Association.

British universities took very little part in this development. There were and are one or two scattered and isolated figures teaching sf in English departments at British universities (which, however, have proved much less receptive than American universities to departures from the Great Tradition); and one or two in departments of Sociology or History. But it was perhaps inevitable that when sf did become established as an academic force in the British system, the crucial institution came to be founded in the less hide-bound environs of a polytechnic. Determined pressure by such sf enthusiasts as George Hay and sf writers such as James Blish, John Brunner and Kenneth Bulmer resulted in the creation in 1971, at the North-East London Polytechnic (now, since 1989, the Polytechnic of East London), of the Science Fiction Foundation. The SFF is run by a Council made up of sf writers, publishers and critics, together with interested academics from the Polytechnic, and is under the patronage of Arthur C. Clarke and Ursula K. Le Guin, two of the best-known of modern sf writers. The SFF has been involved in teaching and supervising students at the Polytechnic, although the educational cuts of the last decade has deprived it of full-time teachers. But it remains the major centre in Europe for academic research into sf, with the most extensive collection of books, magazines and papers relating to the field in any institution outside North America. It was instrumental in setting up the Arthur C. Clarke Award, thanks to the generosity of Arthur C. Clarke himself: a money prize given to the book the selection committee regards as the best original sf novel published in the UK each year. And, finally, it publishes *Foundation: the Review of Science Fiction* – the third serious journal of sf history and criticism to be founded (the other two have been mentioned above). Between the first issue in 1972 and the end of 1990, fifty issues have appeared – over 5000 pages of articles, debates and critical reviews, which together form a major contribution to the development of an understanding of the sf phenomenon. *Foundation* is currently edited by Edward James, an historian from the University of York, together with Features Editor Ian Watson and Reviews Editor Colin Greenland (both of them better known, no doubt, for their sf novels and short stories). Two things distinguish *Foundation* from its rivals: the space it devotes to lengthy reviews by a knowledgeable reviewing team which includes both critics and active sf writers, and its relative freedom from academic jargon. *Foundation* has always welcomed contributions by enthusiastic amateurs and by active writers as well as by academics.

The very first issue featured the start of a series called "The Development of a Science Fiction Writer"; John Brunner and Ursula Le Guin were among the first to contribute. After five such articles the series' name was changed to "The Profession of Science Fiction". Over forty articles have been published so far in the series; the present collection has been selected from amongst them. Sf authors were asked to write about how they came to start writing sf, what they value in science fiction, what they feel about the field today, and, indeed, whatever else they felt like. The result has been a fascinating variety of styles and approaches, giving some flavour of the variety of science fiction today, and considerable insight into the nature of the profession.

Most of the major contemporary sf authors have contributed to *Foundation*'s "Profession of Science Fiction" series, and the following selections are only a tip of the iceberg, with many notable articles sadly omitted, because of length, topicality or ulterior inclusion in the authors' other books/collections.

The following sf writers have also penned "Profession of Science Fiction" articles (many of which can be obtained in back issues of *Foundation*): Brian W. Aldiss, Poul Anderson, Gregory Benford, John Brunner, L. Sprague de Camp, Samuel R. Delany (a massive, fascinating, almost book-length contribution which had to be published over two issues), Philip K. Dick, Phyllis Eisenstein, Harlan Ellison, Raymond Z. Gallun, R.A. Lafferty, Fritz Leiber, Stanislaw Lem, Alexei Panshin, Christopher Priest, Kim Stanley Robinson, Bob Shaw, Robert Silverberg, John Sladek, Bruce Sterling, George Turner, A.E. Van Vogt, Jane Yolen and George Zebrowski.

Like all academic magazines, *Foundation* is not in a position to remunerate its contributors and it is certainly a tribute to the magazine that so many world-famous sf authors have been willing to spend their time writing for it; and, further, the esteem in which the Science Fiction Foundation is held is confirmed by the fact that all contributors to this volume have kindly agreed to donate their royalties to the SFF, which like all academic bodies is, as ever, sorely in need of funds to ensure its upkeep and survival.

In addition, the editors of the present volume, author, critic and publisher Maxim Jakubowski and Edward James, current editor of *Foundation* (in succession to Charles Barren, Peter Nicholls, Malcolm Edwards and David Pringle) have also waived their editorial fee.

If you are interested in learning more about the Science Fiction Foundation, or if you wish to subscribe to *Foundation*, please write to the Science Fiction Foundation, Polytechnic of East London, Longbridge Road, Dagenham, RM8 2AS, UK. Current basic subscription rate for the UK and Ireland is £8.50 (individuals) or £20 (institutions). Further information can be obtained from Friends of Foundation, 75 Hecham Close, Walthamstow, London E17 5QT.

Notes

1. Brian Aldiss, with David Wingrove, *Trillion Year Spree: The History of Science Fiction* (Gollancz, 1986), p. 25.
2. As is argued by Gary Westfahl in two articles published in *Foundation* 47 (Winter 1989–90) and 48 (Spring 1990).
3. Cornel Robu, "A Key to Science Fiction: the Sublime", *Foundation* 42 (Spring 1988) pp. 21–37.
4. Brian Stableford, reviewing *The Queen of the Springtime* by Robert Silverberg, Foundation 47 (Winter 1989–90), pp. 70–1.

1

The Way it Was, 1933–1937

Jack Williamson

1 FREELANCE, 1933–1935

Wolfgang Pauli, in 1931, had found that atomic theory required the existence of the chargeless and massless particle that Enrico Fermi later named the neutrino. The next year James Chadwick, working at the Cavendish Laboratory in England, discovered the neutron. Two more long steps into the hazardous mysteries of the atom.

Most men, in those grim times, found no cheer in such triumphs of science. The grip of depression kept closing tighter, and people were yearning for any escape. Briefly, in the fall in 1932, Howard Scott caught the public imagination with Technocracy. Perhaps the technicians could manage production and government well enough to save us.

Hope of that soon flickered out. By March of 1933, when Franklin Delano Roosevelt took over from Hoover, most of the nation's banks were closed. Industrial production was just over half its precrash level, and 13,000,000 were unemployed.

With the ring of confidence in his radio voice, Roosevelt proclaimed that all we had to fear "was fear itself". Desperate for anything, the nation believed him. In the dramatic actions of "the hundred days", he called Congress into special session, outlawed the exportation of gold, and launched the New Deal. The Century of Progress opened that summer in Chicago, with Sally Rand stealing the show with her fan dance. Seeking escape from the tragedy of their murdered son, Charles and Ann Lindberg flew north to Greenland and back across half the world.

My own situation had begun to improve. A handwritten note from Desmond Hall brought cheering news. Street and Smith, an older and stronger firm than Clayton's, were reviving *Astounding*.

F. Orlin Tremaine was the new editor, and they promised quick money for short stories, though at only one cent a word. Before the end of 1933, they had taken the last two stories Harry Bates returned when Clayton went under, as well as a new one, "The Flame from Mars", grown out of a hike with my brother into Meteor Crater. At *Weird Tales*, Farnsworth Wright and Bill Sprenger had begun making payments when they could, sometimes only $25, for "Golden Blood" and "The Plutonian Terror" and "Invaders of the Ice World".

Records are lacking and my recollection uncertain, but after another stint of work I was off again, by bus to Chicago. Ed Hamilton rejoined me there; we stayed at the "Y". E. Hoffman Price was back from New Orleans. We saw him again and met Wright and Otis Adelbert Kline and a few others of the *Weird Tales* brotherhood – they were an engaging group, full of obscure occult and Oriental lore, happy with one another, drawn to *Weird* as the early science fiction fans were to Gernsback and *Amazing*. Never close to many of them, I was proud to be admitted as at least a 'prentice member.

After a few days in Chicago, I went on to visit Ed at his home in New Castle. That was a new world to me, older than my own, ethnically different, northern instead of southwestern, with wooded hills instead of treeless flatness, grimy urban shabbiness instead of hardscrabble farms. Through the next few years I was there several times at different seasons, enjoying a new milieu, enjoying Ed's family, enjoying Ed himself for his sharp intelligence and his sardonic wit, his professional competence and all he knew of books I hadn't read.

Ed had a car, and sometime before Christmas we drove to Florida. Al Greco, another young friend of his and I think a better friend of his sister Betty, came with us as far as Miami. We went on to Key West, which was still deep in depression. The Florida boom was long dead by then, and the overseas highway had not been rebuilt since the last hurricane. We crossed one long gap by ferry, almost the only outsiders who did. The big resort hotel was closed. With the sponge fishers gone to better grounds, the cigar industry dead, and the naval base abandoned, half the population was unemployed that winter. By summer, the city was in receivership, begging for New Deal aid.

That sleepy stagnation only heightened its allure for me. It was still another world, new to both of us, fascinating for its history and its blending cultures, and tropical enough, with its palms and white beaches and the coral reefs around it, to have come out of my old romantic dreams. For eight dollars a month, we rented a house near Ernest Hemingway's big place on the beach – he was away hunting lions in Africa. We had our own cistern and our own tropical orchard. Ed got the use of a boat for equipping it with mast and sail. We spent the winter on the beach or in Ed's boat or writing science fiction.

A dream vacation, yet not quite the fun I had expected. My energies were ebbing; I didn't know why. Key West isn't really tropical, and our house had no heat. I remember shivering through the miserable chill of the northers, when the wind was too cold for the beach and we had no way to get warm. Ed spent a lot of time fishing, mostly alone. I remember the time he let the sail jib and the boom swing back across us to capsize the boat. We were close to the beach and I waded ashore, leaving him to gather up the wreckage on his own.

He was more outgoing than I; he found friends among the native "conchs", Captain Robbie Whitehead among them. We knew an eccentric old German who, I think, had been a lab technician in the navy hospital. He was building an odd-looking airplane near the old slaughterhouse on the beach where Ed kept his boat, and I remember his anxious way of peering out at people who came near. His plane was never meant to fly; we learned later that it held the body of a Cuban girl he had loved, which he had stolen from her grave.

The only story I recall writing there is a novelette, "Born of the Sun". My favorite way of plotting in those days was to begin with something staggeringly impossible and find a fictional way to show it happening. Suppose the sun were a huge living creature? Suppose our planets were eggs it had laid? Suppose the Earth were to hatch?

I remember discussing the notion with Ed. He scoffed at it, but Tremaine had announced that *Astounding* would now feature "thought variant stories" developing startling new ideas. My idea seemed startling enough. To keep the story going until the planets began hatching, I added a cult of evil Orientals and a lovely heroine abducted. All pretty improbable, but our readers then were mostly young and forgiving. Isaac Asimov, fourteen that year, recalled it to be included in his *Before the Golden Age*, and

Forry Ackerman reprinted it again in his more recent *Gosh Wow! Science Fiction*.

With spring coming, we took steerage passage on a steamer to Cuba and spent a week or so in Havana. Once again, a different world. We rented a big, high-ceilinged room off a narrow street in the old colonial city; it had noisy antique plumbing and brilliant bougainvillaeas all around the window. Drinking a very few Cuba Libres and a lot of orange juice, we went to the races and a *jai alai* game and made bus expeditions into the suburbs and tried our little Spanish on clerks and waitresses. I remember the ancient walls of El Morro and the magnificent harbour at night, the black water glittering with the lights of the Malecon. A little more wistfully, I recall the vivid dark charm of the Cuban women, sadly untouchable for me and I think untouched by Ed.

Back from that expedition, we drove north again to Georgia. I caught a train home from Valdosta, arriving underweight and ailing. One doctor gave me quinine for malaria, but I imagine my troubles were mostly psychosomatic. Eye strain, sinusitis, indigestion, a general malaise. My scanty records show nothing at all finished and sold in 1934. I was becoming increasingly unhappy with myself and my writing career.

In those first few years, I had achieved most of what I thought I wanted. *Argosy*, of course, had kept turning me down, and the high-paying slicks were always out of reach, but I had earned something of a name in the science fiction pulps. Though my travels were never made in luxury, I had managed to see a little of the world. Now, more and more clearly, I was beginning to see that what I had won wasn't enough. Yet I knew nothing else I could do.

Most of 1934 has dimmed in my mind; perhaps there wasn't much worth remembering. But my health got better. I began gaining two pounds a week after another doctor took my tonsils out again – they had been painfully cropped some years before. A little later, on a diagnosis of "chronic appendicitis", I also let him remove my appendix – that was probably ill-advised surgery; it left adhesions that strangled a gut and nearly killed me in a VA hospital in 1946. Both Ed and Al Greco had appendectomies soon after mine. That seemed oddly coincidental to us, but when I happened to mention that to my analyst a few years later he didn't seem surprised.

Trying hard to get back into production, I built a little cabin on the ranch where I could work without interruption. Only one small room at first, but large enough for desk and files and bookshelves and bed. Later I added a tiny bedroom, a little windmill for electric lights, and even a sort of bath – though water for it had to be carried two hundred yards, and the toilet was still anywhere about the farm where you could hide from public sight, with sagebush or new corncobs or whatever for tissue.

Fiction markets were still dismal. *Weird Tales* was overstocked with serials for years to come – Wright had run "Golden Blood" ahead of several he had already accepted, including one of Ed's, something unlikely to happen again. With *Wonder* and *Amazing* deep in trouble, that left only *Astounding* and my dwindling hope of cracking *Argosy*. Reading the letters from Ed that survive, I find us discussing collaborations that always came to nothing. I was also working on ambitious but ill-planned projects that kept bogging down before I got them finished, failing for reasons I could never see. My income for 1935 was only $540, down from $1157 the year before.

Yet life went on. Coached by my sisters, I was learning to dance. Never very well – and I never knew much to say to the girl – yet I enjoyed it. Neighbours – those to whom dancing wasn't a mortal sin – took turns as hosts on Saturday nights. We danced waltzes, two-steps, sometimes a schottische. The music was fiddle and guitar, sometimes a banjo, the musicians rewarded with whatever fell into the hat when it came around. Outside in the dark, there was a little cheap wine, cheap whisky, sometimes moonshine. We used to drive many miles to dance most of the night and get back home at daylight, with cows needing to be milked.

Late that summer, still enamoured of ships and the sea, I took a longer voyage, from Houston around to New York, a trip I enjoyed. Though I was in steerage, I had bought an impressive-looking Korelle Reflex camera that I could carry as a disguise on the first-class deck. I remember dancing one night with a tall attractive housewife from Wichita; her husband was genially tolerant – I suppose he saw how harmless I was. The ship's engineer turned out to be a fan who liked my work; we talked science fiction, and he showed me through the ship.

In New York, trying to meet the editors, I found a less eager welcome. Though *Amazing* had published a lot of my work, all I saw of the venerable T. O'Conor Sloane was a momentary glimpse through his office door. Gernsback gave me a few minutes of his time and a sample copy of *Gadgets*, his newest magazine. The people at *Argosy* were so friendly on my first call that I went back again, and failed to get past the receptionist. Somewhat more warmly, Tremaine took me to lunch and reported that "The Legion of Space" had been well received.

Westward bound, I stopped in New Castle for another good visit to Ed Hamilton. In Chicago, I saw Wright and Sprenger, and spent several days at The Century of Progress. I remember walking through the exhibits with "Jack Darrow", whose frequent letters in the magazines had made Chicago famous in fandom.

The next summer, Ed and Betty drove out to spend several weeks with us on the ranch. Their letters seem to show that they enjoyed the West as much I had Pennsylvania. The rest of the family and some of the neighbors helped me entertain them. One rancher friend, Finus Tucker, had wit and imagination enough to play cowboy for Betty, rolling his own Bull Durham smokes and assuming a bow-legged roll and an exaggerated drawl that impressed her immensely.

That year, 1935, the writing went better again. Tremaine bought two more novelettes for *Astounding*. "Born of the Sun" grew from an unlikely notion about the origins of the planets. "The Galactic Circle" had a more striking idea, a circular flight through size – the explorers in their ship shrink into infinite smallness; still shrinking at the end of the story, they return out of cosmic immensity to the same world they had left. I suppose I tried too hard to make it something serious, with too many characters of types I didn't know. Some readers praised it, but Asimov calls it "rotten" in a fan letter he wrote me in 1939 – he had rated eighteen of my stories; "The Cometeers" and "The Legion of Space" were graded "super-perfect", with five stars each, and I was ranked third overall, behind E.E. Smith and John W. Campbell, but "The Galactic Circle" stood alone at the bottom of the list, with only a single star.

Weird Tales accepted "The Ruler of Fate" that year, to run as a serial in 1936. Welcome news, even though they were still in trouble, paying Ed only $25 a month on a debt of some seven hundred dollars. I think they were doing a little better by me, but I was happy that fall to find another market, one that reported and paid with less delay.

It was the "Thrilling" group, published by Standard Magazines.

The chain was owned by Ned Pines and very efficiently edited by Leo Margulies and such associates as Mort Weisinger. Ed was writing detective stories for them, and I think he helped open the way for me. By the end of 1935 I had begun selling occasional horror novelettes to *Thrilling Mystery*.

Gernsback's floundering *Wonder* became *Thrilling Wonder* when Pines bought it in 1936. I sold a few stories there, and two unmemorable novels to *Startling Stories*, the lower-paying companion magazine launched in 1939. Though checks were almost instant, at a full cent a word for *Thrilling Mystery* and *Thrilling Wonder*, Leo required every story to fit a very rigid pattern. Mort told me once that they had no actual objection to good writing, but all that really mattered was to fit the formula. I learned the horror pattern well enough to invent a variation on it that I wrote up for *Author and Journalist*, but writing for Leo was never much fun.

Ed, evidently, enjoyed it more than I did. He wrote all but two or three of the Captain Future novels, which began appearing in 1940 in their own magazine, more juvenile than *Thrilling Wonder* and even more rigidly formulistic. A master of the pattern, though its restrictions used to chafe him, he kept on pounding out repetitions of it for a good many more years after the magazines were dead, in his scripts for *Superman* and *Batman*.

In the fall of 1935, I undertook a more ambitious project. Others besides Asimov had liked "The Legion of Space" – another fan a few years later tabulated the comments in the published letters and reported that my antiheroic Giles Habibula had been the most popular character of the 1930s. When Tremaine asked for a sequel, I plunged eagerly into "The Cometeers". The manuscript I sent him was 65,000 words. He had me cut 10,000 words, but generously paid me for them. His check for $650, received in early 1936, was the best I had received; it brought that year's income to $1430.

A nice burst of prosperity, but not enough to content me. Wanting more out of life than I had found, I was beginning to think of psychoanalysis.

2   UNDER ANALYSIS, 1936–1937

Ernest O. Lawrence patented the cyclotron in 1934. On May 8, the Dionne Quints were born. On July 22, John Dillinger walked out of a Chicago movie theatre into a hail of gunfire from the FBI. His only Federal offence seems to have been driving a stolen car across a state line, but J. Edgar Hoover had seen the way to make himself a national hero.

Nylon was invented in 1935. Streamlining had become the newest technological fad, applied even to stationary buildings. The *Normandie* made her maiden voyage to New York. The *Queen Mary* followed in 1936. In October, the China Clipper finished its first roundtrip flight to Manila. Mae West earned $480,000 in 1936; Shirley Temple was seven years old; Margaret Mitchell published *Gone with the Wind*. Hitler fortified the Rhine.

Though FDR was trying hard, with the NRA and the CCC and the TVA and the AAA and the WPA, the Great Depression had been hard to cure. Even in the mid-1930s, twenty million Americans were still on relief, perhaps twenty-five million. Nature had conspired to compound disaster. Years of drought blighted farmlands. I remember the Okies trekking west across New Mexico, and the great clouds of dust that rolled after them out of the north and east, settling over everything and turning the whole landscape a dull blue-gray. Through the searing Kansas heat wave in the summer of 1936, my analyst tried to cool his office with a fan blowing air against a block of ice. That winter the Ohio valley suffered the worst flood in history.

I've sometimes wondered if I might have been happier, coming of age in better times. Probably not. Within my own narrow limits I had been pretty lucky, able to escape hard labour and hunger, as free as my own nature allowed to do what I wanted. Yet, with 1936 beginning, I felt as deeply troubled as the whole world was.

There's a glimpse of my own private depression in a scrap of journal I kept that year, from February through March. The entries are rigidly inhibited, though written for "my eyes only", and bleak enough to explain why I quit them so soon, but they do describe my unhappy situation and document my efforts to escape.

I've been reading Spengler's *Decline of The West*, a massive work which is hardly lively or cheering. I'm still a virgin, haunted with longings for sex and fears about it. Living and trying to work in that narrow cabin on the ranch, I'm recovering from flu, limping about on painful arches, suffering from frequent colds and eyestrain. Most of my projects are horror stories aimed at *Thrilling Mystery*, bits of hackwork designed to fit a stifling formula.

"The Cometeers" was more fun to do, but Tremaine has been silent about it. In mid-February he returns two instalments to be condensed into one, but he's buying it. The revisions take five days; I mail them back to him on February 19. His check for $650 arrives the same afternoon, but the journal reports no elation. Nor much more when Leo Margulies writes that he has bought *Wonder Stories* and wants novelettes at a cent a word. Instead of plunging into one, I'm buying a chromatic harmonica that I hope to learn to play by note – a doomed undertaking, because I've no ear at all. Jo, my older sister, is gravely ill when the journal opens, though soon improving. A slice of Tremaine's check goes for her hospital bills, and worry over her future is one more burden.

An attractive neighbour girl has been going with me to movies and dances. I learn now that she has just married a man I didn't know about; he has been away somewhere in military service. Though I wanted her, my sense of loss is soon blunted; I've always known she really wasn't for me; we have too few interests in common. Yet I've quit going out with Jima and my sister Katie. In early March I mail "The Ice Entity" to Leo Margulies and begin a series of eye treatments with an optometrist at five dollars a visit.

As well as Freud and a bit of Jung. I've been reading Karl Menninger's *The Human Mind* and *Facts and Theories of Psychoanalysis* by Dr Ives Hendricks. On February 29 I write Dr Hendricks to ask about coming to Boston for analysis with him. He refers me to Menninger in Topeka, who agrees to see me at the Menninger Clinic in Topeka on April 13. The April 4 entry, the last until 1938, reports two checks from Margulies, $100 for "Death's Cold Daughter" and $80 for "The Ice Entity".

Topeka is the capital of Kansas, but far overshadowed by Kansas City, which is only 70 miles away. Some of my own impressions of it, a few years later, went into *Darker than you Think*. I recall it as a quiet little city, half asleep in those hard times. Its best-known citizens were Senator Arthur Capp, publisher of the daily *Capital* and *Capper's Weekly*, and Alf Landon, governor of the state. Out of mere curiosity, I called on Landon the morning after the Republican convention nominated him to run for the presidency against FDR. His secretary let me in. I found him alone in his office, with time to shake hands and inquire about Republican power in New Mexico, of which I knew nothing. When election time came, he carried only Maine and Vermont.

The Menninger Clinic occupied a big aging building with lawns and trees around it. I took physical tests that included a head X-ray and talked to a good many psychiatrists; most of them must have

been interns. One of them commented that writing science fiction
was symptomatic of neurosis. His promise that I could be cured
became one more mental problem, because I wanted no remedy.
When the tests were over, I began analysis with Dr Charles W.
Tidd, meeting him five hours a week at five dollars an hour – a low
fee, even in those times, though it was finally too much for me. I
liked him at once, and I'm grateful for all he did for me.

Before I left the clinic I wrote an article about that first year.
Turned down without comment by *Atlantic* and the like, perhaps
because it offered too much clinical detail, the piece has never been
published, but bits of it may show something of what the analysis
was for me. The lead paragraph is about the Kansas River, which
runs through Topeka.

> It must once have been deep and clear; but now it is choked
> with bars of mud, red-stained with the lifeblood of the despoiled
> and dying land, turbulent with whirlpools that make it danger-
> ous for swimmers . . . Sometimes I have imagined myself leap-
> ing down into that murky stream . . . There are several reasons
> for this fearful covert wish to die: a blind savage anger at my
> own failings, with the guilty need of self-punishment; a childish
> irrational desire to injure the analyst by my death; the fact that
> the leap stands for impulsive abandonment, for the final fatal
> rebellion against the old false tyranny of self-control.

> This year I have learned all these things, and now I shall never
> kill myself . . .

> It has been a lonely year. I am sitting, this quiet April after-
> noon, in the upstairs front room that costs me ten dollars a
> month – I had neither the money nor the need to live in the
> sanitarium. The room is furnished with two chairs, bedstead,
> dresser, and my typewriter on the table. It sometimes seems
> chill and bare, and during the winter I was driven to various
> ingenious expedients to keep my feet warm as I worked. Habitu-
> ally I eat down at the Greek's place, where a square meal is
> fifteen cents. My clothing was shabby at the beginning, and
> becomes inevitably more so. I have made few friends, in spite of
> fumbling efforts, because of the intangible barriers of fear.

> My profession is the writing of adventure stories for certain of
> those rough-paper magazines known as 'pulps'. One of them

now lies on my desk, with my name in white letters across a garish cover illustration. Beside it is a note from the editor, asking me to do another yarn. Almost desperately, I need the cent a word he would pay. Hopefully, I run a sheet of clean paper into the machine and begin:

> Martin Drake listened in terrible apprehension to the heavy footsteps coming up the stair. His breath stopped, at the abrupt harsh grate of the key in the lock. Cold with a sudden sweat, he crouched beside the door.

From years of practice, I have gathered many technical tricks that build simple interest and suspense. Familiar word-patterns rise mechanically. But even a "wood-pulp" story must be the expression of genuine feeling: words are valueless without emotion. And this story has no reality for me; I care nothing for Martin Drake and the cause of his trepidation. My feelings are confused and turbid as the river.

Still I try to make myself go on. I stare at the sheet of paper, knot my hands, double up as if with cramping agony. I begin to weep, out of sheer helpless frustration.

This is all childish, I say; silly. I want to write, perhaps more than anything else I could do. There is no visible reason why I can't, and every necessity that I should. So I try again. But the machine mocks me. The few words I write are dry and empty . . . I rip the page out . . . Baffled, defeated, I throw myself down on the bed. But I am too tense to relax, too bitter. I get up and try to read, try to study some other man's story. But it seems as hollow as my own. And I know the tricks well enough, if I could only muster up the feeling.

Hence the little essay, an effort to record my own real emotion.

Five times a week I go for the fifty-minute "hour". I always start thirty minutes early, lest I be delayed. The old fear strikes me when the girl at the desk calls my name. (She's a pretty girl, and I've learned that part of the fear is due to desire for her, and my unconscious jealous apprehension of the analyst.)

Walking lightly and hastily, a little breathless, sometimes with a pounding heart, I climb the stairs and walk across the hall and enter the office of the analyst. He has laid a paper napkin ready for me across the pillow on the couch. He stands and bows to meet me, a handsome man with an easy, friendly smile – and yet I feel confused and afraid.

Quickly, feeling a self-conscious restraint, I lie supine on the couch. It is difficult to begin speaking. I delay: my hands ball into fists; my body tenses; I make aimless striking motions.

"Just say what you feel," the analyst prompts me quietly. He is sitting relaxed in his chair behind my head. His manner is always easy, unsurprised. His low voice is sympathetic, encouraging. "Just tell me all your thoughts."

With a convulsive effort, I begin. I try to talk rapidly, because there is so much to say; because the time is so costly, and I do not wish to waste it; perhaps because I wish to hurry over some painful, shameful thing; also because the talk eases tensions and sometimes I become relaxed and comfortable toward the end of the hour.

My hurried voice is low – all through life I have spoken softly, as I have stooped, to make myself inconspicuous and avoid aggression and danger. Sometimes I become inaudible. The analyst asks me to repeat, and I make a brief effort to speak distinctly.

Continually, too, he must urge me to go on. For when I have come to a difficult matter, my voice checks and stops. To speak each word takes a desperate new effort. I catch a deep breath or make random body-movements to delay the need to speak. I search for painless asides and diversions. Often the thoughts themselves flee away and leave my mind a blank. Hopefully, I inquire if the hour isn't already gone.

The analyst usually says little, except for his continual, sometimes tormenting pressure to "go on . . . Yes . . . Yes . . . Just tell me all about it." But his rare pointed questions, his suggestions and disarmingly tentative explanations tear the veil from many a disguised expression. Slowly I have come to understand myself, though I know even less psychoanalytic theory than when I came. Such words as 'libido' and 'id' seem strange when I recall them, for I was requested at the beginning to stop reading Freud and his followers.

There have been dramatic moments. Once in the middle of the hour I began to cry, and talked through my sobs about 'my little black doggie.' The dog, I said, had been mine when I was a tiny child, and I had caused its death. When the hour was over, I walked away from the clinic into a nearby cemetery, where I could cry like a heartbroken child. That abandonment of grief was the most complete I have ever known, and it became more grist for the analytic mill. Because it seems that this little black dog never actually existed; it was only one more disguise for things still too painful for me to face.

It had been a lonely year. I remember walking the river bridge many times that dry summer, when low water wandered between red mud banks, and again on bitter winter days when the river lay frozen under drifting snow, and in the spring when it ran high, choked with drifting rafts of dirty ice. Sometimes in the afternoon, when movies were cheap, I could escape into other dreamlands. Back from a week at home at Christmas, I moved into that ten-dollar room; through the first months, before I found the fifteen-cent meals at Nick's place, I had lived a little better in a boarding house. The budget allowed me a nickel for an ice cream cone or a candy bar when I walked out alone in the evening. I haunted the candy store, searching the racks of pulp magazines for clues to writing skill. The owner was a lecherous old man with designs on young Mexican girls. Once a young fan I met there went with me to hear a hell-fire evangelist preaching in a tent; I had gone as a casual people-watcher, and I felt amazed and a little appalled when he found God. Out of boredom more than talent, I took WPA courses in tap dancing and drawing; for a long time I kept my sketch of one classmate, an attractive girl I never really knew. I paid a few precious dollars for a night flight over Topeka in a Ford Trimotor that took off between two rows of lanterns across a wheat field. The only friend I recall was an able but troubled newspaper-man who left Topeka before I did; he was a homeless drifter, the last I knew, searching the nation for jobs he never found.

In spite of all my painful money-pinching – which became, of course, one more goal for Dr Tidd's probing – the year had been good for me. Somewhat to Ed Hamilton's surprise. In a letter written when I first came to Topeka, he says he's "mystified and a little alarmed". He admits that I'm introverted, but he says I need analysis "no more than a fencepost". In later letters he keeps urging me to give it up and come on to Pennsylvania for another visit with him. But I stayed on as long as I could – until my payments to the clinic were three months behind, with another fifty due my brother for money he lent me to live on.

In theory, I should have turned out fiction enough to meet those modest fees, but my writing had gone badly, with only one novelette sold to Tremaine and a couple of horror yarns to Margulies. Most of my effort had been wasted on two or three longer projects that I must have known were hopeless, because, secretly, I wanted them to fail. Such "unconscious resistance" became more grist for the analytic mill.

In spite of all such problems, I had made a little progress, at least against the barriers to sex. Prostitution was still wide open in Topeka, and I was lucky enough to find a patient girl already familiar with the hangups of Menninger patients. Without money and a car, however – and with hangups enough still remaining – I felt helpless to attempt much more along the private sector.

My health was improving. On Dr Tidd's advice, I had taken my eye problems to Dr F.C. Boggs, an opthalmologist, who gave me a special stereoscope with which to treat myself for exophoria and fitted me with new glasses that I wore comfortably for many years. A podiatrist threw away the arch supports that had kept me limping and taught me how to care for my feet.

More than that, I was escaping some of my old internal conflicts, correcting my old notion that will and feeling and reason must be always at war. Slowly, uncertainly, I had begun to find a less divided inner self that I could like, and to accept parts of me that I had always tried to deny.

No analysis ever ends. As Dr Tidd once put it, the process is like peeling an infinite onion. Everything becomes symbolic of something deeper, with no final truth ever revealed. With inner conflicts not half resolved, I – one part of me – wanted to stay on with Dr Tidd. But the outlaw self, still spoiling my work, made that impossible. In April, Dr Tidd agreed that we had reached a dead end.

When Ed Hamilton heard that we were breaking it off, he wrote that if I could raise the fare to New Castle and fifteen or twenty bucks to support me for a week in the big town, he would take me with him for a trip he was planning to New York. Then, if I would stay with him till June, I could ride west again with him.

I accepted that generous offer.

2

The Development of a Science Fiction Writer

James Blish

In *The Shape of Future Things*, Brian W. Aldiss notes that his future was largely shaped by the discovery of magazine science fiction at the age of thirteen. The same thing happened to me, when I was nine, and I can even place the date: June, 1931. And it seems to me that the half of the Twentieth Century that I have seen, fifty years plucked out of the middle of it, has been science-fictional from first to last, for non-readers as well as for me. There have been very few exterior events, even including some political ones, which cannot be found earlier in the pages of some sf story. My sense of wonder seems to lie pretty near the surface, for it is capable of being turned on by almost anything; but one of the chief marvels of my existence has been the feeling that for me, events did not so much happen as come true.

Curious; I cannot suppose that I'm unique in looking at events in this way, and yet though I have met about seventy-five science fiction writers, many of whom I know or knew well, and uncountable hundreds of its readers, nobody has ever mentioned having this sensation. It is like looking at history standing on one's head. I suppose it is easier to be put off by the enormous numbers of sf predictions which *haven't* come true – its reputation as a literature of prophecy is vastly overblown, and survives only by ignoring its misses – but it seems to me that even in the 1930s it was possible to exercise a sort of common sense about the future, and to pick out the virtually inevitable coming events from the welter of sheer romancing. Speaking about some successful forecasting of his own, Robert A. Heinlein has described it as about as startling as for a man to look out of a train window, see that another train is coming head-on toward his own on the same track – and predict a train wreck. Just so; but the trick requires an instinct for the probable that doesn't seem to be very widely distributed. It has to be regarded as a gift, since I had it at the age of nine: the ability to see, for example, that interplanetary travel was as inevitable as Mr Heinlein's train wreck, whereas time travel was just a romancer's game.

I had played at being a writer even earlier. I was given my first typewriter, a second-hand Smith-Corona portable badly out of alignment, when I was about six. On this I produced single-copy booklets containing lurid but mercifully short stories of fire, war and other disasters, featuring myself and imaginary companions, as well as, later, some verse. But my major ambition in those days was to become a scientist. Astronomy attracted me most, although my arithmetic marks would have discouraged me had I really known anything about the science, and it was not until I was in college that I got my first look through a telescope. I was, however, given a microscope, a small Wollensak which was not much more than a toy but nevertheless work quite well, and discovered the protozoa to be quite as exciting as the planets. Around this instrument a basement laboratory started to grow (and continued to do so for the next ten or more years).

The collision between the laboratory and the typewriter, now so inevitable in retrospect, was in reality curiously muffled and was a long time in producing any visible consequences. It was begun in 1931 by one of my block friends who knew of my interest in astronomy, who offered to give me a book that told all about life on other planets. This turned out to be the April, 1931 issue of *Astounding Stories*.

I still have a copy, although of course not *the* copy. The cover, by Wesso, shows two men in tight-fitting jodhpurs jumping with apparently suicidal intent at three much bigger crocodile-men, against a nocturnal background of cone-shaped buildings whose triangular openings glow an ominous orange. In the background, too, there appear two other crocodile-men who seem to be trying to catch the humans in the red rays of some kind of electric torch. Seven years later, Brian Aldiss was to encounter magazines of this sort with covers bearing only marginal relationship to the contents; but this Wesso cover faithfully represented a scene in the lead-off story, *Monsters of Mars*, by Edmond Hamilton, in which the human explorers are transmitted by radio to Mars just in time to stop an invasion of Earth by the crocodile-men. The issue also included two other space-travel stories, a story about a visit to another dimension, one about a descent four miles into the earth, a fantastic story with a South Polar setting, and the beginning of a serial about time travel – a very good sample, luckily, of the range of science fiction subjects at the time. (Two of the authors, Mr Hamilton and Jack Williamson, are still active producers in the field.)

Thanks to previous reading in the then proliferating air-war pulps (which was eventually to lead me to learn to fly, though that's quite another story), I knew these pieces to be fiction at once – though the opening instalment of the serial, Ray Cummings' *The Exile of Time*, depicted a robot invasion so realistically that I decided then and there not to be anywhere near New York City in the year 1935, which did not seem even to me to be very far in the future. I think I must have been a little disappointed, but if I was, I was also sufficiently entranced by the stories so that all memory of disappointment has vanished. I promptly drummed up 20 cents (*Astounding's* successor, *Analog*, today costs 60 cents for about half the amount of wordage) for another issue, only to find that the one on the stands by then was the July issue – I had missed the two middle instalments of the serial. At the time, I looked about also for other magazines of the same sort, but I found these to be larger, stodgier, and, crucially, more expensive. Conversely, I found the *Buck Rogers* comic strip too unsophisticated, though I liked the drawings.

I learned a lot from these magazines, including a lot that wasn't true, such as that some asteroids had atmospheres and were inhabitable, or that the gravity of Jupiter is crushing; and what I learned that *was* true had about as much applicability to my daily life as the knowledge of how to bail out of an aircraft which has been shot down in flames. But the power of subsequent events to surprise me and/or take me aback was much diminished by the magazines, and much of my daily life now might have come right out of one of them. In this, of course, I do not differ from many thousands of other sf readers. But I think our understanding of this process gives us a slight edge over our fellow-citizens who didn't acquire our addiction, many of whom are now blundering about dazedly in the throes of what has been dubbed future shock. We may not like everything that's happening – I certainly don't – but we're a little less likely, perhaps, to be bowled over.

I had a letter published in *Astounding* when I was in seventh grade, but for reasons I don't at all understand it didn't occur to me to try to write a sf story until I was in high school. My then English instructor was duly astounded, but to his eternal credit, encouraging, a very rare attitude in that era. With a classmate, I started an all-fiction fan magazine, *The Planeteer*, mostly written by myself and about up to the usual fan fiction standards, that is, vile. (We did buy – yes, *buy* – two stories by professionals, one from Laurence Manning and one from Edmond Hamilton. They weren't much of an improvement.)

I didn't actually sell a story until I was a sophomore in college (1940), and of the first ten I had published, only one had any merit whatsoever. The eleventh, however, "Sunken Universe" (1942) contained the germ of, and eventually was incorporated into, "Surface Tension" (1952), by far the most popular single story I have ever written. Together, they reflect, the most directly of all my works, my continuing interest in microbiology, which I pursued formally in university; but I think it is fair to add that the biological sciences play important roles in more of my output than in that of any other living sf writer known to me.

I was drafted soon after I graduated, in 1942, and during my two years in the Army, spent entirely Stateside as a medical laboratory technician, I wrote nothing. Once out, however, I went back into production with a vengeance, not only of sf, but of almost every other kind of thing for which a market existed, including westerns, detectives, sports stories, popular science articles, and even poetry and criticism for the literary quarterlies (these last two still make up an important part of my output, although, of course, not of my income). It was during this period (1945–6) that I wrote my first sf novel, *The Duplicated Man*, in collaboration with Robert W. Lowndes, with whom I was sharing a New York City apartment while I did graduate work at Columbia University; but it didn't see publication until 1953, and then in a magazine Bob himself edited. By 1948 I was selling so much – though to be sure at pretty tiny rates – that I was emboldened to try becoming a full-time free-lance author.

My timing couldn't have been worse. I had by that time also acquired a wife, an infant and a mortgage; furthermore, that was the year most of my non-sf markets chose to collapse. Defeated, I got a job as a trade newspaper sub-editor, continuing to write nights and weekends. I was also forced to sell the house.

Nevertheless, 1948 was an important year for me in another way besides teaching me some bitter economic lessons; it was then that I wrote the first of my stories about space-flying cities. John Campbell of *Astounding* rejected this but with an enormously detailed commentary, the gist of which was that what I had submitted couldn't be an independent story but a rather late stage of a series, made possible (the series) by the fact that I'd failed to consider almost all the implications of the central idea. The series was written, and bought, and the rejected story did appear in its proper order. (That story, *Earthman, Come Home*, is to be in Volume II of *SF Hall of Fame*, as "Surface Tension" is in Volume I). By 1962, the original 15,000 words had grown into four novels, now published collectively under the title *Cities in Flight*, and I hope to add a coda for the forthcoming Campbell memorial volume. In addition, the motion picture rights have been sold and I have myself written the shooting script for the first of the films.

These books, despite some novelties *en passant*, are rather old-fashioned, essentially slam-bang interstellar adventure in the direct line of descent from E.E. Smith (and, for that matter, early Campbell). Yet despite their actual age – the most recent of them is now a decade old – and their more fundamental mustiness, they're still bringing in substantial royalties and subsidiary sales; and the popularity of Larry Niven's *Known Space* series more recently would seem additional evidence that the mode of the interstellar epic is still viable. (*What are you guys going to write about now they've actually landed on the Moon?*).

I think, however, that I have done much more original work, which will in the end also prove to be more lasting. In order to keep this essay down to manageable length (and in part, I suspect, because I seldom enjoy reading autobiography and actively loathe writing it), I have barely managed to mention literary interests of mine quite outside sf, and among these is philosophy. A number of them surfaced at the same time in *A Case of Conscience*, which began its quite astonishing publishing history – at the time I was writing it, I was convinced that it was unsalable – as a 23,000 word magazine story in 1953. Later, against stern resistance from me, Frederick Pohl and Betty Ballantine persuaded me to make a novel of it, which appeared, under the same title, in 1958, and won me my only Hugo. It has stayed in print ever since and has been translated in many unlikely places, including Japan – I very much wonder how an Asiatic audience, even as thoroughly modern a one as the Japanese, could make much sense of a novel the central problem of which is presented in terms of Christian theology, and sectarian Christian to boot.

I do not claim that I invented the theological sf story – in fact, I took pains to point out my ancestors in one of my two books of critical essays on sf, *The Issue at Hand* (1964) – but mine seems to have been the first to have captured and held the attention of what seems to be a majority of the modern sf audience. One reaction why this happened may be that I took what had been for me, up to that time, quite exceptional pains to make it full, well rounded and rich *as a novel*, so that it might hold the reader to whom its decidedly Scholastic theological involutions might prove dull or even outright repugnant. I have since discovered what I think may be an even more important reason, which I shall have to approach roundabout by way of a long anecdote, for which I ask forgiveness; I can see no other way to clarify it; as follows:

With some exceptions, I do not like fantasy, but I have had a lifelong affection and admiration for E.R. Eddison's *The Worm Ouroboros*, and had often thought of trying to write a novel in which the rituals of ceremonial magic as it was actually practiced would play a similarly important part. In 1957, the same year in which I wrote what is now the final novel of *Cities in Flight* and the novel version of *A Case of Conscience* – as well as a sort of novelised monster movie called *VOR* – I decided to try this, and for my central figure settled upon Roger Bacon, of whom I knew very little except the rather Faust-like legend best exemplified in Robert Greene's Elizabethan play *Friar Bacon and Friar Bungay*. When I began to investigate the historical Bacon, however, I found first of all that he had been an *opponent* of magic all his life, and second that his actual life as a pioneer of scientific method – perhaps its inventor – and his complex career and prickly personality made him far more interesting to me than he would have been as a magician. The outcome, years later, was a straight historical novel, *Doctor Mirabilis* (Faber & Faber, 1965; Dodd Mead, revised, 1971).

Doctor Mirabilis is my choice as the best book I have ever written, but it left unscratched the original itch to write a novel about magic. I finally (as I thought) satisfied this with a book called *Black Easter* (1969, after a magazine appearance), which generated more reviews than anything I had ever written before, most of them in newspapers which previously had been quite unaware of my existence. This was gratifying, but for me *Black Easter* had a much more important outcome: when I had just finished it, I realised that I had now written three novels, widely separated in times of composition and even more in ostensible subject-matter, each one of which was a dramatisation in its own terms of one of the oldest

problems of philosophy: *Is the desire for secular knowledge, let alone
the acquisition and use of it, a misuse of the mind, and perhaps even
actively evil?*

I would not suggest for an instant that any of the three novels
proposes an answer to this ancient question, let alone that I have
one now or indeed ever expect to find one. I report only that it
struck me that in each of the three books the question had been
raised, from different angles and without my being aware of it
while I was writing them. I therefore noted, in the third one to be
written, that in their peculiar way they constituted a trilogy, to
which I gave the over-all title *After Such Knowledge*, and subsequently explained my reasons (including acknowledging that the
concept of making them a trilogy had been hindsight) in a fan
magazine article. Thereafter, and this time in full awareness of
what my theme was, I wrote a fourth novel for the group, but since
this was a direct sequel to *Black Easter*, I still regard it as a trilogy
and hope that some day it will be republished as such, although at
present it includes four titles: in the order in which they are best
read, not in order of composition, *Doctor Mirabilis, Black Easter, The
Day After Judgement* and *A Case of Conscience*.

I don't like propaganda disguised as fiction and have never
written any – though one recent story of mine, "We All Die Naked",
has been widely mistaken to be such a hybrid; though sf has been
extensively exploited as a vehicle for social criticism, from Swift on,
my own credo is that I am a sort of artist (a severely crippled one,
as nobody can know as well as I do) and that whatever the artist's
positive function in society may be, he has the negative obligation
to avoid carrying placards and to stay off barricades. I think this
may apply with special force to the science fiction writer, part of
whose stock in trade it is to imagine many different kinds of
futures most of which will contradict each other and in none of
which he can invest more than a temporary acceptance for the sake
of the story and the people in it, which is where his primary
allegiance must remain. I have never seen a Utopia or any other
kind of fictional future, including any of my own, that on inspec-
tion did not turn into something I would hate to live in, or want
anybody I cared for to have to live in; and much more pragmati-
cally, I've observed that every example of what is now being called
relevant sf (in the social political sense) that I have ever read has
been turned into unreadable nonsense by subsequent history
unless it also contained and indeed depended upon some essen-

tially timeless riddle of the human condition, one still capable of invoking wonder, joy or sorrow as no amount of technological ingenuity or future shock can ever do.

And this, I flatter myself, is what explains why *A Case of Conscience* and its three successors had so extraordinary and unexpected an impact on the sf audience and widely beyond it, despite the fact that they belong to different genres and are all packed with esoteric details about subjects – thirteenth century politics and theological disputes, modern black magic, and far future technology – which seem to have nothing in common and should have split the readers into utterly disparate groups which might like one of the books but have no use at all for the others. But that's not what happened, and I now think I know why: the problem of the misuse of secular knowledge, and the intense distrust of it, runs through all four novels . . . and without any such intention on my part, it turned out to be relevant as well as timeless.

I'm through with that problem now, since I'm not a philosopher and have nothing more to contribute to it. But I've got another one of that kind on the fire, and though I've no idea what fictional form it will take, I know now that this has become my metier – though I'll continue to write sf novels which are only games, because I like to and I still seem to be good at it – and I think I've found, at long last, why I wanted to be a writer in the first place, and why I continue to be one.

3

Wonderful Deathless Ditties

Naomi Mitchison

We had more time in the thirties. Olaf Stapledon and I discussed everything from growing potatoes to world politics and back again, but mostly science fiction. His own work was mounting up, increasingly fascinating to the real scientists, especially the younger generation, including my brother J.B.S. Haldane who told me I must immediately read *Last and First Men*. I hadn't started writing sf yet, but I was thrilled with his. We met in the Cafe Royale, where one sat on plush benches and had a good three course lunch with coffee and I think a glass of wine for half a crown. It was full of highbrows but Olaf Stapledon didn't look like one. He was strong and stocky, with light brown hair cut short and very blue eyes; he often looked worried, perhaps because he was looking too far into the future or perhaps because he was onto a problem of which the scientific solution was not visible.

He was very conscious too of the social problems of the depression and understandably doubtful whether the political solutions suggested would have the intended effect. All the time he went on reading solid science and listening to scientists, many of whom were glad to talk with him sensibly and intelligently. We swapped books and he wrote to me often in his small, exact, completely legible handwriting, the lines always going straight across the page. He went very deep and influenced many people, especially perhaps those who had fallen under the spell of D.H. Lawrence and his community mysticism as Aldous Huxley and I myself had done. He wrote to me as somebody who cares very much but keeps his head:

Don't you go the pace too much in everything you do? It's so tempting because it gives one the sense of being effective. But

34

it's dangerous for people whose real function is to use their minds because it blots out all the more delicate reactions and makes for bad work . . . I suspect that you have come up against a most serious flaw in the modern spirit . . . it alone is not good enough to live by, it has to be supplemented by something else perennial . . . all this longing not to be separate is a weakness. You *must* be yourself as precisely as possible otherwise you're no good for community. You are different, "special" and you must not funk the fact and try to bury yourself in the herd . . . Community means being intensely oneself and intensely aware of other bright individual selves and acting accordingly. It doesn't mean all howling in unison in a trance. That's what it is in fascism and the worst sort of Communism . . . as for books, it's ridiculous to say they're no good. The right ones are just about all that really matters these days. (But there one goes and writes a wrong one! But my next will be a right one and much bigger than me which is odd. But you see it's *making* me bigger.)

Olaf Stapledon was a prophet but these are the words of a moralist. He knew that his writings were part of change and he was intent on making it a good change. He didn't want just to amuse people or gratify a publisher out for big sales. He was dead honest about his writing when it was not "scientific" in the sense of rational. He had just written *Waking World* which, he was afraid, "damned me in the eyes of the scientists. It's sad because I have usually a dog-like respect for them". But he defended himself: "I may have madly mis-described what I feel but what I describe is at least as immediate as the warmth which I attribute to a fire. I don't believe I am warm; I just am warm. Similarly with the 'worship' experience. But interpretation of the experience is sure to be mostly false." If only more people could manage to separate the experience from its interpretation! It's too easy to run them together. Olaf comes back to it when he talks of the negative bad of the modern spirit: "What would have been called godlessness formerly but the word is no good today. It's what Spinoza had amongst others and it kept him straight and at peace always."

To be a moral being not because one is told to but because one wants to be: that's what some of the sf writers in those early days were after. That's how H.G. Wells was – another old friend but somehow we never talked about sf! Sometimes H.G. was so enchanted with the new material he had to play with that, as in so many of his short stories, what he gave us was sparkling, intelligent – above all new – entertainment. It wasn't until *The Time Machine* and *The War of the Worlds* that the social doctrine came in. Odd how, in spite of being technologically out of date, those stories are so deeply readable. I wish we were still allowed to believe in the Grand Lunar!

Story telling and morality have gone together since the beginnings of time. The story is more potent than the adjuration. It must have been so since the beginnings of what we think of as human life. What else kept them going? We can see the illustrations to the stories, no odder than many a book jacket, in the caves of Lascaux. These stories told people how to behave, what magic to use. And also they fulfilled curiosity, that natural curiosity that exists in all sentient beings, though mostly about food and danger. When curiosity takes shape in a being with a big brain and clever hands that can twist and shape and alter and uncover, when he begins to look up at the stars and wonder, then the seeds of science are sown. And also the seeds of story telling.

Look at the Australian Dream Time; our own beginnings may have been like that. In one sense it is an enormous bundle of stories about exchanges between gods and animals and people, difficult for us to make sense of – which meant that the incoming white Australians gave up or attempted to substitute their own god-story. But in another sense Dream Time is a coherent moral universe where all who are called into it from the very beginnings have their proper place and are fulfilled. If people lose the sense of their Dream Time it collapses into mere stories. But there are those who still know themselves in what is in many ways a logical sf construct, more elaborate and full of difficulties than *Dune* or any of Ursula Le Guin's worlds, and containing the whole of life. The Australian skeletal and shadow illustrations help but do not explain to the outsider who does not know the stories. Doubtless our ancestors had equally complex worlds with their prohibitions, exchanges and encouragement, out of which were born the great world religions, rising enormously and then collapsing.

The centuries of reason came and the moral and prophetic stories no longer made sense. What magic would help? It was dead. The churches took over, but they were not entirely acceptable; they only had one story. Where was fantasy, where magic, where colour? Science was magic at first, then shook itself clear. Can one imagine the great nineteenth century scientists expressing themselves in terms of fiction? No. They were sufficiently occupied with the astonishing panoramas which were opening in front of them, and also the fight with the stupider theologians who saw themselves supplanted. But there was an outpouring of a whole new stock of scientific images and the poets at least with their airy navies grappling in the central blue had some idea of what was going to happen and drew some quite important morals.

Think now of William Morris who did more than any other single figure, including Karl Marx, to shape British left-wing politics. He was no scientist but he was a craftsman; he knew the detail of wood-working and printing, weaving and masonry, pottery. All this had developed out of scientific technology. All his stories have a continual moral and prophetic thesis. A tale of another world, as so many of his were, must have a hard core. Today's other worlds have a hard core of science. His hard core was that of a craftsman, and the two run together.

Some of the early twentieth century sf writers seem now to be out of date, but I wonder. Most of them took the trouble to write well; not so a hundred per cent of their later followers. But, after Stapledon there was something of a gap. The prophetic strain died out. A major war focuses people's minds on the immediate present rather than the future. The first thing was to survive. Olaf wrote to me in the darkest time: "I think the country is learning its lesson fairly rapidly and there may really be a chance of something better after the war if we are not wiped out". We forget now what a near thing it was. He wrote to me again after *Sirius* came out, Methuen having turned the book down as obscene. In fact the published version had been cut rather hard; it would doubtless have passed now. He was worried about it, partly in case he had been – as the publishers said – wrong in writing it as he did, and yet equally aware that he had been right to do so.

There were two more books after that and then he died, suddenly, perhaps worn down by the hard physical work he had been doing during the war, getting food from a difficult piece of land, travelling uncomfortably, worrying. It was like part of oneself dying.

But gradually the prophets and teachers came back: first of all, I think, Clarke, and the major American writers. All of them had a moral outlook and this goes on with our good writers, more and more strongly. It is now only too obvious that we have made a nasty mess of our home planet, and there isn't much time for putting it right. One writer after another has expressed this forcibly. Few sf writers would catch themselves forseeing anything except an international world government, unless, like Wyndham, they are concentrating on a local disaster.

But should all this warning and teaching be in the form of fiction? The other possible packaging is in mathematical symbols. Oddly enough these are both an international language and a strictly minority one. Fred Hoyle could of course lay out the possibilities of any of his books in terms of strict anatomical observations and conclusions, but no, no, give us another story please!

So, who better to bring the disasters which we are making for ourselves forcibly home to voters and opinion-makers than committed sf writers? They have taken over so much both from the politicians and the churches just because they can and do express themselves more forcibly and perhaps because they can upset people and make them wonder what they're doing. That's their job and their success. Some do it because they have been struck by some particularly unpleasant examples of human intelligence gone wrong. I suspect this of Silverberg, probably Bradbury. Look in almost any anthology of sf writing; a quarter at least are parables, perhaps about man-made pollution or the terrifying possibilities of monopoly capitalism, perhaps about the growth of drug-taking or pleasure in violence. We are constantly being taken by the hand and made to face something we would much rather not be aware of – but it has to be done if action is to be taken.

Perhaps one of the inevitable failures is that it is almost impossibly hard to imagine what human beings will be like in the remote future, or what they, or other life forms, may be like in other worlds. Most of us avoid bug-eyed monsters, good fun as they are to invent, but we all like interplanetary contacts, though we begin to realize the immense difficulties. Then comes the technical difficulty of speech forms, something which also hits historical novelists. The mere fact that the characters in deeply other worlds or far into the future have to talk English makes them English – or American – or whatever other nationality the writer starts with. This reacts in the imagination of the reader but also that of the writer. We are bound to identify fully with some of the people we write about; we have to, for we are using them to speak through; but can they avoid having the kind of thoughts and reactions that we have? However much we are aware that they are different, have completely other work, love and community relationships, we still can't keep ourselves out. Sf writers try different dodges. One is to invent a social set-up something like earlier ones in our own history. Hence the mock mediaevalism of some writers, including princesses and dragons. My own dodge in *Memoirs of a Space Woman* was never to allow actual speech to extra-terran life forms, but instead have the "I" in the story put into words what they are communicating. Yet this could be made into an interesting platform for moralizing!

It doesn't really make things very different if the characters are given exotic names, though it may well make a good story a bit harder to follow, especially if the pronunciation is ambiguous. Ursula Le Guin sometimes makes unnecessary difficulties for us, though I can appreciate why she does it. Tolkien got away with it – or didn't he?

But the main argument and moral must be inherent in the plot and in what feelings and thoughts it excites in the reader, who has to get used to the diction and appearance of the characters, whatever way this is worked out. Then comes the big question: is even a tiny percentage of readers influenced, perhaps in the direction of taking political action to curb powerful monopolies, even though these are not yet galactic? Or, more simply, what percentage has stopped throwing plastic bags or old tins into bushes or has decided never to use any product based on whale oil? Unfortunately these statistics don't exist. We have to be content to shove at the old zeitgeist not knowing if we are getting anywhere. But this is what happens to all prophets from Ezekiel on.

Yet is straight propaganda, the sock in the reader's lazy old ego, the best way to get things moving? Results are more likely from a story with a moral outlook but not too obvious a text and sermon. Let's get the reader musing and reconsidering, and then finding that old attitudes have shifted just a little. One method is to produce an acceptable alternative or future world not utterly remote, but something which the reader might feel he or she might be, or already was, working towards. A world of this kind is postulated in J.B.S. Haldane's *The Man With Two Memories*. The interest here is not so much in the plot as in the historical working out of how it came into existence.

Serious sf writers in other countries are doing the same kind of thing as the British and Americans. It is quite clear that this is so for at least a couple of the authors in the Penguin *Russian Science*

Fiction. In fact it looks as though things could be pointed out, and social and moral attitudes expressed, which might not have been taken kindly in another literary form. We first heard of Stanislaw Lem, from Poland, as the author of *Solaris*, which in turn became the most moving and beautiful sf film that has so far been produced – and packed with prophetic and complex morality. He is not the only good sf writer from the Debatable Land between East and West, and it would be surprising if there was nothing excellent coming out of Spanish-speaking South America.

When it comes to our prophetic ideas, we sf writers must remember the good guys, those who are deliberately trying to make the right choices, social and political. They need our help. It can be more than a little un-nerving to feel we are heading towards an inevitable dark age, a chaos in which it doesn't matter if Shakespeare, Donne or Blake, or Michael Angelo, Carl Milles and Pablo Picasso had never existed. This isn't so. It does matter and sf writers should not pretend that the human spirit is useless although, as in more than one book, we encounter higher intelligence and although, as most of us are deeply aware, we humans are only in the dawn of our history. We have made terrible mistakes; we have had knowledge and lost it – I think of the increasing evidence for competent mathematicians and astronomers working in our own island between the Orkneys and Stonehenge long before the building of the pyramids. Perhaps much else has been lost, even earlier, and exchanged for – what? There are human gains not to be reckoned in terms of air travel, the amusement industry and contraceptives, but in the wakening of the spirit which Stapledon foresaw – but in 1939 with the shadow of World War II already over him. The reckoning must be remade over and over and the gains and losses made clear. This is one of our jobs and can only be done if we have a moral framework, fully believed in by ourselves, within which to make it.

Now let us be careful. A moral framework is not the same as a religious framework, though there is some overlap and many of us move from one to the other and back. But our moral framework as sf prophets and shakers must be rational, based on the human spirit but stretching reason and humanity beyond their present bounds. We must foresee, but without the aid or hope of miracles. It is the lapse from a humanist moral framework into a narrowly Christian one which makes the C.S. Lewis series, even *Perelandra* with its lovely opening chapter, unacceptable as prophetic sf.

There must at least be some solid evidence of the possibility of what we describe or infer in our stories. Anything beyond is fantasy.

But here we are in something of a puzzlement and we do not always recognize it ourselves, even while we are writing. Harry Harrison put it very well in his diagram of the sf circle inside the fantasy circle, but which sometimes coalesces until there is nothing of the original circle left. Wind-steeds for instance, delightful as they are, must count as fantasy; in fact so must most of the fauna and flora with which we bedeck our alternative worlds. Almost any author other than the real hardliners like Asimov, Heinlein, Van Vogt and Clarke falls into f for fantasy more or less, perhaps for a whole book. Sometimes Bradbury does it so continuously that we only get glimpses of the s behind the f. Or take an author of considerable literary talent and a violently lively inventiveness, Josephine Saxton. What she writes is fantasy but without benefit of kings of fairies; yet we feel somewhere at the back a hard scientific impulse and she must certainly class as an sf writer. There is yet another pitfall, rather an unfair one. Something which, when it was first published, was deemed scientifically possible, as well as imaginatively plausible, ceases to be so. All the fiction we pinned onto Mars has become increasingly unreal with every bit of evidence which comes back from the space probes. This is sad, as some of the Mars stories were so good!

Now there are certain assumptions which most sf writers make and which are perhaps a little shaky and need examining. One is the weapon category, the ever more efficient gun which can in its simplest form destroy space monsters, including ships pouring out of further galaxies, or even black holes, and more sophisticated versions which merely anaesthetize or immobilize. Counter-armour of course exists. Considering what a shockingly high percentage of today's technological ingenuity goes into the designing of new methods of destruction, this is probably legitimate.

Another assumption is in dealing with time in terms of light years and human years during space flight. We get round it by using words like hyperdrive, time-blackout and so on. Only the mathematicians and astronomers among us really try to work it all out and they are not always totally convincing. But something of the sort must come about sooner or later.

Another general assumption which almost all sf writers make sooner or later is about psi. It is assumed that "mind-speech" of

some kind is a faculty which exists to some extent now among
some individuals and is likely to be developed. I am myself inclined to think this is correct, partly from my own early experiences with Prof. Gilbert Murray and with my brother, and partly
from the experiences of other people, who, I believe, are intelligent
and totally honest. It appears to be almost always a young person's
ability, usually lost later on. But there is certainly considerable
scientific scepticism about this, especially among the tough boys of
the *New Scientist*. Our present methods of verbal communication,
even with translating computers, which do make the oddest mistakes, are inadequate even in the world as it is. Words are made
even less meaningful when used as a private language of science or
economics. Linguistics is a delightful branch of science, but real
communication is something else. I think it may not be long before
something serious comes up in the psi field, bringing with it very
genuine moral problems.

But what about the really disintegrated sf? Is it prophetic? Does
it have a shape, even in the writer's mind? Clearly for some people
it is the picture of things to come. It may be marginally valid for a
period of change which the rest of us only sense uneasily. We have
certainly not forseen all the changes which are going to come. Does
Doris Lessing's *Memoirs of a Survivor* count as sf? From time to time
I recognize something happening which is in that book, not anything as simple as an incident, but a ripple of social behaviour out
of the new morality or moral collapse – but can we be sure which is
which, and, if collapse, can we see beyond?

This means that the moral basis on which we build our lives,
which for writers is essentially what we write, is in a state of
change, parallel with the changes in technology. A very unrestful
state no doubt, but surely by now we know that God changes with
Man? So we are on a permanent edge. Now, this change in
morality cannot be directly argued, mostly because we know what
it was and to some extent what it is, but not what it will be, even
when we try to glimpse it. But it is also because only a minority of
the well-educated, themselves a minority, are interested in argument for its own sake. So this groping towards a view of change
must be put some other way. How? That, surely, is where sf comes
in. We can and must attempt to make a picture of the new
morality, the kind of society which it might make at its best and
with luck. Alternatively, the kind which it can make if it goes
wrong.

How far forward can we hope to foresee? Classics like *Childhood's End* or the Stapledon books take us a very long way and there may be other turns on the journey which no prophetic vision has yet encountered. Indeed this is quite certainly so. We are far from possessing all the evidence necessary for accurate extrapolation. But our guesses are warnings. If things go along road X this may be the result: if along road Y that. What is our own stand-point? I think we must admit that a few human categories are valuable: courage, though not necessarily physical: kindness, that is to say empathy with the not-self in any life-form-curiosity kept within a framework by courage and kindness. But how to rate that difficult abstraction truthfulness, without which curiosity can hurt rather than help? How to rate aesthetic perception and creation? How to rate patience, or is it essential to kindness? Loyalty is a difficult one and honour can be twisted. There are also social virtues, including freedom which is scarcely a meaningful concept any longer, so much has it been used as a political stone to sling at our opponents. If we intend to be prophets and moralists we must make our own moral mixture and live by it ourselves.

And yet, yet, the main thing is the story, the inspired story, the serious sf of the prophets and movers who never know what effect they are having. They only know that reviews and sales mean little in the sense of our hopes, our shy and delicate hopes. Have we contrived to send out our antennae to meet with reciprocal thought of change? Have we been so well able to point the choices for mankind that some people, only so far a very few but they could swell to armies, have thought and done something which leads to a better future and which they would not have done but for the stories which we, the far-sighted, have written for them?

4

From Shanghai to Shepperton

J.G. Ballard
(with David Pringle)

Shanghai was an American zone of influence. All the foreign nationals there lived an American style of life. They had American-style houses, air-conditioning and refrigerators, and American cars. I never saw an English car until I came to Britain in 1946. We had Coca-Cola – and American-style commercial radio stations. We used to listen to the radio a lot. Shanghai itself had about ten English-language radio stations, and they were blaring out American programmes and radio serials. (I think there were sf serials.) And of course there were American films on show in the cinemas which I went to from a very early age. I started going to the movies when I was six or seven, something my own children didn't do (they had television). One had a peculiar cultural diet, in a way. I spent a great deal of time reading as a child – all the childhood classics, like *Alice in Wonderland*, *Robinson Crusoe* and *Gulliver's Travels*, as well as American comics and the American mass magazines of the day, *Collier's*, *Life* and so on. I don't think I read any Jules Verne, though I certainly read H.G. Wells. There were popularized versions of Wells's novels in the American comic books, and those things called Big Little Books. I must have read a bit of science fiction in book form, but I certainly didn't buy the sf magazines until much later, when I went to Canada.

Shanghai itself was one of the most extraordinary and bizarre places on earth, a place where anything went, completely without constraints. Every conceivable political and social cross-current was in collision there. War in all its forms was institutionalized in Shanghai, after the Sino-Japanese War began in 1937. I remember in 1938 or 1939 having to leave our house on the outskirts of the city, and move into a rented house in the centre of Shanghai, because the Chinese and Japanese forces were firing shells whose trajectories went right overhead . . . I remember seeing a lot of troops, and going out frequently to the battlefields around Shanghai where I saw dead soldiers lying around, dead horses in the canals and all that sort of thing. The Japanese were sitting around the city, and in fact occupied all but the International Settlement. Our house was on the western outskirts of Shanghai, actually outside the International Settlement and within the area controlled by the Japanese. The whole business of checkpoints and military occupation had been there since the earliest days I can remember. Huge armies engaged, naval forces came up the river, and large sections of the city were under air attack by Japanese bombers. This had been going on for years, so Pearl Harbor wasn't that big a surprise . . .

My father was a chemist originally. He joined a big Manchester firm of textile manufacturers – this was before I was born – and he moved into the management field. They had a subsidiary in Shanghai of which he was the chairman and managing director throughout the 1930s and into the 1940s. I was sent to the Cathedral School in Shanghai before the war. A very authoritarian English clergyman was the headmaster there, and he used to set lines. It's the most time-wasting enterprise one could imagine, but he would say "500 lines, Carruthers! 600 lines, Ballard!" for some small infringement. 500 lines was about 30 pages of a school exercise book. You were supposed to copy out school texts, and I remember starting to copy from a novel about the Spanish Armada. It was something like G.A. Henty, or it might have been Kingsley's *Westward Ho!* (I remember that. It has a marvellous last paragraph which has stayed with me all my life; the last paragraph of that novel is a fine piece of prose, and you ought to find echoes all over my fiction!) Anyway, I started copying out this high adventure narrative. I suddenly realized – I was only about nine or ten – that it was easier, and it would save a lot of effort, if I just made it up, which I did. So from then on I would make up my own narratives. I think the authoritarian clergyman must have scanned my lines because he reprimanded me by saying: "Ballard, next time you pick a book to copy your lines from don't pick some trashy novel like this!" He didn't realize I'd written it myself. I think there's a judgment on my whole life and career there – I've gone on writing within that sort of seditious framework! I went on writing little short stories and pieces, even when we were in the prison camp –

just adventure stories and thrillers, my own variants on whatever I
happened to be reading.

> From that hour Ayacanora's power of song returned to her;
> and day by day, year after year, her voice rose up within that
> happy home, and soared, as on a skylark's wings, into the
> highest heaven, bearing with it the peaceful thoughts of the
> blind giant back to the paradises of the west, in the wake of
> the heroes who from that time forth sailed out to colonize
> another and a vaster England, to the Heaven-prospered cry of
> Westward Ho![1]

I remember the very first little book I produced. Of course it was
never printed, but it was my first effort at a book. It was about how
to play contract bridge. I learned to play the game at an early age,
because bridge-playing was all the rage. I must only have been
about 11, because this was before the camp. My mother used to
hold bridge parties, almost every afternoon it seemed. To a child
the bids conjure up a whole world of mystery because they don't
seem to be related to anything. "One heart, two hearts, three
diamonds, three no trumps, double, redouble – what the hell does
all this mean?" I thought. I used to pace around upstairs listening
to these bids, trying to extract some sort of logical meaning. I
finally persuaded my mother to explain how contract bridge was
played. I was so impressed by the discovery of what bidding
meant – deciphering these cryptic and mysterious calls, particularly when I discovered they relate to the whole world of conventions so that they are a code within a code – that I wrote a book. I
think I filled a school exercise book on the basic rules of contract
bridge and what the main conventions were – I even had a section
on "Psychic Bidding", which was pretty good for an 11-year-old! It
was quite an effort of exposition. I haven't played bridge for years
and years now, though I used to play chess with my son before he
left home. I've always been very interested in chess; it's more of a
solitary man's game.

The Japanese didn't intern everybody simultaneously. It was
staged, and I think it took six months or so before we were
interned. We had very hot summers and cold winters in Shanghai,
and I remember wearing light clothes when we arrived in the
camp. Pearl Harbor was in December 1941, so it must have been

the following summer. To me, the period of internment wasn't a huge surprise as my life had changed continuously. From a huge house with nine servants, a chauffeur-driven Packard and all the rest of it, I was suddenly living in a small room with my parents and sister. Although that may seem an enormous jump, in fact it was all part of a huge continuum of disorder . . .

I have – I won't say *happy* – not unpleasant memories of the camp. I was young, and if you put 400 or 500 children together they have a good time whatever the circumstances. I can remember the acute shortage of food in the last year, and a general breakdown of facilities. Drinking water was no longer brought in by road tanker to the camp for the last year or more, once the tide turned against the Japanese. I remember a lot of the casual brutality and beatings-up that went on – but at the same time we children were playing a hundred and one games all the time! There was a great deal of illness, and about three-quarters of the people in the camp caught malaria, though not my family, thank God. My sister, who is seven years younger than me, nearly died of some kind of dysentery. I know my parents always had very much harsher memories of the camp than I did, because of course they knew the reality of the circumstances. Parents often starved themselves to feed their children. But I think it's true that the Japanese do like children and are very kindly towards them. The guards didn't abuse the children at all.

I saw it all from a child's eye, and didn't notice the danger. Right next to the camp was a large Japanese military airfield (I think it's now Shanghai International Airport). This was under constant attack in the last year or so from American bombers and low-flying fighters. The perimeter fence of the camp was in effect the perimeter of the airbase. We looked right out over the airfield. Although we had a curfew imposed by the Japanese during the air attacks, they became so frequent – almost continuous towards the closing stages – that we were often out in the open with anti-aircraft shells bursting over our heads. I daresay my parents were driven frantic by all this, but children don't remember. It wasn't like a dream, because dreams often *are* unpleasant and full of anxiety. I had no sense of anxiety, I don't remember any fear, but I look back now and I think "My God, why didn't I turn and run!" I was totally involved but at the same time saved by the magic of childhood.

Most of the British nationals there were people from the

professions, senior management personnel, and most had university training of various kinds. A school was started in the camp, and the headmaster was a missionary called Osborne (oddly enough, I discovered years later that he was the father of Martin Bax's wife, Judy – Martin Bax is the editor of *Ambit*). There were a lot of missionaries like him, who had been teaching all their professional lives. So a school was started and ran most of the time – though towards the end, when the Japanese wanted to penalize the adults in the camp, the first thing they did (with a sort of fiendish logic) was to close the school and impose a curfew. All the parents were stuck in their tiny little rooms, trapped with their noisy offspring! But I think that people like Osborne did a very good job, because I didn't feel when I got to England, despite very nearly three years in the camp, that I was much behind. I think in many areas I was absolutely up to scratch, for all the interruptions.

Outside a relatively few enclaves in Western Europe and the United States for the past few decades, the vast majority of the world has always lived the sort of life I lived in Shanghai, in that close proximity to violence, death, disease and the like. On the whole, we live enormously protected lives in Europe and the States, and children are particularly well protected here. In the historical sense of how most people have lived, my own life has probably been very close to . . . How can I put this? My life is probably much closer, in its proximity to death, disaster and destruction, to that of any Elizabethan poet or dramatist, than it is to that of most people living in this country today. If you'd been brought up in Renaissance Italy, say, or in France under the Ancien Régime, you'd probably have lived in a world very similar to that in which I was brought up. Most people in the world still do! Coming to England in 1946 was a shock that I've never re-covered from. Even though Britain was directly involved in World War II – this island had been the springboard for the invasion of Europe – English life as a whole in 1946 seemed enormously detached from reality. It seemed a world of self-enclosed little suburbs and village greens where nothing had ever happened.

My father stayed in China, and I came over with my mother and sister. We had friends who lived down in the West Country, near Plymouth, and my mother rented a house there for a couple of years. We lived in a sort of Daphne du Maurier-land – in fact, there was a little creek which was reputed to have been the source of inspiration for her novel *Frenchman's Creek*, only a few hundred yards away. There was indeed the remains of a great old wooden ship lying there in the mud: it's quite possible that it gave her the idea. It's full of little smugglers' coves and caves, that part of the world . . In about 1948 my mother and sister went back to China, and – when I wasn't at school in Cambridge – I stayed with my grandparents near Birmingham. My mother came back from China, but my father was still there in 1949 and he was caught by the communist advance from the north. He was held in Shanghai for about a year after the communists arrived, but eventually he was released and was able to make his way to England. That was in 1950, and they bought a house in the Manchester area. By then I was at university. When he arrived here, my father became a consultant in the pharmaceutical field; he became director of European operations for an American pharmaceutical company, a big Boston firm – which he remained until his retirement, shortly before he died in 1966.

My mother's maiden name was Edna Johnstone. Her parents lived in West Bromwich, near Birmingham (I never met my father's parents: they lived in Blackburn in my father's youth). They were teachers of music. I remember my grandfather, with whom I stayed in the late 1940s for about a year when my mother went back to China, as a very straightlaced puritanical Edwardian gentleman. My grandparents were in their 70s, I think, after the war, and were rabidly right-wing Conservatives. They were faced with the apocalypse of the post-war Labour Government, which shattered everything in their world. But in *fact*, according to my mother, my grandfather was a bit of a maverick. He shocked his very bourgeois family, round about the turn of the century, by forming his own band! It may be that the maverick tendencies of my own come through him . . .

A man of vigorous and stubborn temper, the Reverend Johnstone was one of those muscular clerics who intimidate their congregations not so much by the prospect of divine justice at some future date but by the threat of immediate physical retribution in the here and now. Well over six feet tall, his strong head topped by a fierce crown of grey hair, he towered over his parishioners from his pulpit, eyeing each of them in their pews like a bad-tempered headmaster obliged to take a junior form for one day and determined to inflict the maximum of benefit upon them.[2]

I went to the Leys School in Cambridge for a couple of years in the late 1940s. I disliked it intensely, but I'd been through so many strange experiences before and during the war that it was just another strange experience that I coped with. I wasn't unhappy there, actually. I had a great deal more experience of life in general than almost all the boys that I met there. Although they'd lived in Britain during the war, they'd had very sheltered lives (the school had been evacuated to Scotland). I didn't have anything very much in common. The big saving for me was that the Leys School was in Cambridge itself. I'd sneak off to the Arts Cinema to see all the French films of the 1940s. I'd go to the Cambridge Film Society and soak myself in *The Cabinet of Dr Caligari* and all those experimental films of the 1920s. And there were always art exhibitions of various kinds on in Cambridge. Also I had two or three friends among the boys in the class above mine who went up to Cambridge University to read medicine, and through them I had an early entry into Cambridge undergraduate life. I used to visit the colleges. If I'd gone to a school out in a remote corner of Dorset or somewhere it would have been a bit of a strain, but being in Cambridge it was like being a member of a junior college there, which was a big help to me.

I became very interested in psychoanalysis while still at school, and read almost all the Freud I could lay my hands on. In fact my chief reason for reading medicine when I went up to King's College was that I wanted to become a psychiatrist – a sort of adolescent dream, but I was quite serious about it. England seemed a very strange country. Both the physical landscape and the social and psychological landscapes seemed fit subjects for analysis – extremely constrained and rigid and repressed compared with the sort of background I had. To come from Shanghai, and from the war itself where everything had been shaken to its foundations, to come to England and find this narrow-minded puritanical world – this was the most repressed society I'd ever known! I became intensely interested in psychoanalysis and began to devour every library I could lay my hands on when I was 16 or 17. I read a good number of Freud's major works then, plus a lot of other works on psychoanalysis and psychiatry. Jung, of course, who was really a great imaginative novelist (in a sense, Freud is too!). But while I was still at school I was reading not just psycho-analytic texts but all the leading writers of the day – Kafka of course, and Hemingway – the strange sort of goulash of writers and poets that you read when you're that age.

I was already writing experimental fiction, what might be classed as avant-garde fiction. I'd been writing bits of fiction ever since I was quite a small child. I wanted to become a writer, there's no question about that, but I didn't see writing and a medical career as mutually exclusive. I wanted to study psychiatry professionally, and first of course I had to gain a medical degree – which was five years ahead, then two years doing the Diploma of Psychological Medicine: seven years in all. That seemed a lifetime away, and I took for granted that I would write my own fiction throughout this period. I didn't see myself as a professional writer; it didn't occur to me that I could become one just by *decision*. I was writing a lot of fiction – I don't say it was particularly naive – but it was very experimental and heavily influenced by all the psychoanalysis I'd read, by all the Kafka and so on . . .

> Popularly regarded as a lurid manifestation of fantastic art concerned with states of dream and hallucination, surrealism is in fact the first movement, in the words of Odilon Redon, to place "the logic of the visible at the service of the invisible". This calculated submission of the impulses and fantasies of our inner lives to the rigours of time and space, to the formal inquisition of the sciences, psychoanalysis pre-eminent among them, produces a heightened or alternate reality beyond and above those familiar to either our sight or our senses. What uniquely characterizes this fusion of the outer world of reality and the inner world of the psyche (which I have termed "inner space") is its redemptive and therapeutic power. To move through these landscapes is a journey of return to one's innermost being.
>   . . . At the same time we should not forget the elements of magic and surprise that wait for us in this realm. In the words of André Breton: "The confidences of madmen: I would spend my life in provoking them. They are people of scrupulous honesty, whose innocence is only equalled by mine. Columbus had to sail with madmen to discover America."[3]

I'm almost certain I became interested in the surrealists at school, because I know that by the time I went up to King's I was already very interested, going to exhibitions and so on. I read medicine, and my interest in psychoanalysis abutted surrealism at all sorts of points. When I was in my early 20s, long before I started writing sf, I had reproductions of surrealist paintings pinned up wherever I was living. They were totally out of favour then and it was difficult to get hold of works by the surrealists. If there was an exhibition somewhere or another – usually in a small commercial gallery in London – it wasn't well reviewed. If you wanted a reproduction of the latest painting by Dalí or Magritte you stood a better chance of getting one in something like *The Daily Mirror* or *The Daily Mail* than you did in the serious papers. They were hardly mentioned in the columns of papers like *The Observer* or *The Times* – if they were, it was always in a derogatory way. I didn't give a damn about that; I was absolutely convinced that this was one of the most important schools of painting in the 20th century, one of the most important imaginative enterprises the century has embarked on. I felt that then and I still do.

Salvador Dalí has still not been welcomed into the fold of critical respectability. Good – I'm glad in a way, and I don't think it matters a hoot. His recent exhibition in London was enormously successful, and I think that speaks for itself. There's a continuing public interest in Dalí which makes the responses of the critical bureaucracy totally irrelevant, as they always have been. The triumph of the surrealists in the 1960s, when they really arrived for the first time, was a triumph of their own talents. No critic discovered the surrealists and persuaded the public that here was something worth looking at. They did it themselves. Their hour came, and quite rightly. I remember being interested in Francis Bacon in the very early 1950s, when he was virtually unknown and painting most of his early masterpieces, and he was treated with the same sort of disdain that the surrealists received until about 15 years ago (and Dalí still does receive). There's an enormous resistance here to certain categories of imaginative work, both in the visual arts and in the novel. This is a very puritanical country. The Protestant non-conformist hatred of the imagination – of symbolism as a whole, let's say – runs through the whole of English life, and a large section of American life too for the same sort of reasons. Great works of the imagination, of the 19th and 20th centuries, are far too seditious of the bourgeois certainties.

But there *were* surrealist works in the Tate Gallery in the early 1950s. I remember seeing Delvaux there, along with a few Chiricos and Ernsts and Dalís. They were in a sort of little dark ante-room. I know that before I went to Canada with the RAF, and when I came back, in the early years of my marriage, I was intensely interested in the surrealists – and in the Pop Artists as they emerged. I don't think my attitude to the surrealists has changed. My whole imaginative response to them was fully fashioned by the time I started writing science fiction. And although the surrealists in particular were regarded as totally disreputable by the guardians of bourgeois culture there were still exhibitions. I remember going to an exhibition of new Magrittes in a little gallery near Berkeley Square – this was in something like 1955 – which included many paintings of his which are now world-famous. They were openly derided, and not just by art critics: no literary reviewer would refer to the surrealists at all. When I wrote my first serious novel, *The Drowned World*, somebody at Gollancz suggested to me that I delete the references to surrealist painters – this was 1962 – because, it was felt, the references diminished my own novel by association. He regarded my novel as a serious piece of imaginative fiction, and by bringing in the surrealists, these references to Ernst and Dalí and Delvaux, I diminished my novel. I refused of course. But that was 1962!

I wasn't acquainted with literary surrealism. The French texts probably weren't translated. I remember reading Edmund Wilson's *The Wound and the Bow* as a student, his accounts of writers like Joyce and Hemingway. His chief interests were Eliot, Pound and so on. The Paris in which those writers for the most part lived was also inhabited by the surrealists, but they figured in the margins of the text, in the margins of the biographies of those writers. It was primarily the artists who were referred to. I've never really been interested in literary surrealism – in Jarry and Appollinaire, yes, but they're not strictly speaking surrealists.

J. Graham Ballard who shares the first prize of £10 with D.S. Birley in the *Varsity* Crime Story Competition is now in his second year at King's and immersed in the less literary process of reading medicine.

He admitted to our reporter yesterday that he had in fact entered the competition more for the prize than anything else, although he had been encouraged to go on writing because of his success.

The idea for his short story which deals with the problem of Malayan terrorism, he informs us, he had been thinking over for some time before hearing of the competition.

He has, in addition to writing short stories, also planned "mammoth novels" which "never get beyond the first page".[4]

I remember submitting one or two of my early short stories to *Horizon*. There weren't many places to be published then. There were very few magazines at all, and the experimental, impressionistic prose poetry I was writing – free-form – was the sort of thing that was just turned down without a second thought by people in charge. That very early story of mine, which won the Cambridge competition when I was 21, was done as almost a pastiche of a certain kind of Hemingwayesque short story. It certainly wasn't typical of the other material I was writing at the time. I wanted to win the competition, actually: that was my intention, but I knew that I wouldn't win unless I wrote a story of that kind.

I went to London University for a year after I left Cambridge and I read English. This makes me sound like a medieval scholar, moving from bench to bench, but it wasn't like that. I'd won this story competition, and I thought I'd studied enough medicine for my purposes. The next phase was the clinical phase. I'd been in and out of clinical hospitals as part of the two years I did at Cambridge, and I knew that clinical medicine was enormously demanding in time and energy. Young doctors work long hours, and though they may over the years accumulate an enormous amount of fascinating material they have no time for anything else. In a way I felt I'd completed the interesting phase of studying medicine. The pre-clinical phase is almost pure science; it's anatomy, physiology, pathology. I felt I'd already stocked my vocabulary enough for me to move on. I wanted to write – I felt the power of imagination pushing at the door of my mind and I wanted to open it.

My Father said, with a chemist's logic, "Well, if you want to be a writer you should study English". So I went to London University, read English, and they turfed me out at the end of the year, deciding I hadn't got what it took to be a student of English Literature. I was then about 22. I went to work for an advertising agency called Digby Wills Ltd., where I wrote copy, for lemon juice among other things. I was there for three or four months. Then I worked as an encyclopaedia salesman. That was fascinating, one of the most interesting periods in my life. It lasted about six months, I think. Simply going into so many people's homes, I was conducting my own Gallup survey of English life. An encyclopaedia salesman has to start at No. 1 – knock, knock – and then go on to No. 2. You must knock on every door and try to get in. You have to overcome the feeling that because the lace curtains look a little intimidating you won't knock here – you must go in. And it's quite extraordinary, the variety of human lives . . . It was fascinating.

My father certainly disapproved totally of my wanting to become a writer (in exactly the way I would if one of my children wanted to be a writer!). He regarded it as not really a profession at all, didn't think one could make a sustained career out of it. It would take years to discover whether one had the sort of talent the world would pay attention to. In many senses of course, he was absolutely right. But even with the benefit of hindsight I wouldn't change things. It would have been much easier for me if I had, say, graduated as a doctor. I then would have been financially secure, and given the sort of imaginative pressures I was feeling I think I probably would have written – though nowhere near as much as I did. But I'm glad I approached it the way I did. I was a late starter, but that may have been necessary.

My mother agreed with my father, but I don't think either of them had much influence on me. I don't think parents do have as much influence on their children as people imagine. I have three children, a son and two daughters, all of whom are in their 20s now. I don't think I have any influence on them whatever. In fact we agree about a great number of things, but where they disagree with me they follow their own paths.

My real problems began when I was thrown out of London University, because that had been a year's grace. I still wasn't ready to do anything remotely like becoming a professional writer. The opportunities didn't exist. My father gave me a small allowance, but it was *hard earned*. It was a tricky time. But the sort of pressures that make an imaginative writer, as opposed to say a naturalistic novelist, the pressures are so strong they must come from some source deep within the mind that's been forming itself since the very earliest days. It's part of one's fundamental apparatus for dealing with reality. It's not in any way the exercise of some social art. One might almost say it's part of some neurological apparatus for coping with the experience of living – everything from the most humdrum event like crossing a room and opening a door to the most important and richest events in one's life, like being married and having children. The whole spectrum of one's experience is obviously integrated with something deep in the mind, and if somebody feels that sort of pressure – this is obvious if you read the biographies of surrealist painters or imaginative writers in general – there's nothing really that's going to deflect him. It's like breathing . . .

There were periods, I suppose, when I just drifted. I was discovering London for the first time. I'd come down from Cambridge and had a year as a student. I lived in a very shabby cheap bedsitter in South Kensington. I spent a lot of time in Chelsea, a world that's vanished now. It wasn't a bohemian phase, though. I was writing a lot of short fiction of various kinds, but I was still waiting for that discovery of science fiction. I think I would have made it if I'd not gone to Canada in fact, because round about the mid-1950s the sf magazines began to be distributed over here, and I'm sure I would have come across them.

I went into the Air Force on a strange sort of impulse, I think. I was suddenly keen to fly. I always have had a keenness to fly, all my life. It's a strange thing running through my mind, and I think it comes out in my writing. I've always been interested in aviation, and the 1950s was an exciting time. The first advanced postwar jets were appearing on the scene, supersonic travel was here to stay, the world was being changed by aviation. Also in the field of weapons technology there was a whole new world, huge bombers carrying atomic weapons everywhere. I suddenly felt "I want to be part of this" – I was very young. I'd had a great deal of experience as a child and also as a medical student, but I needed something more. I wanted that experience and it was a chance also to get out of England, because the RAF's flight training was done in Canada. I'd been to Canada and the United States on a trip with my parents in 1939, but only had hazy memories. I wanted to get out of England desperately. So after my basic training I went. I was sent to the RCAF flight-training base at Moosejaw, Saskatchewan, which is quite a place to be! That's where I discovered science fiction, in the magazine racks of the airbase cafeteria, and I've never looked back since!!

Already one can see that science fiction, far from being an unimportant minor off-shoot, in fact represents the main literary tradition of the 20th century – a tradition that runs in an intact line through Wells, Aldous Huxley, the writers of modern American sf, and such present day innovators as William Burroughs and Paolozzi.

The main "fact" of the 20th century is the concept of the unlimited future. This predicate of science and technology enshrines the notion of a moratorium on the past . . .

In the face of this immense continent of possibility, all literatures other than science fiction are doomed to irrelevance. None have the vocabulary of ideas and images to deal with the present, let alone the future . . .[5]

"Passport to Eternity" was the first sf story I ever wrote – again, written as a kind of pastiche. I think I slightly embroidered it when I came to sell it to one of the American magazines some years later. But I was still in the RAF when I wrote that story. I wrote it at RAF Booker, which was a base for cashiered air crew, for people being thrown out of the Air Force. We sat in this airfield, near High Wycombe, a sort of transit camp, straight out of Kafka in a way. There were great gloomy huts by the pines on the edge of these empty runways where we reject aircrew sat around, trying to keep warm by the one stove. They didn't bother to keep us warm, and there was nothing to do. There were two squadron leaders who were in charge of processing us, and they had to wait for various documents to arrive. As mine had to come from Canada, I spent a long time there. Weeks went by and I sat around waiting for my name to be called. Suddenly a name would be called out the man in question would go to meet these squadron leaders, and five minutes later he would be a civilian and leave the base forever. One didn't know when this was going to happen, so with all this spare time on my hands I thought "I'll write a science fiction story!" Which I did. I'd been reading all this stuff in Canada. For some reason, I wrote "Passport to Eternity", which was a sort of summary of it all in a way.

It was influenced by a story by Jack Vance, which I remember vividly from a magazine, called "Meet Miss Universe". That was a biological fantasy about a beauty contest; it impressed me enormously with its wit and cleverness and inventiveness – the best of that sort of American science fiction. As I say, "Passport to Eternity" was a summary of all the American sf I'd been reading over the past year in Canada. It's a kind of spoof, indistinguishable really from the American sf. It didn't occur to me to submit it – I don't know why, I think I had other problems on my mind. I already knew that I wanted to write a different kind of sf – that story may have been my first, but it isn't in any way typical. A few years later I typed it out again from the original typescript, the basic story unchanged, and sent it to – Cele Goldsmith, I suppose.

I wanted to write for the American magazines. It didn't occur to me to write to British ones, I don't think I even *knew* about *New Worlds*. The American magazines of the day were much more widely distributed. I'd been reading them in Canada, and I was familiar with the writers – the level of professionalism was far higher in the American magazines. The magazine that I admired most (sadly, I never had a story in it) was *Galaxy*. I admired it tremendously, and read every issue for a couple of years. *Astounding* was terribly *heavy*, it seemed to be mostly planet yarns, and the stories had very little wit. Wit was the great strength of *Galaxy* – there were stories by Sheckley there, and other things which I relished at the time, like Leiber's "The Big Time". My ambition was to be published in *Galaxy*. I think I submitted some stories, but they all came back. When I wrote "Prima Belladonna" I knew that I couldn't adopt an American manner and tone of voice, and I didn't want to. I couldn't use an American location for Vermilion Sands, although nominally in some respects it is American . . . I was forced to invent a kind of international version of a decaying resort in the desert. Thank God I had to, because if I'd been able to use Palm Springs or wherever I would have slipped into a lot of clichés, all the conventional clichés of the American landscape. I had to invent my own landscape, and I invented something which was much truer to myself and also much closer to the surrealists (who were my main inspiration). In fact, I had to invent my own America.

I got married in 1955, I suppose. Time went by very rapidly, with the baby around . . . I worked in a couple of libraries for about six months – Richmond Borough Library, or Sheen Public Libraries, I can't really remember. But I spent a lot of time writing, and of course I had a young wife and child . . . The period of greatest financial stringency was after I got married, that *was* the difficult period.

After winning the annual short story competition at Cambridge in 1951 he wrote his first novel, a completely unreadable pastiche of *Finnegans Wake* and *The Adventures of Engelbrecht*. James Joyce still remains the wordmaster, but it wasn't until he turned to science fiction that he found a medium where he could exploit his imagination, being less concerned with the popular scientific approach than using it as a springboard into the surreal and fantastic.

Outwardly, at any rate, he lives quietly in Chiswick with his wife and baby son Jimmie. He admits that though she doesn't actually write his stories his wife has as much to do with their final production as he has himself. She hopes to have his novel *You and Me and the Continuum* finished by the end of this year.

. . . Of the genre in general he says "Writers who interest me are Poe, Wyndham Lewis and Bernard Wolfe, whose *Limbo 90* I think the most interesting science fiction novel so far published."[6]

I think I did write some pastiches of *The Adventures of Engelbrecht*, though I was gilding the lily a little to refer to it as my first novel. When you're 21 or 22 thirty consecutive pages feel like a novel! I'd accumulated a great mass of experimental prose, certainly heavily influenced by *Finnegans Wake* and *Engelbrecht*. Maurice Richardson's book was, I won't say a *big* influence on me, but I loved it. It's a marvellous book, with terrific panache and swing – very nicely illustrated in the published edition. Moorcock's a great admirer of it too, I'm glad to say. Richardson wrote a science fiction story in fact, which was published in *Horizon*, Connolly's magazine. A fine sf story. I met him for the one and only time about two weeks before he died, and I'm glad I did because I was able to tell him, for what it was worth, how much I admired his *Engelbrecht*, and that sf story he wrote in the 1940s (the only one, he said).

As for this *You and Me and the Continuum* – I did write a sort of experimental novel, nothing like the subsequent story of that name or any of the *Atrocity Exhibition* stories. At the time I wrote the story "You and Me and the Continuum", in 1965, I'd completely forgotten this – ten years in your 20s and early 30s is a long time – but the phrase must have stuck in my mind. That was a long time ago, I can't really remember. I suppose it was fiction of an impressionistic nature, no attempt at straightforward narrative or story-telling – a highly stylized mixture of dramatic dialogue, in some ways rather like a film script, with interludes of prose poetry, a very hot steaming confection with bits and pieces from all quarters. The sort of thing you produce if you're a great devotee of *Ulysses* or *Finnegans Wake* when young . . . Of course, Joyce was a totally different sort of writer. I think I simply hadn't found the narrative conventions which would carry my real interests, and when I stumbled on science fiction I realized "Ah! – this is the right vehicle for my imagination." Remember, in the early 1950s I was writing against a background of English and American fiction at the height of the naturalistic novel, in which I felt no sympathy whatsoever. I can't remember who the dominant English writers of the day were – most of them have vanished into oblivion. Not just the novel, but criticism and the English cinema – I had no interest in that whatever. I read on what I'd call the international menu, not the English menu.

I was as impressed by Wolfe's *Limbo 90* when I reread it a year or so ago as I was when I first read it in 1954 or 1955. It certainly was one of the books that encouraged me to write sf. Much as I admired Ray Bradbury – he was almost alone among sf writers of the day – I didn't feel that my own sf would follow in Bradbury's direction at all. It was tremendously encouraging to read *Limbo 90* and to see a powerful imagination given full rein. I was impressed by the power of the central imaginative idea, and Wolfe's lucid intelligence at work. It stands head and shoulders above anything else, in a similar vein, by any science fiction writers I've read. To some extent it reminds me of the huge disservice which American writers of the old *Analog* school, Campbell chief among them, have rendered to the cause of sf. They virtually seized a monopoly interest in a social and political sf, which they reduced to a series of comic strips. Wolfe's novel is a sophisticated, anti-utopian piece of fiction which stands comparison with anything written by mainstream writers of the mid-20th century. It may not be as great a book as *1984* or *Brave New World*, but it's certainly worth judging by the same yardstick.

I was about to start writing sf myself. *Limbo 90* was a great encouragement to me, because here was a writer who had the courage to follow his own imagination to the limit, without any concern for the commercial constraints and conventions that I felt severely handicapped the American and British writers of the early 1950s (they only went so far and then stopped). Wolfe's novel has a literary and imaginative dimension that's explored for its own sake. I was struck by the huge vitality of the thing, and by his central image – self-amputation as a metaphor for the castration complex, with the whole apparatus of neurotic aggression, wars themselves, struggles for power and so on, flowing from that. I think he brilliantly sustained the idea both on the imaginative level and on the conscious and intellectual level. That's something that's very rare in anti-utopian fiction, where you tend to get one or the other. I think the book was above the heads of most sf readers of the 1950s. It's a shame that it's out of print.

> Jim Ballard sent me a story, "Escapement", in the summer of 1956, when I was editing *New Worlds SF* and *Science Fantasy*, which I liked and offered to buy. He then followed it up with a personal visit to my office, bringing with him a fantasy story titled "Prima Belladonna", which I liked even better. The chemicals had begun to catalyze. In a very short time, stories were flowing steadily from the versatile mind of Jim Ballard . . .[7]

I remember submitting stories to Carnell's magazines only out of desperation. And of course he bought the very first one. I think "Prima Belladonna" was the first I wrote, although it may not have been the first I submitted. Whatever the case, it and "Escapement" went to him within weeks if not days . . . In fact, I'm certain it was "Prima Belladonna" because I remember getting a very, very encouraging letter from him, which he wouldn't have sent if it had been "Escapement" (that was rather a humdrum story). He wrote to me saying "Extraordinary story, with fascinating ideas – I'm going to publish it and will pay you £2 a thousand . . ." I was amazed. I was 25, married by then of course, and it was an extraordinary event. To have your first published work in a commercial magazine . . . I was overjoyed. I sent him the next story, which I'm almost certain was "Escapement", and he took that and I was well away. I never thought about submitting stories anywhere else for years, simply because Ted Carnell was sitting there. He never rejected a single story, ever. He must have taken 30 or 40 from me. In one or two cases he suggested alterations, that certain sections could be expanded, and I think I always took up his suggestions, expanded a particular scene or made something slightly clearer. But he never really wanted any rewriting. The only things he sometimes changed were the titles, but not too often. There was a little story called "Track 12" – that was his title, not mine. We had an argument over that, because he'd just taken "Manhole 69" without querying what *that* meant . . . I can't remember my original title in fact, but it contained the word "Atlantis", as the story is all about a drowning, and he said "we can't use this title that includes the word Atlantis because that suggests a different kind of story to our readers".

After I'd written about three or four stories he suggested "Why don't you come into the office – we can meet". I went along. He had offices somewhere near the agents A.P. Watt, just around the corner from the Strand. He had rather a big comfortable basement office, full of sf posters and artwork for the magazine. I liked him enormously. He struck me as a very likeable, sensitive and intelligent man, whose mind was above all the pettiness in the sf world. I think he recognized what I was on about from a very early stage and he encouraged me to go on writing in my own way.

In 1957 Ted said "I can get you a job on one of the journals upstairs". In fact it was round the corner at McLaren's offices where all these technical and trade journals were published. I jumped at it. I worked there for six months, and then somehow I heard that there was a vacancy as assistant editor on *Chemistry and Industry*, at a much better salary, and I went there. That was a very good choice – apart from anything else, because of all the scientific journals which came into the offices and I devoured. And the hours were pretty lax. I was even able to do a bit of writing in the office, which was a big help. *Chemistry and Industry* was published by the Society of Chemical Industry, in Belgrave Square. I was there for three or four years as assistant editor. I did practically everything. The editor was a chemist but he was not a journalist, and he knew nothing about magazine production. This was a weekly journal, of about 50 pages, including a mass of formulae and tabular material. It was quite an enterprise, and I enjoyed it. I did all the basic subbing, marking copy up for the typesetter, dealing with the printers, doing make-up and paste-up, dealing with the artists who drew the scientific formulae. I used to go on works visits, visits to laboratories and research institutes. I wrote a few articles – scientific reporting – and I reviewed scientific books. But most of it was straight production. I enjoyed being at the centre of a huge information flow. A leading scientific journal like *Chemistry and Industry* is on the mailing list of every conceivable scientific body in the world. I think one of the reasons my fiction of the early 60s has a high science content is because I was immersed in scientific papers of all kinds continually.

The exhibition "This is Tomorrow" was staged at the Whitechapel Art Gallery in 1956. The exhibition consisted of a dozen stands, on each of which a different team of architect/painter/ sculptor had collaborated. Richard Hamilton was teamed with

John McHale (now an associate of Buckminster Fuller) and John Voelker; together they produced an environment which has been called the first genuine work of Pop. It combined a large-scale use of popular imagery with an imaginative exploitation of perception techniques. Prominent were a 16-ft robot – with flashing eyes and teeth – making off with an unconscious starlet; a photo blow-up of Marilyn Monroe; a gigantic Guinness bottle. These large objects were placed at the rear of the exhibit . . . Another section of floor – part of a sci-fi capsule – was painted with flourescent red paint . . . In a tall chamber some of Marcel Duchamp's rotor-reliefs spun in a setting which was itself compounded of optical illusion. Smells drifted about the whole exhibit; several movies were projected at once while a jukebox played in front of a huge collage of film posters which curved round like a cinerama screen.

To a large extent this concept grew out of the activities of the ICA's Independent Group in which Hamilton had been a notable participant along with Eduardo Paolozzi, the architects Peter and Alison Smithson and the critics Peter Reyner Banham and Lawrence Alloway . . . [8]

I was always interested in the visual arts. I bought a lot of art magazines, and I used to go to all the new exhibitions on in London. I spent a lot of time haunting the National Gallery and the Tate Gallery – at times I used to go every day. I was interested in the old ICA. I wasn't a member, but I used to go to exhibitions there. That was a hothouse of ideas, and pop art was born there. Some people whom I subsequently got to know – Paolozzi, Reyner Banham, Hamilton and so on – formed the so-called Independent Group there. They were interested in a fresh look at the consumer goods and media landscape of the day, regarded it as a proper subject-matter for the painter. I felt that their approach had a certain kinship with that of science fiction (in which they were all extremely interested) and I went along to the "This is Tomorrow" exhibition at the Whitechapel Gallery in 1956. That was really the birth of pop art, the Americans hadn't started then. Richard Hamilton had on show his famous little painting, I can't remember the exact title – "What is it That Makes Today's Home So Exciting?" The first pop painting, though in fact it's a collage. And there were a lot of other pop artefacts there, which impressed me a great deal. It struck me that these were the sorts of concerns that the sf writer should be interested in. Science fiction should be concerned with the here and now, not with the far future but with the present, not with alien planets but with what was going on in the world in the mid-1950s. I still feel this, of course, but it was even truer then than it is now, because the world we live in now was being *born* in the postwar period. Then, if you looked at sf magazines, both British and American, they were almost entirely concerned with inter-galactic adventures which struck me as rather juvenile and irrel-evant to the lives that most people were leading.

What was so exciting about pop art was the response it elicited from the public. People were amazed by it. Here for the first time was an art actually about what it was like to buy a new refrigerator, what it was like to be in a modern kitchen, what modern fabrics and clothes and mass advertising were about, the whole world of the communications landscape, TV, radio and movies. I mean, the pop artists (and pop is an unfortunate term to describe them) were taking the world they lived in seriously, at its own terms. I thought the sf writer needed to do the same, to get away from interplan-etary travel and time-travel and telepathy and all this nonsense.

I first met Eduardo Paolozzi with Michael Moorcock, much later. When Mike took over *New Worlds*, after a year or two and with my encouragement he adopted a large format and he wanted articles on the visual arts. I knew that Paolozzi was interested in sf, and I suggested that we have an article on him. So I got his number from somebody, rang him up, and we went along to his studio. This was in something like 1966. We all got on famously together, and he became a contributor to *New Worlds*. I've known him very well in the years since, and through him I've met people like Hamilton and Reyner Banham.

By the late 1950s pop art was well on its way. I don't think it was a big influence on the fiction I was writing – if you read my early stories and novels there are very few traces, if any at all. (The dominant influence, if there *is* an influence from the visual arts, was that of the surrealists.) It wasn't really until I started writing the stories which made up *The Atrocity Exhibition* that I began to make direct references to the pop artists. What the pop artists did for me though was to encourage me in my determination to change things. This was more difficult to do than you might realize, because 1957 was the year of Sputnik 1, and this seemed to confirm all the age-old dreams of the old-guard sf writers, editors and readers. In the next two or three years there was Gagarin's first flight and the launch of the American space programme. But the pop artists and their interest in the present, all the excitements of the media landscape around us, helped convince me that the course I'd set myself was the right one – sf needed to be about the present day, so much more interesting than this invented realm millions of years in the future and on other planets . . . All that struck me as nothing to do with science fiction.

ZERO SYNTHESIS . . . COMA: THE MILLION YEAR GIRL . . . KLINE: RESCORING THE C.N.S. . . . MR F IS MR F . . . XERO: RUN HOT WITH A MILLION PROGRAMS . . . "I am 7000 years old" . . . T – 1: EMERGENCY MEGACHANNEL . . . THORACIC DROP . . . PROGRAMMING THE PSYCHO-DRILL: CODED SLEEP AND INTERTIME . . . AM: BEACH HAMLET . . . PM: IMAGO TAPES . . . THE EXISTENTIAL YES! . . . TIME ZONE . . . PRE-UTERINE CLAIMS: KLINE . . . THE A-GIRL: COMA . . . TIME PACK: MR F . . . COMA SLID OUT OF THE SOLAR RIG . . . T – 12 . . . TIME PROBE . . . VOLCANO JUNGLE: VISION OF A DYING STAR-MAN . . . "Coma," Kline murmured, "let's get out of time . . ."[9]

Martin Bax has that now. It was a sort of collage of things; a lot of them were clipped from journals like *Chemical Engineering News*, the American Chemical Society's journal – I used them a lot because I liked the typeface. I wanted to publish a novel that looked like that, you see – hundreds of pages of that sort of thing. Get away from text altogether – just headlines! I was very proud of those pages. Moorcock published them in *New Worlds* three or four years ago. They were like chromosomes in a way, because so many of the subsequent ideas and themes of mine appeared in those pages. Kline, Coma, Xero – they're all there. I don't know. I used to make these things up!

I wasn't satisfied just by writing sf stories, you see. My imagination was eager to expand in all directions. The sf magazines only allowed me a limited amount of scope. Ted Carnell was tremendously generous, but as soon as I started writing for the American magazines, which I began to do in about 1961, 1962, I started to get a lot of rejections. People like Cele Goldsmith and the man on *Fantasy and Science Fiction* accepted some of my stories and published them, but they rejected a lot too. It was obvious to me that the conventions of American sf were far tighter, far more prescriptive,

than anything Carnell laid down. He was remarkably flexible . . .
Some people think there always has been a new wave, there
always has been total freedom to write anything you like in sf.
What they don't realize is that this had to be *earned*, the breakthrough had to be made – and it didn't start in 1965.

In those days, when I started writing science fiction, I would like
to have written stories such as I wrote later in *The Atrocity Exhibition*
– not those stories in particular, but similar ones. I would like to
have written those *long* before they finally began to appear, but I
didn't have the freedom to do so. The kind of narrative breakthrough, or whatever you like to call it, that I launched myself on
in the *Atrocity Exhibition* stories from 1965 onward wasn't just a
sudden event, a blinding light on my own little road to Damascus.
I was interested in writing experimental fiction (though I hate the
phrase, in fact) when I was still at *school*. But one has to work
within the possibilities available. Ted was reluctant to publish
"The Terminal Beach". I think he only published it, to be honest,
because *The Drowned World* had just had a big success, and he
knew that I had put "The Terminal Beach" into a Gollancz collection, under that title. I remember him saying to me: "Oh, Gollancz
are publishing it, are they? Right, I'll do it." But up to that point I
had to work within the possibilities. If I'd had the freedom to do so
I'd have been publishing experimental sf long before the
mid-1960s.

But I think it was remarkable of Ted to publish "The Terminal
Beach" in what was, after all, a commercial magazine. I remember
sending that story to America. I think I sent it to *F & SF*, and
certainly to Cele Goldsmith, who turned it down. My then agents,
the Scott Meredith agency in New York, refused to handle the
story. It was one of the very few stories of mine that they actually
returned to me, saying there was no scope for it. Subsequently, of
course, they've sold that story umpteen times to American anthologies. Very funny!

The grand occasion in 1957 was the holding of the World
Science Fiction Convention in London – the first time this annual
event had been allowed to stray outside the North American
continent . . .

Was that nondescript year really 1957, and not 1947? The
convention was held in a terrible hotel in the Queensway dis-
trict. A distinctly post-war feeling lingered. Bomb damage was
still apparent . . .

I went to the bar and bought a drink. Standing next to me was a slim young man who told me that there were some extraordinary types at the convention, and that he was thinking of leaving pretty smartly. He introduced himself as J.G. Ballard.[10]

I didn't really have that much to do with Ted, on a personal level. I would talk to him on the phone and write him letters but I didn't go to his offices very often. For one thing I was very busy, and for another a lot of the British sf writers of the time used to hang around there and I didn't like them very much. I don't mean to be offensive personally – can't even remember their names – but to my young, arrogant mind they struck me as being hacks who were only interested in their two guineas a thousand, or whatever. They had no interest whatever in what they were writing, and regarded anybody who was trying to do anything different as just affected or wasting his time. I had brief discussions now and then with one or two of them, but I didn't have anything in common. I took sf seriously, I thought it had great possibilities . . .

I produced quite a lot of stuff in 1956, 1957, and then I went to the Science Fiction Convention in London. That shattered me, and then I dried up for about a year. For over a year I didn't write any sf at all. I was disillusioned and demoralized. I only went to the Convention for one day, actually, or maybe I went on a couple of days. But I won't repeat all that. Carnell was the only person in the sf world I ever met, because I never went to any meetings or anything like that. The fact that I was writing and being published in *New Worlds* and *Science Fantasy* from 1957 to 1963 didn't alter my life in any way. It was just something I did: I wrote a story, put it in the post, got a small cheque, and the story in due course was published. Then I wrote another. It wasn't really until 1963, after *The Drowned World*, that I began to meet people in the sf world – Moorcock, Brunner, Aldiss and various other people (though I'd met Aldiss at the Convention in 1957, and John Wyndham).

I've had problems since – not recently, but in subsequent years. I came across philistine attitudes in many of the American writers in the 1960s when I began to meet them. Certainly at a place like the big sf conference at Rio that I went to in 1969 (I met practically all the American writers there) I came across the same attitudes, though by and large they were far more talented writers than the ones Carnell had around him in the late 1950s.

We moved to Shepperton in 1960, and one drawback was the enormous journey, to and fro, from central London. It was difficult to help in bringing up a family of young children *and* to travel this distance to work *and* to secure enough time and energy for oneself to go on writing. Though I produced short stories at quite a steady rate, I think, in the late 1950s and early 1960s. By the time I was in my early 30s I was beginning to feel that I couldn't see any opportunity for a radical break – another ten years would go by and I'd still be churning out short stories. It was difficult to seize enough time to write, and I couldn't visualize myself being able to write a novel, given all this endless commuting. When I got home I had a tired young wife who wanted to go out for a drink, or round up a baby-sitter and see friends, or do whatever one did then. With three young children she was absolutely exhausted anyway, at the end of a long day. It was difficult to visualize actually writing . . . When I think of the leisure I have now: it's beyond my wildest dreams! I couldn't conceive of myself writing a serious novel, so I wrote *The Wind from Nowhere* very quickly in my fortnight's annual holiday, simply to make that break and become a professional writer.

Which I managed to do. And of course *The Wind from Nowhere* opened a few little doors. It led to my tie-in with Berkley Books and to short-story collections. It was a convenient arrangement because they published almost everything I'd written, volumes of stories which were then republished all over the world and gave me the income to make the final break. But they were hectic times. My stories were written in snatched minutes, snatched half hours here and there, scribbled on the backs of envelopes . . . I'm not, for God's sake, inviting pity, but it was all done in a kind of spur-of-the-moment, knocked-out-rapidly fashion. This continued to be true until quite recently. My youngest child is now 22, but it wasn't *that* long ago that I had three teenagers at home and domestic life going at full blast!

There can be no question now that J.G. Ballard has emerged as the greatest imaginative writer of his day. This latest collection of stories is profoundly stimulating and emotionally exciting. It shows us a writer whose intellectual control of his subject-matter is only matched by the literary giants of the past, and it shows us a writer who is developing so rapidly that almost every story he writes is better than the last. He is the first really important literary talent to come from the field of modern sf and it is to his credit that he is as popular with his magazine audience as he ever was. He has shown that sf need make no concessions to the commercial publisher's idea of what the public wants.

. . . Buy this one – as an investment if nothing else, for there will come a time when a Ballard first edition will be valuable.[11]

I have no feelings about first editions. I don't think there's anything magical about a first edition. Obviously, if you gave me a first edition of *The Ancient Mariner* I would look after it because it would have a sort of iconic value, but a first edition of *Our Lady of the Flowers* or *The Naked Lunch* would mean no more to me than a tenth edition. I was annoyed recently. Some of my own books are more valuable now than I realized. Somebody sent me a parcel of books, asking me if I'd sign them. There were a couple of the original Berkley paperbacks of *The Voices of Time* and *The Terminal Beach*. They were just paperbacks that retailed at 40 or 50 cents in the early 1960s. And *The Voices of Time* was marked at £6 and *The Terminal Beach* at £4! It put me in a terrible temper for the whole of the day! I thought this was outrageous. I got a 5% royalty on those, so if it was a 50 cent paperback I got the princely sum of 2½ cents – which in those days was probably about a penny. Now somebody is getting £6 from these things, and that's extraordinary. I suppose one ought to be grateful; in a way it's a reflection of the continuing interest that people have in the stuff . . .

There's an illustrated edition of *The Drowned World* coming out soon. It's being done by those Dragon's World or Dragon's Dream people, the company started by Roger Dean. Two artists were commissioned. One did a whole mass of wonderful huge paintings, six feet by five feet, illustrating *The Terminal Beach* stories. I thought they were superb paintings. The other artist did *The Drowned World*, and they appear to be publishing this illustrated large-format version any time now. I've seen most of the artwork, and it seemed to me rather good. I assume that if they do all right with that they'll then issue *The Terminal Beach*. Roger Dean, when he was all excited about it three or four years ago, had a group of artists who were eager to do everything – *Crash:* there was one man doing huge paintings of crashed cars . . . But commercial considerations tended to cool their ardour. Illustrated books are enormously expensive to produce.

My original idea for *The Atrocity Exhibition* was that I would do collage illustrations. I put that up to Cape. I originally wanted a large-format book, printed by photo-offset, in which I could prepare the artwork – a lot of collages, material taken from medical documents and medical photographs, crashing cars and all that sort of iconography. It wouldn't have been any more expensive for them to photograph the pages of collages than the pages of text. But to them illustrated books meant six pages of line drawings by some distinguished artist, Felix Topolski or somebody. So that fell through. I would still like to do it . . . Well, I don't know. My mind has moved on. Time goes by, one loses contact with one's previous incarnations, one's previous selves.

The pain in this book is overwhelming, the impact devastating . . . Like "The Terminal Beach" it is absolutely cold, contained, final and *sui generis*. In short, it is a masterpiece . . . It is impossible not to realize confronting it that one is in the presence of perhaps the major figure in western literature of our time.[12]

My wife died in 1964, so I was a single parent as well as a full-time author. If I had not been a full-time writer I couldn't have brought up my children. Somebody else would have had to do it for me, at least during the daylight hours. Conversely, if I'd had to go out to work I couldn't conceivably have written. If I had not been here with the children all day long I would not have been able to write. When I think of the *Atrocity Exhibition* stories, written between 1965 and 1970 – that's 16 years ago. Bea, my youngest daughter, who is 22 now, was six when I started writing them – so Fay was seven and Jim was nine. Children of that age, I drove them to and from school, I did everything. We had an integrated rich family life blazing away 24 hours a day!

I wrote *Crash* with three children running around. It *was* worrying. I wrote that between 1970 and 1972, when Bea was ten. And they were crossing the road about 20 times a day, on the way to wherever children go. I didn't want a knock on the door and see a bobby or a policewoman come to tell me some unpleasant news. That really would have been life's most bitter joke . . .

As recently as five or six years ago I had two teenage girls here doing 'A' levels, with all the fuss involved in exams and their school activities which I took part in. So most of my fiction has been produced out of the huge harum-scarum of domestic life! It's none the worse or better for that. But the domestic aspect of my life has been tremendously important.

My next book will be a short-story collection, *Myths of the Near Future*, which will contain two new novellas (nearly half the book is brand new), plus stories from the last three or four years which have appeared in *Ambit, Bananas* and *Time Out* – ten stories in all, and I think one of my best collections for a long time. I hope to write some more novellas, as I seem to have a lot of ideas in that sort of range.

I think a new science fiction magazine is needed now. There are very powerful political, economic and social currents flowing. You see them at work in this country – all these riots, the polarizing of political forces – and all over the world for that matter, between the haves and have-nots. All these topics such as how do you run a society where a large proportion of people will never work, these are the sorts of themes that classic sf treated. I think a new sf magazine would do a marvellous job, and have a market of concerned readers. If you read papers like *Time Out* or *The New Musical Express*, for example . . . A paper like *NME* is full of anguished concern with the great issues of the day – unemployment, science and technology, the nuclear arms race – a range of social and political issues moves through the pages. These are the sort of topics that sf writers should be working on. We now have all these political currents that are flowing ever more briskly, a clash of radically opposed ideologies. I don't just mean party political, but fundamentally opposed interest groups on the most basic of levels. I think this is an extremely interesting time. Western Europe – and Eastern Europe to some extent – is a huge cauldron that's coming up to the boil. (I don't think there's any politics at all in the United States. There's a scramble for power up the greasy pole, but there's no clash of political ideologies there.)

Overlaid on this are all the changes in advanced technologies, communications, the video revolution, which are going to change enormously the way people see everything. I think these are fascinating times, and just the times that demand a good sf magazine to comment on them.

Notes

1. Charles Kingsley, *Westward Ho!*, 1855 (final paragraph)
2. J.G. Ballard, *The Drought*, 1965 (Chapter 5)
3. J.G. Ballard, "The Coming of the Unconscious", *New Worlds* 164, July 1966

4. Profile accompanying "The Violent Noon", *Varsity*, 26th May 1951
5. J.G. Ballard, "Salvador Dali: The Innocent as Paranoid", *New Worlds* 187, February 1969
6. Profile in *New Worlds* 54, December 1956
7. from "Preface" by E.J. Carnell, *J.G. Ballard: A Bibliography*, compiled James Goddard, 1970
8. Christopher Finch, "A Fine/Pop Art Continuum", *New Worlds* 176, October 1967
9. Phrases from a collage, *New Worlds* 213, Summer 1978 (described in the editorial as "J.G. Ballard material originally done in 1958 and published here for the first time")
10. Brian Aldiss, *The Shape of Further Things*, 1970, (Ch. 11)
11. Michael Moorcock, reviewing *The Terminal Beach* in *New Worlds* 144, Sept./Oct. 1964
12. Barry Malzberg, reviewing *Love and Napalm: Export USA (The Atrocity Exhibition)* in *F & SF*, September 1976

5

A Citizen of Mondath

Ursula K. Le Guin

One evening when I was about twelve I was looking through the living-room bookshelves for something to read, and pulled out a little Modern Library book, in the old limp leather binding; it had a queer title, *A Dreamer's Tales*. I opened it, standing beside the battered green armchair by the lamp; the moment is perfectly vivid to me now. I read:

Toldees, Mondath, Arizim, these are the Inner Lands, the lands whose sentinels upon their borders do not behold the sea. Beyond them to the east there lies a desert, for ever untroubled by man: all yellow it is, and spotted with shadows of stones, and Death is in it, like a leopard lying in the sun. To the south they are bounded by magic, to the west by a mountain . . .

I don't entirely understand why Dunsany came to me as a revelation, why that moment was so decisive. I read a lot, and a lot of my reading was myth, legend, fairytale; first-rate versions, too, such as Padraic Colum, Asbjornsson, etc. I had also heard my father tell Indian legends aloud, just as he had heard them from informants, only translated into a rather slow, impressive English; and they were impressive and mysterious stories. What I hadn't realised, I guess, is that people were still making up myths. One made up stories oneself, of course; but here was a grown-up doing it, for grown-ups, without a single apology to common sense, without an explanation, just dropping us straight into the Inner Lands . . . Whatever the reason, the moment was decisive. I had discovered my native country.

The book belonged to my father, a scientist, and was a favourite of his; in fact he had a large appetite for fantasy. I have wondered if there isn't some real connection between a certain kind of scientific-mindedness (the explorative, synthesising kind) and

73

fantasy-mindedness. Perhaps "science fiction" really isn't such a bad name for our genre after all. Those who dislike fantasy are very often equally bored or repelled by science. They don't like either hobbits, or quasars; they don't feel at home with them; they don't want complexities, remoteness. If there is any such connection, I'll bet that it is basically an aesthetic one.

I wonder what would have happened if I had been born in 1939 instead of 1929, and had first read Tolkien in my teens, instead of in my twenties. That achievement might have overwhelmed me. I am glad I had some sense of my own direction before I read Tolkien. Dunsany's influence was wholly benign, and I never tried much to imitate him, in my prolific and derivative adolescent scribblings. I must have known already that this sort of thing is inimitable. He was not a model to me, but a liberator, a guide.

However, I was headed towards the Inner Lands before I ever heard of them. I still have my first completed short story, written at age nine. It is about a man persecuted by evil elves. People think he is mad, but the evil elves finally slither in through the keyhole, and get him. At ten or eleven I wrote my first science fiction story. It involved time travel and the origin of life on Earth, and was very breezy in style. I submitted it to *Amazing Stories*. There's another vivid memory, my brother Karl on the stairs, looking up at me on the landing and saying reluctantly, "I'm afraid this is your story come back." I don't remember being very downcast, rather flattered by a real rejection slip. I never submitted anything else to anybody till I was twenty-one, but I think that was less cowardice than wisdom.

We kids read science fiction, in the early 1940s: *Thrilling Wonder*, and *Astounding* in that giant format it had for a while, and so on. I liked "Lewis Padgett" best, and looked for his stories, but we looked for the trashiest magazines, mostly, because we *liked* trash. I recall one story that began, "In the beginning was the Bird." We really dug that bird. And the closing line from another (or the same?) – "Back to the saurian ooze from whence it sprung!" Karl made that into a useful chant: The saurian ooze from which it sprung/Unwept, unhonour'd, and unsung. – I wonder how many hack writers who think they are writing down to "naive kids" and "teenagers" realise the *kind* of pleasure they sometimes give their readers. If they did, they would sink back into the saurian ooze from whence they sprung.

I never read only science fiction, as some kids do. I read everything I could get my hands on, which was limitless; there was a house full of books, and a good public library. I got off science fiction some time in the late 1940s. It seemed to be all about hardware and soldiers. Besides, I was busy with Tolstoy and things. I did not read any science fiction at all for about fifteen years, just about that period which people now call The Golden Age of Science Fiction. I almost totally missed Heinlein, *et al*. If I glanced at a magazine, it still seemed to be all about starship captains in black with lean rugged faces and a lot of fancy artillery. Possibly I would never have gone back to reading science fiction, and thence to writing it, if it hadn't been for a friend of ours here in Portland in 1960 and 1961, who had a small collection and lent me whatever I glommed onto. One of the things he lent me was a copy of *Fantasy and Science Fiction* containing a story called "Alpha Ralpha Boulevard", by Cordwainer Smith.

I don't really remember what I thought when I read it; but what I think now I ought to have thought when I read it was, *My God! It can be done!*

After that I read a good deal of science fiction, looking for "that kind" of writing; and found some, here and there. Presently it seemed that since there was so little of it, why not do some myself?

No, that is not true. It is much more complicated, and boring.

To put it briefly, I had been writing all my life, and it was becoming a case of publish or perish. You cannot keep filling up the attic with mss. Art, like sex, cannot be carried on indefinitely solo; after all they have the same mutual enemy, sterility. I had had a number of poems published, and one short story, in little magazines; but this wasn't enough, considering that I had written five novels in the last ten years. I had either to take off, or give up.

One of the novels was set in contemporary San Francisco, but the others were set in an invented though non-fantastic central European country, as were the best short stories I had done. They were not science fiction, they were not fantasy, yet they were not realistic. Alfred Knopf said (in 1951) that he would have published the first of them, ten years ago, but he'd lose too much money on it now. Viking and other publishers merely remarked that "this material seems remote." It was remote. It was meant to be. Searching for a technique of distancing, I had come on this one. Unfortunately it was not a technique used by anybody else at the moment, it was not fashionable, it did not fit into any of the categories. You must either fit a category, or "have a name", to publish a book in America. As the only way I was ever going to achieve Namehood was *by* writing, I was reduced to fitting a category. Therefore my first efforts to write science fiction were motivated by a pretty distinct wish to get published: nothing higher or lower. The stories reflect this extrinsic motivation. They are kind of amiable but not very good, not serious, essentially slick. They were published by Cele Goldsmith Lalli, the kindly and courageous editor of *Amazing* and *Fantastic*, in the early 1960s.

The shift from the kind of writing I had done before to categorisable "fantasy" and "science fiction" was not a big one, but I had a good deal to learn all the same. Also I was pretty ignorant of science, and was just beginning to educate myself (a hopeless job, but one which I continue to enjoy immensely). At first I knew too little science to use it as the framework, as part of the essential theme, of a story, and so wrote fairytales decked out in space suits. If anything gives these merit, it would be my long apprenticeship in poetry and in the psychologically realistic kind of novel.

The first science fiction story I wrote that begins to break from the trivial became the source, and prologue, of the little novel *Rocannon's World*. I was beginning to get the feel of the medium. In the next books I kept on pushing at my own limitations and at the limits of science fiction. That is what the practise of an art is, you keep looking for the outside edge. When you find it you make a whole, solid, real, and beautiful thing; anything less is incomplete. These books were certainly incomplete, especially *City of Illusions*, which I should not have published as it stands. It has some good bits, but is only half thought out. I was getting vain and hasty.

That is a real danger, when you write science fiction. There is so little real criticism, that despite the very delightful and heartening feedback from and connection with the fans, the writer is almost her only critic. If she produces second-rate stuff, it will be bought just as fast, maybe faster sometimes, by the publishers, and the fans will buy it because it is science fiction. Only the writer's own conscience remains to insist that she try *not* to be second-rate. Nobody else seems much to care.

Of course this is basically true of the practise of all writing, and all art; but it is exaggerated in science fiction. And, equally of course, it is not true in the long run, of science fiction or any other form. But it is an awfully long run. One can trust in the verdict of posterity, but it's not a handy tool to apply in specific instances. What almost all of us need is some genuine, serious, literate criticism: some standards. I don't mean pedantry and fancy academic theorising. I mean just the kind of standards which any musician, for instance, has to meet. Whether she plays rock on the electric piccolo or Bach on the cello, she is listened to by informed, profoundly interested people, and if she's second-rate she will be told so; ditto if she's good. In science fiction, sometimes it seems that so long as it's science fiction at all, the fans will love it – briefly; therefore the publishers will put it in print – briefly; therefore the writers are likely to settle for doing much less than their best. The mediocre and the excellent are praised alike by aficionados, and ignored alike by outsiders. In such a situation it is simply amazing that writers like Philip K. Dick continue in excellence. It is not at all amazing, though very sad, that writers like Roger Zelazny may be forced into a long period of floundering and groping, after initial sureness. After all, writing is not only an originative act, it is a responsive one. The lack of genuine response, and therefore the lack of the sense of responsibility, is painfully clear in those writers who simply go on and on imitating themselves – or others.

I think the standards are rising, however. In fact I know they are, when I think back to the saurian ooze from whence we sprung.

Along in 1967–68 I finally got my pure fantasy vein separated off from my science fiction vein, by writing *A Wizard of Earthsea* and then *Left Hand of Darkness*, and the separation marked a very large advance in both skill and content. Since then I have gone on writing, as it were, with both the left and the right hands; and it has been a matter of keeping on pushing out towards the limits – my own, and those of the medium. Very much the largest push was made in my last (not yet published) novel, *The Dispossessed*. I hope rending sounds and cries of dismay are not heard when it comes out. Meanwhile, people keep predicting that I will bolt science fiction and fling myself madly into the Mainstream. I don't know why. The limits, and the great spaces of fantasy and science fiction are precisely what my imagination needs. Outer Space, and the Inner Lands, are still, and always will be, my country.

6

Backwards across the Frontier

Richard Cowper

The title I have chosen for this piece was not intended to be fanciful: I was searching for some phrase which would capture the "Who? Me?" sensation I experienced when Peter Nicholls suggested I might contribute to this series. I felt deeply flattered – who wouldn't? – but I was also conscious of the sort of misgivings familiar to a man who arrives at a party and finds he is wearing the wrong clothes. Let me try to explain what I mean.

All the science fiction novelists I have ever spoken to seem to have entered the field by way of the main gate; they cut their milk teeth, as it were, on *Astounding/Analog, Amazing, Fantastic* and *Fantasy and Science Fiction*. I crept in over the back fence using an 80,000 word novel called *Breakthrough* as my step ladder. At that time (1964) I had published three previous novels under the name "Colin Murry". The reason I chose a pseudonym for *Breakthrough* was, quite simply, that I desperately needed a change of luck. Various Freudian friends of mine have hinted that there were other, darker, psychological motives, but I still prefer my own explanation if only because it appeals to my superstitious nature.

For all those *Foundation* readers who have not read *Breakthrough* I should perhaps point out that its ostensible subject is ESP – a phenomenon which had fascinated me for many years before I got around to writing the novel. As a matter of fact I had already made fringe use of parapsychology in two of my previous "straight" novels. The difference between them and *Breakthrough* was purely one of emphasis. Even so I had considerable difficulty in getting the book accepted. My previous publishers rejected it out of hand on the grounds that they had no sf list, and when I tried the main British sf houses they shot the manuscript back at me with such alacrity that I doubt if it ever got beyond the office boy. Finally, after its fourth or fifth refusal, I handed the script to a friend of mine who was an ardent sf reader and asked his opinion. He read the book and told me he thought it was a good novel (which was heartening) but that it wasn't what *he* called sf (which was not). Nevertheless I parcelled it up and cast it once more upon the waters, depressingly aware that, at this rate, I would soon have run out of possible publishers.

But my friend's criticism bothered me and finally I sought him out and taxed him with the question: "How was it possible for *Breakthrough* to be (a) a good *novel* about ESP and (b) not a good *sf* novel?"

His reply completely floored me. "Your problem", he said, "is that your characters are too real. They dominate the ideas. Hell, I almost found myself *believing* in them!"

My reaction to hearing this is best summed up in the words of the Victorian "Punch" caption: *Collapse of Stout Party*. It was, I think, my first indication of how thin the ice was on which I had chosen to skate. What I appeared to have produced in *Breakthrough* was the sort of hybrid which would satisfy nobody. And yet it had satisfied *me* when I was writing it. There was no question but that I had willingly suspended my own disbelief. In that book I had been able to say things about the nature of the human psyche which I could have said in no other available literary form. But if I had not written an sf novel and I had not written a "straight" novel either, what, in God's name, *had* I written?

I was still trying to decide on the answer when I learnt that the book had at last been accepted – as sf. It appeared in print about a year later and such press notices as I saw treated it kindly. The publishers asked me for another and I offered them the one I have called *Phoenix*. That too got a friendly reception. I was even written to by a couple of people who had read the books and appeared to have enjoyed them. At first it felt rather odd being addressed as "Dear Mr. Cowper", but I got used to it. Yet, at the back of my mind lingered the uneasy suspicion that I was engaged in perpetrating some outrageous confidence trick and that one day I would be exposed for the fraud I was. Maybe this essay is just a way of crying out: "Believe me, I am innocent!"

There now follows a straight autobiographical section for which I feel bound to apologize because, although it has undoubted relevance to the question of why I came to be a writer of science fiction, it cannot, such is the nature of things, concern itself specifically with my first tottering footsteps in that exotic field. After all, "Richard Cowper" was "born" in 1964 – Colin Murry first saw the light of day in 1926, and it is way back in the early 1930s that the seeds of Cowper's science fiction were first sown.

Those seeds were, I'm almost certain, the stories of Hans Andersen and the tales, myths and legends collected by Andrew Lang into his multicoloured anthologies. As a child I devoured fairy stories voraciously, possibly as an avenue of escape from a rather Grimm family situation. Yet I was far from being a bookish child. If anything, quite the reverse. I was blessed (or cursed?) with an extraordinarily vivid visual imagination and had somehow acquired the ability to identify effortlessly with whatever caught my interest. I don't think I was ever *bored* in my life. I was forever pulling machines to pieces and putting them back together again – not always so successfully. Academically I was the archetypal drop-out. Hopeless at Maths; an imbecile at Latin; and, for the first fourteen years of my life, seemingly incapable of writing any sort of imaginative composition. Since my father had been a child prodigy, an Open Classical Scholar and heaven knows what else besides, there was probably a psychological block somewhere.

At about the age of ten I stumbled across the work of H.G. Wells, I gulped down the *Complete Short Stories* and thought *The Time Machine* and *The War of the Worlds* the most marvellous tales ever written. The same year I read James Jeans' *The Mysterious Universe* and built myself my first telescope and a crystal set. Another landmark was *The Modern Boy*. I can still recall a "Captain Justice" serial in which the members of a mysterious South American civilization were kept in a state of zombie-like subjection by means of some sort of radio-receiver(?) bracelet clamped around the biceps. Come to think of it, there must have been a good deal of quasi-sf in those boys' magazines between the wars. The *Wizard*, the *Hotspur*, the *Rover* and the *Adventure* were frequently trotting out something rich and strange to pep up their usual bland fare of public school, sport, and healthy high jinks on and above the Western Front. There was also a library of fourpenny paper-back novels – weren't they called *Tales of Science and Wonder?* – which purveyed a pretty hair-raising line in covers if little else.

However, at no time did science fiction dominate my reading. All was grist to my insatiable mill. As well as my never-forsaken H.G.W., I went through a Rider Haggard period; a Conan Doyle period; an M.R. James period (terrifying!); a Karel Čapek period

(why, oh why doesn't somebody reprint *The War With the Newts?*);
a Richard Jefferies period; a John Buchan period; a Sax Rohmer
period and several others. In between were always the legends
and the fairy tales to which I returned again and again. What I
demanded of a book was that I could lose myself in it – dive deep
and live it out in my own mind. Nowadays few things make me
more depressed than those people who affect to sneer at "escapism". I think I realized early on in life that the ability to "escape" is
but to exercise the divine faculty of the human imagination. A
great writer lends us his whole sensibility. The intensity of the
imaginative experience communicated is what counts. This, basically, is what distinguishes the first rate from the second rate – or
worse. The rest is peripheral.

I emerged into adolescence to find myself in a rather peculiar
psychological state. For one thing I had considerable difficulty in
distinguishing between what was real and what was unreal. Very
Berkeleian, to be sure, but also unsettling. Fortunately I had also
discovered that I could write. I wrote furiously; desperately: stories,
sketches, poems, plays, anything. I lived in a sort of hazy dream –
rather isolated but not unhappy. I also discovered Walter de la
Mare's poems. One in particular opened a door through which I
wandered. It was called *The Song of Shadows* and began:

Sweep thy faint strings, Musician,
  With thy long, lean hand;
Downward the starry tapers burn,
  Soft sinks the waning sand . . .

Some quality in those lines really haunted me and started me off
writing a series of fairy tales. Most of them were sad; a few wildly
funny. Tragedy and farce were the two poles between which my
creative compass needle lurched dizzily back and forth. When,
many years later, I told someone that I regarded my science fiction
as "fairy tales for adults" he accused me of denigrating the genre.
He could not have been more wrong. I was, indeed, awarding it
my ultimate accolade. By then I had discovered in sf the sole extant
literary form which would allow me the *total* imaginative freedom I
craved, without the inevitable limitation upon adult experience
which the fairy tale proper must of necessity impose.

Having reached this point I find myself in something of a
dilemma. Do I now skip forwards some twenty-odd years and

emerge fully-fledged in 1964 as "Richard Cowper", or do I try to show how he came into existence? Consoling myself with the reflection that the original title of this series was *The Development of a Science Fiction Writer*, I press on regardless.

I managed somehow to scrape through my senior grade exams, specializing in Art, History and Literature, left school and found myself in the lowest possible rank of the Fleet Air Arm. The war still had a year or so to run and I was dimly aware that I might be unlucky enough to get killed. I don't think the prospect worried me unduly. Anyway my spare time was fully occupied in writing and falling romantically in love with a married woman. Then, in 1946 I think it was, a magazine called *Lilliput* accepted one of my short stories. They actually *paid* me for it! Aha, says I to myself, Messrs. Greene and Waugh will be sleeping uneasy in their beds tonight: this, my friends, is *it*. However, the walls of literary London remained strangely impervious to my Lilliputian trumpet blast. During the next two years I sold perhaps half a dozen stories to little magazines and then, suddenly, the magazines weren't there any more. The party was over and with it my hopes of taking the literary world by storm. Talk about waking on the cold hillside!

A *deus ex machina* in the guise of the Welfare State now came to my rescue and informed me that, by reason of my skill in having avoided a hero's death, I had qualified for a financial grant if I should choose to go to a university. To be frank I didn't fancy it particularly but at least it seemed preferable to any alternative course of action I could think of. Consequently, in October 1948, I found myself at Oxford studying English Literature. The facility in stringing words together which I had by then acquired helped me to squeeze by, and I surfaced eventually with an honours degree and a lot more unpublished stories. That same year (1950) I married a girl who had been so improvident as to allow me to fall in love with her two years previously. She was now studying science at Leicester and thither I sped to join her, having, with commendable forethought, signed myself on in the Leicester University Education Dept. for a teacher's Diploma Course. Anything to postpone actually having to *earn* my own living.

Unlikely though it must seem, I was by now firmly convinced that I would be a professional writer one day. My conviction seemed to grow in direct counter-proportion to my literary success. Nothing seemed able to deter me though my constantly rejected stories came thumping on to the doormat with monotonous regularity. Eventually I read the message between the lines of the rejection slips: magazine editors, one and all, were moronic, purblind, deviant idiots. Obviously the time had come for me to write a novel. So I did just that. It was called *Before the Snows* and was prefaced by an enormously long quotation from *The Research Magnificent* by H.G. Wells. Its style was an undigested mixture of E.M. Forster, Aldous Huxley, dos Passos, H.E. Bates, various Russians, Flaubert, Maupassant and just about everyone else I had read. Here and there were a few fugitive fragments which seemed to have got in by mistake. These were my own. Its ostensible subject (surprise! surprise!) was a young man's falling in love with a married woman. It was pretty bloody awful, but at least it *was* a novel – all 75,000 words of it. Naturally I thought it was a masterpiece. I wrote it in six weeks.

When it had been typed out I sent it off to Messrs. Curtis Brown, having selected them as worthy recipients of my august patronage. That they did not immediately consign my novel to the incinerator now strikes me as wholly remarkable. In fact they even wrote to say that the considered it showed promise while, at the same time, hinting delicately at certain "flaws in the construction". I would, I am sure, have contested the point vigorously had I not by then been fighting desperately to hold down my first job as a teacher in a school in Brighton.

In the summer of 1952 I started work on another novel. It was better than the first but also a good deal longer. This meant that I couldn't finish it in one summer holiday. Although I did not realize it at the time, this break was to prove fatal. If I am anything at all I am an *organic* writer. I tell myself the story as I go along. I want to find out what happens next: what my characters are going to say. Each book is in the nature of an exploration, sometimes towards a selected point (which is why I am addicted to the "forward-flash" technique), sometimes away from one. The genesis of *Clone*, for instance, was this single gnomic paragraph scribbled on the back of an envelope – "The apple was good", said Norbert. "The apple was *very* good. But bananas are the best yet." I watched the novel grow towards that point of post-lapsarian revelation like a plant searching for the light.

Time to Recover – my second attempt at a novel – died from lack of nurture just when it was bursting into flower. So involved in the story had I become that I went on writing the book in my head while I was back teaching at school again. When I eventually came to take up the story where I had left off, the vital impulse had died. I knew what was going to happen and there was nothing left for me to discover. The sense of real *loss* I experienced might well have been comic if it hadn't been so painful. But at least it taught me a valuable lesson about the *kind* of writer I was. Since then (with one exception) I have finished the first draft of every book I have written in a single burst – usually within five or six weeks. The second draft (longhand like the first) may take anything up to two or three months. Such art as I can command goes into the first draft; the craft into the second. Shaping the first draft – assuming the writing has gone well – is rather like riding a surf-board just ahead of a breaking wave-crest, very much a matter of balance and instinct. My first drafts tend to sprout wild metaphors in pro-fusion. I let them come, knowing that on the second go through I can weed and prune to my heart's content. Probably I'm far too self-indulgent and don't cut severely enough, but I persuade myself that weeds are only flowers growing in the wrong place – a sure sign of fertility of some sort.

In 1954 I wrote my third novel, *The Golden Valley*. It was quite short, about 55,000 words, and highly laconic in style. I had at last discovered the value of short sentences. What's more I had dis-covered my own *voice*. It may hearten any aspiring novelist who happens to read this to learn that *The Golden Valley* had been turned down by no fewer than nineteen publishers before it was eventually accepted. It was published in 1958 and got the sort of rapturous press reception which might well have turned my head had it not been for all those previous rejections. Two particularly unpleasant traps await the novelist: overnight, best-seller success with a first book at the start of his career, and, at the other end, recognition too late in life to be meaningful. I suspect that the first has proved to be a kiss of death for a lot of promising young talents.

My publishers were naturally delighted with the reception given to *The Golden Valley* and urged me to write another like it. That's a great drawback in publishers, they tend to want you to go on writing the same book for ever and ever. Reviewers are almost worse. How often they appear to take a perverse delight in casti-gating an author for not having written a book like his last one, conveniently choosing to forget that when that one appeared they lamented that it wasn't like the one before – which, incidentally, they hadn't liked! Rare indeed is the critic who has sufficient sense of perspective to judge a book purely on its own merits. A writer *has* to experiment if he is to grow. His school is failure. What he reaches for must for ever remain fractionally beyond his grasp. Above all he has to believe in himself – in his own judgement. Ultimately, if he is any good at all, he will create the taste for his own work, but only if he has hacked out his own chosen path. This is not to disparage constructive criticism – would there were more of it! – but simply to reaffirm my belief that the only durable touchstone is a writer's own deepest conviction.

Then again there are those things called "rules". Frankly I don't set much store by them. A helpful publisher once showed me a reader's report on a novel of mine which he was in the process of rejecting. Among the reasons for turning it down was the contention that my book broke a "golden rule" of science fiction, which says that a story is not allowed to have two major catastrophes in one book. Now with all due respect this strikes me as nonsense. If need be a novel can have a dozen catastrophes *providing* they have all been sufficiently intensely imagined to convince the reader of their own inevitability. That, I submit, is the only acid test.

In the four frustrating years which elapsed between *The Golden Valley*'s writing and its eventual publication I wandered off and explored various other literary forms. One of these was a quasi-sf radio script called *One Man's Nightmare* about a chap who dreams prophetically that he sees a hydrogen bomb fall on London. It was rejected by the BBC on the grounds that it was too alarming. So I collected together a group of friends and we made a tape-recording of it ourselves. We then played it over to another group of friends and alarmed *them*. Quite pleased with the success of this venture I wrote a second script entitled *Room 2004* about what befalls a disparate group of people *after* they have been killed in a train crash. Quasi-sf again. This one was rejected by the BBC on the grounds that it would be expensive to produce. We went ahead and taped it anyway. By now I had become firmly convinced that I had what it took to write good radio scripts. To prove it to myself I wrote a quite simply non-sf radio play about a sad, middle-aged spinster. I called it *Taj-Mahal by Candlelight*. It was rejected without any reason being given. Ten years later, without a word having been altered, it was to win a prize in a BBC radio play competition and be broadcast. By then, understandably perhaps, I had lost interest in writing for radio.

By this point the perceptive reader (if he's still around) may have observed that though "Colin Murry" is shuffling sideways and backwards across the frontier into sf, "Richard Cowper" has still not been conceived, let alone born. But hang on. We're getting there.

Having failed signally in my attempt to rape the BBC I next wrote a couple of full length stage plays. One of these was called *Living by the State* and was set a hundred years into the future. It too was quasi-sf. Not knowing quite what to do with it I sent it off to Granada TV. They hummed and hawed and made encouraging noises before sending it back to me with various suggestions for improvement. I might well have been tempted to follow these up if *The Golden Valley* had not been published that year. Wisely, I think, I returned to novel writing.

During the next two years I wrote two more novels – *Recollections of a Ghost* and *A Path to the Sea*. They were well reviewed and sold badly. Both, to a minor degree, explored certain phenomena and attitudes of mind familiar to readers of science fiction but they were far from being sf novels. It was almost as if I were reacting to some inner need to stretch the fabric of the "straight" novel until it could accommodate what I felt I had to say about the nature of human existence. The fabric still held – but only just.

At no time did I ever lose contact with science fiction. I have just dug out a diary for 1960 in which I jotted down a list of some thirty odd books which had impressed me over the previous decade. Among them I find *Childhood's End*, *The Illustrated Man*, Anthony West's *On a Dark Night* (an astonishing *tour de force* of a "fringe" sf novel), *Tiger! Tiger!*, *A Case of Conscience*, *A Voyage to Arcturus*, *Earth Abides*, *Fahrenheit 451*, *The Lord of the Flies*, *The Chrysalids* and *More Than Human*. Had I made another such list in 1970 it is quite likely that several of those would have reappeared because I am addicted to re-reading. But alongside them would feature Arthur Koestler's great *Act of Creation* triology, Mumford on *Cities*, *A Canticle for Leibowitz*, Zelazny's *A Rose for Ecclesiastes* (now there's a man who ought to be paid a fat retainer on condition that he wrote no more than one book every three years!), *Future Shock*, Ballard's *The Drowned World*, William Golding's *The Inheritors* (a *perfect* book and the only sf novel I would love to have written myself), Rosalind Heywood's *The Sixth Sense* and Rattray Taylor's *The Doomsday Book*. The only thing these have in common is that they have all impressed me at one time or another and have, in their different ways, contributed their mite to shaping my own outlook.

Reading back through the list it does not strike me as being in the remotest sense *avant garde* and I daresay I could, if pressed, produce a parallel list which would appear to have no bearing whatsoever upon sf and yet which would contain books which have been equally influential upon my own writing. This one would carry a good deal of poetry, a fair amount of art and literary criticism, some history, archaeology and psychology, and – most recent discovery of all – a totally indescribable but wholly remarkable book by Robert Pirsig called: *Zen and the Art of Motorcycle Maintenance*.

1963 was for me one of those years which, at the time appear to be an unholy and chaotic mess but which, in retrospect, can be perceived as genuine watersheds. I spent most of the spring and summer possessed by a demon. The "art bug" which had been in the habit of biting me from time to time had given me a real working over. I got so badly infected that I didn't want to stop painting even though I had a novel to write. Finally I reached the beginning of September and there I struck a bargain with myself. I would shut myself up in my study for three days. If by the end of that time I wasn't *into* a book I'd call the whole thing off and go back to my paints. In fact the book took off like a rocket from the very first sentence. I all but disembowelled myself in 60,000 words. In three and half weeks the book was finished and so was I. I called it *Man Alive!* (subsequently altered to *Private View*) and waited for the publishers to beat a path to my door. All they beat was a very hasty retreat. I discovered at first hand what it feels like to be called "a purveyor of pornography". As a matter of fact the book came within a hairsbreadth of being accepted by Tom Maschler who had just taken over at Jonathan Cape, but the other directors took fright and rejected it *en masse* as being altogether too erotic for their chaste imprint. My heady visions of myself defending my book from the dock of the Old Bailey, reading out selected passages to the jury and watching them rolling around in paroxysms of mirth, evaporated overnight. Truth to tell I became somewhat melancholy. That book had meant more to me than I cared to admit. It was, indeed, somewhat ahead of its time. Ten short years ago – incredible though it seems today – the one thing a writer could not be about *sex*, in a novel, in England, was *funny*. After all, had we not recently been told in sober judicial tones at the *Lady Chatterley*

trial that sex, like Religion, was a Very Serious Matter? So I dried
my eyes, put *Private View* away in a drawer, and became "Richard
Cowper".

Between 1964 and 1969 I wrote the two more or less mainstream
sf novels, *Breakthrough* and *Phoenix*, and one off-beat quasi-sf story
called *Domino*. In 1967, acting on the sage advice of that supreme
iconoclast and literary lone wolf Edmund Cooper, I had sent the
first two books to the United States where, to my astonishment
and delight, they had been accepted by Ballantine. *Phoenix* was
even picked up for The American SF Book Club. For the first time
in my life I was actually making some real money (as opposed to
pocket money) out of my writing.

Then, at just the right moment, I came across an article in *The
Author* by John Brunner. It was called: "Dealing in Futures" and it
set out in clear, no-nonsense terms the basic economic facts of
science fiction writing in Britain. It was far and away the most
helpful article I had ever read in *The Author* and undoubtedly it
went a long way towards tipping the scale for me. Within a week
of reading it I had made up my mind to give free-lancing a go for
two years. This particular time span was chosen because my wife
and I worked out between us that, if she went back into teaching,
her salary – together with such money as we had managed to save
over the years – would just about keep us and our two daughters
afloat until the summer of 1972 even if the worst came to the worst
and I didn't manage to earn a penny from my pen. Ah, they don't
make wives like that any more!

That July we hauled up our metaphorical anchor and headed out
into the shark-infested seas. In the middle of September I began to
work on the novel I have called *Kuldesak*. I set it two thousand
years into the future and mainly underground. As I went along I
worked out in considerable detail the possible nature of a cultural
dead-end as well as the mores and vocabulary which might ac-
company it. I sometimes think that it is the only novel of mine
which "Colin Murry" was surprised to find that he had written.
The first draft was completed in six weeks and I went straight into
the re-write. A month after that had been completed I dived into
the first draft of *The Twilight of Briareus*. It took me two months and
by the time it was finished my nerves were vibrating like glass
springs. Surfacing from that book was like pulling the plug out of a
deep, deep bath. Of all my novels to date (*Private View* excepted)
Twilight is the one in which I was most deeply involved. What I

was saying in it could *only* have been said through the medium of science fiction. It is my stock answer to all those friends of mine who still persist in lamenting that I have given up writing "straight" fiction (I haven't, but that is beside the point).

I posted *Twilight* off to my agent, convinced that my gamble had paid off and that I could now safely look forward to extending my two years to three. A month later we set off for a long, well-earned holiday in France and Yugoslavia.

I arrived back in Wales to find a stack of mail awaiting me. Among it was a letter from my agent. She informed me, in worried tones, that *Twilight* had been rejected as unsuitable by the very publisher who, three months previously, had accepted *Kuldesak* with cries of joy.

The effect this rebuff had on me was to make me sit down and read the typescript of *Twilight* through again from beginning to end. Long before I had finished I knew that I was right and they were wrong. My conviction was absolute and unshakable. But what now? In an effort to collect my thoughts I set off for a long walk across the top of the cliffs. After a couple of miles I found I was laughing like a maniac – much to the indignation of the gulls. I had just realized that my grandiloquent gesture of chucking up a well-paid job and going freelance was virtually at an end. Either I locked myself in my study and wrote another *Kuldesak* and then another and another, or I had one final quixotic fling before calling it a day and renewing my subscription to *The Times Educational Supplement*. I chose what seemed to me the cleaner death. Next morning I opened a fresh notebook and wrote the opening sentence of *Clone*.

I started that book with no clearer idea in my head than to "send up" sf to the skies – or, perhaps it would be truer to say, to send up the kind of sf mind which could not accept *Twilight*. To relieve my frustration I had determined to push the medium to its absolute limit – and then give it one final shove right over the edge. But it didn't quite work out that way. What happened was that by the time I had written the first five hundred words I was completely hooked on Alvin and Norbert. I fell in love with them: it's really as simple as that. I suppose that if there is a sub-category of science fiction known as "inspired lunacy" that book must qualify for it. And some of the most lunatic episodes are those that are closest to life, which, no doubt, is why it has been classed as dystopic satire. Its literary progenitor was certainly *Candide*. I don't think I have ever enjoyed writing a book more. As I recall it I spent much of the time laughing out loud.

By the time *Clone* was finished I was quite certain that it was now a case of "Come in Richard Cowper, your time is up!" even though *Kuldesak* had by then been accepted for hardback publication in the States. I just could not believe that *Clone* would be wanted by anybody. In fact it turned out to be the book which put me on the map as a science fiction writer and has brought me more friendly letters than anything I've ever written. Which just goes to show. Just *what* it goes to show I'm far from certain.

Since *Clone* I have produced two other sf novels and an autobiographical account of my childhood. Checking back through the notebook in which I jot such things down I find I have brief outlines for at least four further science fiction novels and about a dozen sf stories of varying lengths. None of these theme-notes is longer than fifty words and many of them are records of dreams. The ideas for about three quarters of my fiction ("straight" and sf) have come to me in this way, and I know for a fact that I have lost at least one potential supernova of a book simply because I couldn't find a pencil in the bedside table and was too lazy to get out of bed and look for one. By the time I woke up again that dream was gone beyond recall. Too bad. It might have been another *Clone*.

Having just read through those notes for future work it occurs to me that, if there is one single theme, one subject, which intrigues me above all others it is *the nature of human perception*. I suspect that this preoccupation may well be a hangover from that period in my early adolescence during which apparently solid things had a way of seeming to melt beneath my touch – when I experienced what Wordsworth in a marvellously evocative phrase has called: "Fallings from us, vanishings . . ." In three of my science fiction novels (*Breakthrough, Twilight* and *Worlds Apart*) I set out to explore different aspects of the problem: "What *is* Reality?" and now, with the books written, I feel I am just as far from knowing the answer as I was when I started out. Nor is orthodox science much help. It has a way of drawing down the blinds just when I want them raised. It dismisses ESP on the grounds that it breaks the Inverse Square Law while, at the same time, it blithely accepts the "unthinkable" concepts of modern particle physics. What could be more wilfully perverse? I wish someone would have the courage to write up in letters of fire over the doors of every university in the world Keats' profound observation. "The only way of strengthening the intellect is to make up one's mind about nothing – to let the mind be a thoroughfare for all thoughts. Not a select party." Try telling that in Gath – or publishing it in the columns of *Nature*!

So on to Peter Nicholls' two final questions: *"Where do I feel myself to be right now?"* and *"Where do I think Science Fiction is at right now?"*

The answer to the first seems simple enough: I feel I have at last joined that small, fortunate minority who are able to do what they enjoy doing most *and* make a living of sorts out of it. Indeed, if Public Lending Right ever gets on to the Statute Book in this country, it might even be a reasonable living. For over twenty years I dreamed of being a full-time professional writer. By that I meant being able to earn a living by writing *only what I myself wanted to write*. By nature and upbringing I am a compromiser (it was a pre-requisite of survival where I came from) but over that one thing it seems that I am constitutionally incapable of compromising. Instinct says no. For fifteen years I was able to arrange my life in such a way that I wrote a novel or play at least every other year. I wrote fast – I always have – and was able to get a first draft done in the eight weeks of a summer holiday. Because I did not *have* to sell what I produced I was able to write to please myself. In the end I found I could write no other way. At times this has tended to make me the despair of agents and publishers, though nowadays, I must say, they seem more inclined to sigh philosophically and hope that, though this particular book isn't exactly what they had in mind, perhaps the next one will be. All I can tell them with confidence is that the next one, like the last, will be about human beings and their relationships – for the rest I just don't *know* – yet. However, I suspect that I may shortly be presenting them with a story set within the framework of some awful global catastrophe if only because, in common with that latter-day Ezekiel J.G. Ballard, I find I really do get a kick out of chronicling disaster.

Being a full-time professional in the field of science fiction has certainly alerted me to some very real dangers facing the writer. Unfortunately, awareness does not render one immune. The most obvious threat is the pressure to over-produce. However much creative energy he has a writer simply cannot go on and on turning out book after book without some loss of vitality and quality. To use a homely metaphor the cistern has to be given time to refill before the toilet will flush properly. In the last four years I have written six books, five of them science fiction novels. I *could* have written eight: I would *rather* have written four. Here again I find that having a different literary "persona" provides me with a useful bolt-hole. I am convinced that having spent the last year and a half working on something right outside science fiction I am now in better heart to return to the battlefield. Time alone will show whether I am kidding myself.

Concomitant with over-production is frustration with the genre itself. This is a tricky one but I suspect that a lot of other sf writers will know what I am getting at. In part it stems from the pressure upon the writer to go on repeating himself. Yet each time he does this he inevitably loses a tithe of his freshness of vision and with it a precious fragment of his *respect for himself as a writer*. I liken repetition to drinking hemlock by the teaspoonful. It brings a fatal relaxation of self-imposed critical standards and leads, ultimately, to paralysis of the imagination, for which there is no known cure. We can all name at least half a dozen excellent writers of science fiction who have either opted out of the field or have stopped writing altogether. I am sure their motives for doing so were mixed, but I would be prepared to bet that boredom and frustation were among them. I don't know the answer to this problem and even mentioning it here may seem like biting the hand that feeds me, but I would not like to pretend that I was unaware of it. I am inclined to believe that deepening despair over the general reading public's refusal to take any science fiction writer seriously *as a writer* so long as he works within the genre, may have some bearing on the matter. Jonathan Swift was luckier than he knew!

Last – and perhaps the most pernicious danger of them all – is isolation. A vision that sometimes comes to my mind when I think of the full-time professional writer of science fiction as a *species* of writer is an image of a little spider scuttling back and forth in some obscure corner, spinning endless webs out of its own guts. What nourishes it, I wonder? Are there not times when it pauses to ponder what it is all *for*? Enough! That way madness lies.

"Where do I think sf is at right now?" Publishing crises and the international economic situation apart I feel bound to say that from where I am sitting right now, it seems in a reasonably healthy situation. I should guess that the amount of first class science fiction being written, proportional to the dross, is about the same as first class "straight" fiction to "straight" dross. Anything else would surprise me because, as I have tried to explain in this ill-organized account of my own development, I refuse to recog-

nize a difference in *kind* between the two sorts. Of *emphasis*, yes, but that's only to be expected. After all, historical fiction, spy fiction, war fiction, children's fiction, are all leafy living branches of that gnarled old *genus* "the Novel". Nevertheless, I can't help regretting that Hugo Gernsback saw fit to erect a special artificial category called "Science Fiction" where none was called for. Wells, Stapledon, Čapek, Doyle, Huxley *et al* wrote imaginative fiction in which science played a predominant part. Those books were read by all who read novels. Nowadays one comes across far too many people who say smugly: "Oh, I *never* read science fiction." Well, that's not just their loss, it's ours too. It is a sad reflection on our culture that maybe the only way to undo the damage *is* through the literature departments of the universities, because in the last resort what matters is not what *kind* of fiction it is, but whether or not it is well written. This the literature faculties are (hopefully!) equipped to demonstrate. Anyway it is surely a healthy sign that the pressure is coming up from below. Sf is alive and well and living in the imaginations of the young.

As John Brunner aptly put it – we deal in futures. The "present" is an abstract philosophical concept. In a very real sense all novels which claim to be realistic or contemporary are doing no more than describing what is already past. Now whatever else the future may be it is sure to be uncomfortable for most people. Perhaps that is why there is, in some quarters, such staunch resistance to reading vivid imaginative projections of what lies ahead. Be that as it may, science fiction remains the only specifically *literary* form which tries to probe the future and lend imagination to those who have not got it. And, God knows, never was a loan more badly needed! The professional futurologists from Kahn downwards appal me because, one and all, they insist on dehumanizing humanity. We can at least do something to rectify *that*.

Earth Abides, A Canticle for Leibowitz, Brave New World, Fahrenheit 451, A Case of Conscience, The Inheritors, 1984: these are all fine novels deeply concerned with positive human values. Yet read Adrian Berry's *The Next 10,000 Years* which purports to be about the future of the human race and you will find that, for all its technological ingenuity, its human values are almost wholly negative. Berry sees the future simply in terms of the present – only more and bigger. Well, we all know plenty of sf novels which do just that too – the majority of them I'd say – but now and again one elbows itself above the ruck and protests passionately that there *must* be something better than ITT on a galactic scale, something that can feed that spiritual "hunger of the imagination which preys upon life". And, let's face it squarely, unless that hunger *is* satisfied, there may well be no future for the human race at all.

7

Where I get my Crazy Ideas

Norman Spinrad

Which, of course, is Idiot Question Numero Uno: "Hey, where do you get your crazy ideas?" Matched only, perhaps, by "What is your definition of science fiction?" Harlan Ellison has taken to answering "From an Idea Service in Schenectady, New York, dummy!" But people keep asking him for the address. When asked this question on a panel once, I held up the glass of beer before me and grinned moronically.

Nevertheless, this piece *will* be more or less of an attempt to answer this question seriously. After all, any series of "The Profession of Science Fiction" should make an attempt to say something about the wellspring mysterious core of any novel or story, to wit, the initial inspiration, for without it, the most skilled writer in the world will simply end up staring at a blank piece of paper for months on end, and any further discussion of "how to" will be moot indeed.

Now I'm not talking about hacko plot-by-the-numbers kits like plot skeletons or automatic writing tricks or there's this high-g planet with seventeen Earth-sized moons or hand-held plagiarism computers. I'm talking about the kind of "story idea" that causes you to rap out a short story obsessively or that can kick around in your head for years accumulating material around it before you even begin to spend half a year of your life in the universe of a novel. The real stuff, genuine creative inspiration.

How do you even know when you've got it? You can tell whether you did or not in hindsight, perusing the finished product, or observing the trail of paper leading to never completed works, and sometimes you can realize the awful halfway through and be faced with the moral question of art versus fulfilling that contract. But knowing which of your moment-to-moment obsessions

95

is the true heart of a story or novel – and indeed knowing whether its natural child is short story or novel – is maybe the highest and the deepest of the writing skills that can be taught or learned.

Failing to learn this is probably the cause of most writer's blocks, and regaining the clear vision of your own internal landscape is probably ultimately the only real cure for same. Imagination, synergetic thinking, sheer craziness, whatever the irreducible magic talent may be that allows a statistically tiny proportion of the gene pool to actually be able to write any kind of fiction at all, is a toss of the cosmic dice, not something that can be learned or taught. If you can or have been able to write fiction at all, however, all kinds of "story ideas" are going through your head all the time. When they are shit, and you know it, that's a writer's block. When you don't know it, you end up writing stuff that makes you and the critics wonder whether you may be blown out.

So first of all, you need a shit-detector. What is the difference between a viable idea and smoke-rings in the mind?

If you have to ask that question, you do not have a story idea. In essence, it's simple as that. If an idea doesn't grab you by the throat or start obsessing you for weeks, or roll around in your head for months gathering intellectual moss quite unlike a rolling stone, then you should wait for one that does. If you think you have to write it down so you won't forget it, then forget it.

The subconscious mind is a better processor of data into fiction than any notebook or cardfile or system you can concoct. If you wait for one of its creations to really grab you, you'll *know* when you've got an inspiration for something.

The zen of it is that the way to analyze the worth of your story ideas is to wait for a self-evidence grabber to swim by. You'll know it when you see it. If you don't, you haven't.

You are then, of course, sometimes left sitting there like a frog on your lily pad waiting for months for a succulent mental dragon-fly. But these uninspired periods can be part of their own solution, depending on what you do with the time.

Staring at a dry typewriter for weeks or months or centuries on end, will, of course, drive you crazy. Reaming out pages of desp-erate bibble for the pleasure of wadding them up and building a pile of rubbish on the floor is hardly any better.

One excellent solution to how to occupy yourself during the dry spells is to take vacations. Get out there in the world, travel, get loaded, have adventures, and forget about work until the spirit once more moves you. This is an appealing solution if you are independently wealthy, or believe starvation is good for the soul. That is, unless, the good times come to be seen as the blocked times.

Many of us, however, do not have this option. The rent must be paid, the belly must be fed, and to do this, one must make money. Distasteful but true. We have three options. We can go out and get a job. While my experience with this phenomenon is mercifully limited, it has not led me to believe that a nine-to-fiver is what a writer needs to get the creative juices flowing. Or we can grit our teeth and write formula potboilers out of whatever we can and feed the body at the expense of the soul.

Or write non-fiction.

What a weird term "non-fiction" is, upon reflection! It must have been invented by a fiction writer, because what it means is anything there is to write except this magic fabulation of new realities and actual people out of the thin air of our minds that we call fiction. As if fiction is the lion's share of the craft and art of all possible writings, and everything else is simply non-it.

Perhaps in certain sense this is true. Fiction may be seen as the pinnacle of the writing profession in that it demands access to levels of the spirit by the conscious mind which are *not* necessary to the writing of that other stuff, and in that it creates its own subject matter out of the void. Whereas "non-fiction" is a step further down the ladder of absolute creation since it is always about something and does not create either people or events, a brand new synthetic reality.

Which is why there is so much more of it, and why it is so much easier to write than fiction. The fiction writer must seine his own mind for inspiration, a zen act that cannot be reduced entirely to conscious volitional control. But if you can write fiction, if you have the necessary command of description and language to write short stories, then writing non-fiction is merely a matter of scanning your environment for targets of opportunity. The material of fiction must come from your own head, but the material of non-fiction surrounds you.

Journalism in its most extended sense is the craft of reporting events in the external environment, pondering them aloud, and ideally reaching some philosophic position. In the practical world of publishing, this can mean anything from scientific treatises to jack-off material for low porn magazines, from criticism to sports

writing, from political commentary to gourmandizing, endless
possibilities to write about stuff you don't have to make up and
earn some money doing it.

I've been writing non-fiction intermittently for about as long as
I've been writing novels. I've been a film critic, a book reviewer,
and a science writer. I've done political columns in a men's magazine and the Underground Press. I've interviewed Buckminster
Fuller and done a piece about Chinese food. Whatever. At times I
did it strictly for the money, at times I wasn't hardly getting any
money and did it for kicks or free movies. At times I've written
pieces because there were real things I wanted to talk about
directly, and at times I just felt like being funny.

I guess I started writing non-fiction originally because I wasn't
making enough money out of writing short stories or even my
early novels, and it seemed like a quicker and more enjoyable way
of solving economic crises than getting a job. And it always has
seemed so much easier to write non-fiction on demand. If someone
gave me an assignment to take his story idea and turn it into
fiction, no way. But if someone points me to a subject and says
maybe you'd find that interesting and I do, I have no trouble in
writing about it.

In those days, when science fiction stories were selling for 3c a
word on the average and $1500 was a respectable advance for a
book, journalism was economically attractive because even the
lowest men's magazines paid more than the science fiction mags,
and a sale of an article to a top market could net you more than a
whole book.

Now, of course, the situation is reversed, and there's no way I
could make a living as a journalist doing it full-time one step ahead
of the bill collector, and for the time I spend I can certainly make
much more money writing fiction. Nevertheless, I continue to
dabble in journalism in its varied forms, though there is no longer
an economic necessity.

Because, over the past few years, I've come to realize that fiction
arises not from more fiction, but from all that stuff that is non.
Garbage in, garbage out. Nothing in, ultimately nothing out,
sooner or later. You can't keep writing fiction that lives if you're
not interested in anything else. What's more, sometimes it can be
very rewarding to have your attention focused on something
which you might not have thought you were interested in.

Examples of fiction that had its origins in something that journal-

ism of one sort or another got me into are endless and recompli-
cated. A book review I was assigned, Wilhelm Reich's *The
Psychopathology of Fascism*, came my way about the time I was
writing *The Iron Dream*, and was certainly a significant influence.
Film criticism got me into the process of movie-making as well as
the milieu of the record industry through connection with rock
critics, and a few years later, out comes *Passing Through The Flame*.
A four-hour interview with Buckminster Fuller triggered all sorts
of things that emerged in all sorts of places later. The Fuller
interview led me into writing on scientific subjects which led to the
metapolitics of energy which when combined with a piece I did on
the L-5 proposal and a few other things germinated in the forthcoming *Songs From The Stars*. Some reviews I once did of some
feminist books combined with the usual personal travails led to a
piece in a men's magazine called "The Masculine Mystique" which
led to another piece on the subject of sex and gender for a woman's
magazine and later it all surfaced in *A World Between*.

In terms of your fiction, what is valuable about doing journalism
is not so much what you write as what writing it gets you into.
And what it gets you out of, namely your own head.

Writing is a solitary and solipsistic occupation anyway. You sit
there alone your whole working day communing with the brilliance of your own prose. Fiction writing is even more solipsistic;
there you are in a universe of your own creation playing god to
your creatures. *Science* fiction writing is perhaps the purest form of
solipsism – it doesn't have to have any connection with outside
reality at all.

If you spend all your working hours either creating your own
fictional realities or trying to, you can get pretty weird. If all your
intellectual input is science fiction, if your only mental stretching
exercise is creating it, and if god forbid you don't even read much
of anything else, sooner or later, your fiction will cease relating to
anything but itself, and you'll find yourself either running dry or
crazy.

Worse still, writers tend to rub minds mostly with other writers
and with editors, since those are the only people they tend to have
working relations with. Science fiction writers have a whole world
of fandom they can submerge themselves in during their non-
working hours as well.

I have found that my intermittent non-fiction keeps me in the
habit of being a student of sticking my nose into sometimes

unlikely intellectual crannies sniffing for something that might be worth reporting. I guess I started doing it for money, and now I do it for fun. Although ultimately I know on another level that I can justify my dilettantish pursuits on the basis of supplying the richest possible data-flow for the magic subconscious computer that germinates my fiction.

But the zen of it is, for me anyway, that I can't generate fiction ideas through organized research, the very thought of which fills me with schooltime memories of the horrors of homework. While I consider my fiction the main line of my concern, I never do any research for it beyond what is necessary to avoid factual or descriptive goofs. But that subconscious computer draws on all the stuff I've crammed into it in the pursuit of *other* goals and synthesizes it, transmutes it, and generates fictional creation from it.

And that's where I think I get my crazy ideas.

Of course if you don't believe me, you could always ask Harlan for that address in Schenectady . . .

8

By Chance out of Conviction

D.G. Compton

It would be nice to be able to say that the writing of sf was my profession. Sadly it wouldn't be quite true. Vocation, yes – profession, no. For I'm one of those timorous creatures, a spare-time writer. Most writers are these days, of course, usually as a matter of simply economic necessity. But in my case there's a second controlling factor: sheer lack of ideas.

Already, in my spare time, I put together two books a year, only one of which, if I'm lucky, will be sf. If I'm lucky enough, that is, to have come up with a usable idea in that particular twelvemonth. It's clear, therefore, that I wouldn't be able to increase my sf output, no matter what. Hence the vocation rather than the profession.

Only one idea per year may sound like a pretty poor showing. And so it is. Most self-respecting writers – especially the short story people who flaunt their fertility with almost indecent confidence – can hardly wait to be done with one idea before another is clamouring for their attention. Or that's how it seems to me. And I envy them. For the fact has to be faced that (as a writer at least) I'm as near barren as dammit.

By way of some small mitigation though, it might be wise to explain what I mean by an "idea". Certainly I demand an awful lot of one. Principally I ask that as a result of it the book should more or less write itself. Everything should slip into place: the basic sfish notion; its usefulness as a symbol of something bigger; the interesting story to go with it; the interesting people to inhabit that story; and, most important of all, the significance of whatever theme the idea suggests as something I genuinely want to write about, something about which I believe I have things genuinely worth saying. And all this in at the most two or three blinding flashes . . .

So perhaps it's not surprising that it doesn't happen all that often. In fact, that it happens at all is a flaming miracle.

I'm not suggesting, please, that other writers finally demand less of their ideas. But they're willing, and able, to niggle away at them, turning them over, trying them this way and that, pushing them into shape. Whereas I need to have all that done for me. Or done, presumably, *by* me, but on some subconscious and blessedly undemanding level.

Mind you, it took me a long time to suspect even the existence of this other level. All my life, ever since some repellant poem about snowdrops when I was nine, greatly admired by my doting grandmother, I had known that I would be a writer. School magazines, with their easy acclaim, reinforced that ambition. As did the orgasmic delirium of actually having a play one had written produced as part of the end-of-term show. Self-criticism might never have been invented. Fame, to coin a phrase, was the spur.

A writer, then – no doubt of that. But a writer of what? Well, plays, of course – partly on account of that end-of-term show, partly on account of an actress mother, partly because poems about snowdrops had been discovered to be distinctly un-chic, but mostly for the obvious reason that plays were shorter than books, and therefore easier to write. I was an idle little turd, even then.

Admittedly a novel did get started during National Service, but it never progressed beyond the statutory first three chapters. As I recall, it was all about a conscientious objector with what I now look back on as a most unnatural affection for his cat. A conscientious objector on account of my detestation of what National Service was doing to me, and a cat on account of my backwardness at that time with women. The novel faded out when I was transferred to a psychiatric hospital on Southampton Waters, where the possibility of making a radio-controlled model boat as part of my Occupational Therapy seemed far more attractive.

I was still a playwright, though. And to prove it I composed a send-up of Dick Barton to be broadcast over the hospital tannoy. As if Dick Barton could be sent up any further than he was already. The play was never broadcast, I'm glad to say, but we had a lot of presumably therapeutic fun rehearsing it.

After National Service the real world suddenly loomed. University had already been ruled out – if I was to be a playwright, so my reasoning went, then the sooner I got down to the actual business of writing plays the better. My mother however (being a proper cow) had little confidence in my ability to earn my living as a playwright. With the most cursory of nods in the direction of my ultimate ambition, she shanghied me into a job as Assistant Stage Manager in a provincial rep. Friends in high places, e.g. Leatherhead, helped.

So I went to Leatherhead. And I loved it: the pose of it all, the smell of size and grease-paint familiar from my childhood, the world-within-a-world, the glory, the whole fantasy-feeding she-bang. Plus the fact that I was after all preparing myself in the best way possible for future playwright-hood. I even began to see plays in a new way, from the point of view of the stage staff. I decided that scene one of my next play would end with ten bottles of beer being opened on stage, the entire cast then having to hurry off for a complete costume change before scene two. Assistant Stage Managers were thirsty folk.

The mechanisms of plays, therefore: none of the matter. I don't remember thinking that they needed any.

My theatre career was short, however, for I soon fell insanely in love with the wife of the stage director, and she with me. Exit one ASM, hurriedly. And, such was the nature of our shared insanity, the maturing of a small insurance policy at the time of my twenty-first birthday convinced us both that now was the moment for me to fulfill all my delayed playwriting ambitions.

In retrospect once again, I imagine that the real attraction of that scheme was the romantic cottage in a Cornish fishing village (courtesy of the previously mentioned doting grandmother) that naturally came with it.

Cornwall was nice. My wife, though, quickly not quite so much so. And the children, one of hers and very shortly one of ours, cried all the time and were perfectly horrible. (I was horrible myself, too.) But worst of all was the lovely attic, with a view of the harbour, in which I was to do my writing.

Up there I was daily brought face to face – I did go up daily, for the first few months – with the realisation that there was more to writing plays than putting nice words on a page, or even arranging for beer bottles to be opened at opportune moments. There was also more to it than neatly turned plots. I was quite good at neatly turned plots – but there was still all that space between the exposition and the denouement to be filled in somehow. In short, one had to have something to write *about*. And further, one had to have something one *wanted* to write about.

I was twenty-one. I had precious little of the first, and none whatsoever of the second.

So I packed it in. My first truly wise act in twenty-one years.

Ten years later, when I returned to writing, I was more or less in the same condition. But at least by then I had written two radio plays and one short story, and sold all three. And anyway, life at that time was so utterly bloody that a return to writing could hardly make things worse.

We'd lasted eighteen months in Cornwall, first on my insurance policy, then on making lampshades and raffia bags to sell to the holiday-makers – those were the days before tourists had been invented. And our family was on the brink of being increased to three. It's sad the way people still breed, even when they don't really like each other. *Don't like each other* . . . hardly a sufficient description of the mutual hacking that went on between my poor wife and me. Still, it was, in the long term, educational.

We went to London. I got an office job, and we lived on a houseboat. Next boat but three lived a playwright called John Osborne, whom I didn't resent because he was both unsuccessful and even poorer than we. I'm glad to say he moved away before the opening night of *Look Back In Anger*, otherwise I might have crept out at dead of night and vengefully scuppered his mouldering hulk under him.

I worked in the bedding department of Heals furniture store, where I learned that the best mattresses were filled with the curled manes of white Argentinian horses, and that eiderdown came from the arctic nests of the eider duck, one small handful per nest. She'd tweaked every wisp from her own bosom, poor thing, so it was hardly surprising there wasn't more. I learned also that Dodie Smith, of *Dear Octopus* fame, had worked at Heals before me, so I was in good company.

Later I managed a small furniture factory making hi-fi cabinets in Mortlake – by which I mean assembled the cabinets, polished them, delivered them, and dealt with the subsequent complaints. In short, I *was* the factory.

And so on. Jobs, nervous breakdowns, moves, more jobs . . . Until finally we landed up in Devon, pregnant again, and working as a door-to-door salesman. It was a confused time, and I wasn't always sure which of us was which. Except that it was then that the worm, of which we were the opposing ends, turned.

Clearly I was unfitted to the world of commerce. Equally clearly she was unfitted to be the wife of someone working in a world to which *he* was unfitted. Ergo, change the world. False reasoning, of course, but that's life all over.

So we sold our cottage, rented another, and I set up as a playwright on the balance. At last, a playwright. Again, a playwright? Full circle – even to the cottage which, if not in a romantic Cornish fishing village, was in the next best thing, a romantic Devon muddy field? No, I really do believe there was a difference. I was a hundred years older.

Not that the difference, as far as my writing was concerned, was immediately apparent. Though I did in truth have a few more things to write about, and wanted to write about them, nobody seemed in the least inclined to pay out good money for the results. The radio plays – radio now because I had become more realistic about my chances of a West End stage production – flowed abstrusely from my pen, dropped into the deep dark well of the BBC, and were spat out again at painfully long intervals. Once I was summoned to London – Peter Sellers might be interested in one of my scripts – they'd be in touch. We lived on that hope, dogging the postman, for nearly a year.

Funds ran out. National Assistance supervened, and occasional work on Bideford quay. Perhaps I wasn't, after all, destined to be a playwright. Perhaps I wasn't destined to be a writer, of whatever sort.

I turned to crime. The old joke is that it doesn't pay. Well, it didn't – or at least, only a hundred pounds a book – but even that was better than the poke in the eye with a wet stick that I'd got so used to. And those books did show me that the greater length need be no serious deterrent. One simply began at the beginning and after a while one reached the end. Still, crime novels (those neatly turned out plots again, but with the space between exposion and denouement now quite decently filled) seemed hardly a fulfilment of my writerly destiny, and anyway, at a hundred pounds a time the wolf was still unpleasantly audible on the doorstep.

It was then that German radio discovered me. And my backlog of BBC rejects. And suddenly I ate. We all ate. Not lavishly, but well enough for my crime novel publisher and me to part, with no great expressions of regret on either side. I even sold a couple of TV plays – they were never transmitted, of course, but they were comfortingly paid for.

This, then, was the moment, with things suddenly trickling my way, when I had an idea for a book. Within my own rather special terms of reference, a genuine idea. I'd had ideas of radio plays, admittedly, but little ones, radio play-sized ones. This latest idea was book-sized. It wasn't crime. It wasn't anything. It was just that miraculous thing, an idea: characters, story, theme, the whole glorious kit of parts.

My wife said it was horrible, so I wrote it down. No – that's cheap. Mostly I respected her literary judgement. But I'd have written down this particular idea, whatever she'd said. It interested me. I believed in it.

Which is how, at long last and over my wife's protesting body (if you see what I mean) I became an sf writer.

I called the book *The Quality of Mercy*, and sent it off to Hodder and Stoughton. They accepted it. They even paid me two hundred and fifty pounds for it. And they asked me if I'd mind if they marketed it as sf. I told them I wouldn't – for two hundred and fifty pounds they could market it as fish and chips if they felt so inclined . . . Not that I'd any clear idea what sf was. There were gaudy magazines, weren't there, with rockets and girls in brass bras in their covers. But there was H.G. Wells also, who was really quite respectable. And anyway, my book had an identity of its own, quite apart from either, so I certainly wasn't going to get hung up over a label.

Around that time, also, a worrying thing happened: my supply of radio play-sized ideas dried up. I had a job by then as a part-time postman (4.30 to 9 in the morning) and another as a bank guard two days a week but even these two together hardly produced a living wage. So Hodders' two-fifty soon went, and I was broke again.

Hodder were most understanding. They offered to pay me thirty pounds a month for three years, by way of advance royalties, in exchange for three more sf novels. Was I interested? I did a quick sum. Thirty pounds a month represented three hundred and sixty pounds a year – and all for just one book. I was interested. And besides, I had to do something with my time, now that I was no longer writing all those radio plays.

The only trouble was, my current idea for a book was all about man's need for a rigid framework, all about the stringent circumstances under which I judged him to be happiest. Now, I had no notion that Utopias were part of sf's common currency. But I *did* know that sf was often concerned with outer space. So I placed my ideal society on Mars. Nothing to it. I was in business again: characters, story, theme, the whole glorious kit of parts.

Two more sf novels followed. It seemed, in fact, that my subconscious idea machine had only to be pointed in the right direction, the my-impression-of-sf direction, and out popped the right sort of thing – though strictly on a one a year basis. Plus, as it happened, one totally non-sf idea that refused to be ignored, and produced *The Palace*, which Hodder published more or less as an act of loyalty. So that, what with this and the fact that they had taken me on as a reader as well by now, I was kept fairly busy.

Three years, three sf books, and then my contract ran out. But I wasn't worried. I was well into yet another sf novel, and surely Hodder would be interested. It turned out that they would – none of the last three had earned its three-sixty advance, so by rights I owed them another for nothing. They got it. It broke my bank, but I saw their point.

It didn't, actually, break my bank quite as much as it might have done, for a year or so earlier I'd written a short story, and Terry Carr had picked it up for Ace in America, and had written asking me if I'd done any books. So I met Don Wollheim in London, and handed him a sizable bundle. All of which Ace put out at suitable intervals. Three thousand dollars each. I bought myself a car.

It was 1968, and my marriage of inconvenience had just passed its seventeenth birthday. Enough of a bad thing by any standards, so we quit.

Predictably, though, with two homes to maintain now, the post office job, the bank guard job and my writing were no longer sufficient. I'm sorry to go on about money so, but life's like that. Well, my life was. Still, miracles do happen and, with the help of a recommendation from Hodder, the *Reader's Digest* offered me an editorial position. Not that I knew anything about the *Reader's Digest* – I'd led a very sheltered life. But I knew nothing about sf either, and that hadn't deterred me. So I returned to London, took up my duties in the Condensed Books department of *RD*, found myself the most marvellous wife any man could wish for, and kept up with my writing at weekends. I enjoyed London. I enjoyed my work at *RD*. I enjoyed my wife. I enjoyed my writing. The sun shone.

Except that in England Hodder were growing tired of losing money on me, while in America Don Wollheim had left Ace and set up his own firm, and taken me with him, and then also grown tired of the loss I represented. "You may not sell many books," he told me, "but the very best people will go to your funeral." I bet that's what he told all his authors. But it was a poor consolation when he subsequently rejected two of my books in a row.

By then in England too my writing was having a bad time. I'd been lucky enough to interest John Bush of Gollancz in *The Continuous Katherine Mortenhoe*, but my next two (Don's two) had found no favour with him at all. In the face of such informed and unanimous dismissal my own belief that I was writing as well as ever, if not better, was clearly a delusion. Eight years of writing sf, eight books, and no progress. Scarcely any of these books, in fact, had even earned its advance. A blank wall, therefore. I was forty-five years old. I was happily married. I could live on my *Digest* salary. Time to call it a day. Everybody knew prophets weren't honoured in their own lands. Nor in other people's lands either, if my experience was anything to go by.

Not that I was a prophet. I wrote about today, only very thinly disguised as tomorrow.

Be that as it may, obviously I was wasting both my own time and other people's. So I moved out. But I was still temperamentally a writer, and hopeful, and greedy, so I turned to something else: romantic historical novels. About today again, I suppose, only very thinly disguised as yesterday.

Four years passed. Time for a keen young German agent to take me on, and succeed with my back list, thus reinforcing my gratitude to the German-speaking peoples, already profound from the radio play years. Time also for a small digression . . .

There is, in Southern California, a dedicated sf fan, and equally dedicated sf bibliographer, called Robert Reginald. Back in 1968 he had written to me, requesting information for his current bibliography. I wrote back. It emerged that he admired my work. The correspondence flourished, and has done ever since. For many years, in fact, Rob has been my best – if, admittedly, for most of that time my only – American friend.

Recently (which brings me to the point of this digression) he has entered the field of specialist sf publishing with his own imprint, Borgo Press. And a couple of years ago he approached me in my retirement: putting his loyalty to the ultimate test, he would himself publish one of those books of mine that nobody else would touch. Greater love hath no man.

My tale is nearly told. Picture, if you will, the mildly successful

Condensed Books editor, the mildly successful romantic historical novelist, gazing gratefully at his Borgo Press contract and wistfully wishing that the rest of the publishing world were so kind. Take that same middle-aged gent down to Milford-on-Sea as the flattered guest of an sf writers' workshop there. Introduce him further at a boozy party to the dazzling Judy Blish and engage the two of them in conversation on the hackneyed subject of literary agents. "They aren't necessary," says he. "If a book is good, it sells. If it isn't, it doesn't." "Balls," says Judy Blish. "Oh, but surely –" says he. "Do you mind if I give your address to a friend of mine?" says she, whipping out an empty fag packet to write on.

The party ends, the gent thinks little more of it. Ladies like Judy Blish are dear kind souls. But the backs of empty fag packets are the most forgettable things in the world.

I did Judy scant justice, of course. She remembered her empty fag packet. And she also managed to decipher what she'd written on it. The result of which is that I now have the indomitable Virginia Kidd of that other Milford far across the sea as my American agent, who has recommended me to A.P. Watt in England, and I am, incredibly, back in business as an sf writer.

It's early days, of course. But nice things are already happening. First of all, Virginia's enthusiasm so fired me that I wrote an sf short story, closely followed by a whole new novel, and she sold them both. And the remaining hitherto unloved one. And reprints of others. While in England the new book, aided by A.P. Watt, has got me very happily back on the Gollancz list . . . Which seems to prove that I was totally wrong: it's the agent who has to be good, not the books. Or perhaps, ideally, a bit of both.

There's even a film on the way, with my beloved Katherine Mortenhoe played by my equally beloved Romy Schneider.

So there it is. I always wanted to be a writer and now, fingers crossed, I am one. I only work part-time at the *Reader's Digest*. And I plan to go on writing two books a year for as long as anybody will buy them: one romantic historical because it's fun, and one sf because it's both fun and a way of exploring the truth – about people, and about science's part in shaping them.

If I've stuck with what folk have been kind enough to call sf ("kind enough" because the label makes possible a large and informed readership for stuff that otherwise would probably sink without trace) it's principally because I'm afraid of admitting to commitment, a person who welcomes sf's distancing mechanisms.

After all, it's far safer to dare to care about one's characters when the world one places them in isn't quite "real".

Admittedly the future worlds I choose are always closely tied to my own muddled understanding of the present world about me. But that's because in general terms I don't much like it, and developing it a few years on is as good as way as any of finding out why. And perhaps even seeing how it may be changed.

9

The Writer as Nomad

Pamela Sargent

Not long ago, I was asked to write an introduction to a second collection of my short fiction. Unable to think of anything to say about the stories themselves, I ended up writing about how, for years, even after the publication of a few stories, I couldn't really acknowledge that I was a writer at all. Left unwritten was the explanation of *why* I felt that way. Like the well-bred hostess of a dinner party, I did not want to invite readers to meet my guests, the stories, while bombarding them with too much unsuitable talk. I joked a little, made a few darker remarks, and left a lot of things unsaid.

I did not, in the beginning, choose writing as a profession. Writing was, for me, something I had to do to survive – not economically, but psychologically. Writing was a compulsion, a way to make sense, metaphorically, of various events, to find a purpose in my life, and even, at times, to escape it. One might say that the stories were game to be hunted and tracked, brought down, and then eaten. Publication, like the mounted heads on a hunter's walls, was merely a by-product of the pursuit, one that was not really essential; the act of writing and the mental nourishment gained from that act seemed far more important. Writing was a way of living.

I was, in fact, a kind of nomad, keeping my distance from communities where everything is fixed and settled. There's something to be said for being physically nomadic. I felt most free when everything I owned could fit into a couple of suitcases and a small trunk; this meant I had less to lose, and could always escape. But what I want to consider here is the psychological nomad, which is what many writers are and what science fiction and fantasy writers in particular may be.

At our best, we're trying to seek out new trails and find new game; we see more familiar literary hunting grounds as overhunted.

111

We learn the skills we need from other hunters who keep nearer to their home ground, then move toward unknown lands and hope that some of our tribe will follow. We want a different kind of nourishment, and may also be trying to escape the tribal customs that constrict the movements of many of us.

During my teens, when some of my contemporaries were wrestling with such problems as grades, high school cliques, dates, or preparing for the PSATs, I was delivered into the hands of an institution in the hope that it might keep me from destroying myself. By then, I had two suicide attempts and various other attempts at escape to my credit; my family no longer knew what to do with me.

During the months I was in this place, which was supposedly designed to help me, I learned how to appease one of my keepers with cigarettes, money, and some personal possessions so that she would not report my transgressions to her superiors. I learned how to tell those in authority what they wanted to hear and how to conceal the truth; I have distrusted such people ever since. I endured the assaults of one man, and didn't report them, although that wasn't out of any misplaced concern for him. Either I wouldn't have been believed, and would have had the additional problem of reprisals on his part, or I *would* have been believed, in which case I would be blamed for allowing the assaults to happen and would only lose what little freedom I had.

This sage advice on how to deal with my problem was offered by my friend Gwen, a ghetto kid who knew her way around such institutions and considered this place a paradise compared to the one she had been in earlier. She also gave me a few pointers on how to defend myself in fights, tips that did come in handy.

Some of my other friends were Lydia, whose parents had decided that she needed to be whipped into shape when they discovered she was a lesbian; Raul, an angry young man who had suffered abuse as a child and whom I planned to marry if we could get away and manage to lie about our ages; and Bob, a boy who had occasional blackouts after which he couldn't recall what he had done, but who struck me as one of the gentlest people I had known. My ability to predict a friend's actions was obviously impaired; little more than a year later, Bob was in prison doing time for a murder he couldn't remember having committed.

None of us had any ambitions for the future other than getting out, and couldn't really imagine what would happen to us after that. Bob had a fantasy of running away and finding a house where we could all hide out, but those plans never came to fruition; it was easier to dream about it. Our favorite recreational activity was washing down some of the tranquillizers and psycho-tropic drugs used to keep us malleable with large swigs of whiskey a bribed adult would smuggle onto the grounds. This wasn't hard to do; we pretended to swallow our drugs, spat them out, and saved them for later. We could escape for a little while by blotting out all thought.

The solace of writing, of struggling to recast some of my experi-ences into fictional form in order to make sense of them, or to create the refuge of an entirely imaginary world, was taken away from me. I had to learn how to face reality, my keepers reasoned; therefore, my writing, in which the imagined could take on a kind of reality, had to be discouraged. Clearly, it hadn't helped me before (so they believed), and wasn't likely to aid my adjustment now; I dimly felt that writing was considered somehow dangerous.

I did, however, find a tool to help me in my mental wandering. Someone had left an old, beat-up paperback lying around, a copy of Alfred Bester's *The Stars My Destination*. This story of the tor-mented Gully Foyle, who was able to "jaunt", or teleport, himself from one place to another, immediately spoke to me.

That paperback became one of my treasures; I kept it with me most of the time so that it wouldn't be stolen. I was well aware that I couldn't teleport myself out of the institution, but did begin to imagine a future self, the adult Pamela Sargent who had finally escaped. I visited this self in my mind and saw myself looking back, free at last, safely distant and able to look back with some objectivity. Whenever I was enduring a painful or humiliating experience, or a dark, despairing mood, I tried to jaunt or migrate mentally past that time.

I also told myself that, some day, I would draw on what had happened to me in my writing, find a way to make order and sense of it, find a purpose in what would otherwise be only meaningless, brutal, or random acts. I would gain some freedom inside myself, if nowhere else. It didn't occur to me then that my situation, in an exaggerated way, reflected some experiences common to other girls and women.

I have to consider myself lucky in the end. I returned to a school where a few fine teachers encouraged my intellectual ability, which must have seemed latent at best. I won a scholarship to college and, later, became reconciled with those who I thought had abandoned me earlier.

But for a long time, I was also careful not to get too close to anyone. Close relationships, I believed, would almost inevitably lead to either betrayal or violent confrontations; they meant giving someone else power over oneself. Under the guise of friendship, love, or concern, others could inflict a great number of wounds. I was scarred enough; I was going to travel light.

I continued to write from time to time; the solitude of writing was appealing. But for the most part, I hunted alone, and kept my distance from the rest of the tribe.

Often, I threw away my stories after they were written. Part of this was a natural fear of criticism, or insecurity about having the stories read and judged by others. But I also feared revealing too much of myself to anyone else; the most meaningful stories were the ones I kept hidden.

I ate my game by myself, and didn't think of sharing it with anyone else. Writing was my private act of rebellion, and I had seen what could happen when you rebelled too openly; writing was my refuge, one I might lose if it were revealed. Maybe I should have learned, through my experience with *The Stars My Destination* earlier, that writing could also be a lifeline to others.

During my senior year in college, I managed, to my surprise, to sell a story. This was unintentional; I'd been encouraged to submit it by two aspiring writers I knew, but had not expected that it would be bought. There was some satisfaction in actually getting a check for this small act of rebellion, but also a fear that future game might now evade me.

I reached a compromise, one that would allow me to keep writing while protecting my refuge. I wrote, but did not concern myself with what happened to the stories after they were published; I shared some of my game, but didn't want to hear other people's opinions of it. I put published stories on my shelves, but did not think of myself as a "real" writer.

I kept to my own trails. I stayed away from writers' workshops and other such gatherings, regarding them much the way a hunter would view chattering companions; they might frighten away whatever I was tracking. Gradually, I came to see that a good editor might lead me to a trail or hunting ground I otherwise wouldn't have explored; other writers could suggest new methods for trapping or bringing down my game. Writing remained a solitary pursuit, but there could be companionship after the hunt.

Writing became a way of communicating with others. Given the masks I had learned to hide behind much of the time, it was virtually the only way I had of doing so.

I was extremely fortunate to be doing my early writing at a time when the women's movement was growing, although I didn't see that in the beginning. The early complaints of feminists seemed strange to me at first. Didn't they understand that some things couldn't be changed, and that all we could do was to survive or escape in whatever small ways were open to us? The prospect of exposing oneself in sessions of consciousness-raising seemed re-pellent and threatening; the notion that others might once again tell me what I should think and feel was disturbing. I had found a way to shield myself and did not want to lose it.

It was the writing of feminists that brought about my change of heart and made me see that I did indeed have a bond with other women. In their work and their lives, I came to see, there were other choices besides either surrendering or retreating. I had believed that I had escaped; in fact, I had only imprisoned myself.

Other women were hunting; some of them were following the trails of science fiction and fantasy. The best fantastic literature and the most profound feminism have this in common: they are sub-versive, continually challenging the accepted wisdom of the tribe while seeking change and a new way of understanding and viewing the world. They question, and probe, asking why things are as they are and looking for ways in which they might be different.

I had dreamed of a future self able to look back at the past with some understanding. In a sense, science fiction involves a search for other future selves, imagined people who will look back on our present and near-future as their past, perhaps seeing what we cannot and showing us that there are paths out of the prisons our age has built for us all.

Women writers of science fiction and fantasy encouraged me, by their example, to range farther afield. Some of them were explor-ing territory other writers had avoided. Their stories and novels raised questions, illuminated some darker corners, expressed a rage I had felt but had learned to suppress, pointed the way to new possibilities, or entertained while poking fun at some of our tribal ways. The game they had successfully hunted nourished me.

I began to assemble some of these stories in the hope of putting together an anthology. If writing can be seen as hunting, then editing a collection of stories might be seen as gathering (or, perhaps uncharitably, as scavenging). These stories had fed me, and now I wanted to share them with others.

For a while, however, as I went from one publishing house to another with my proposal, I felt that no one wanted to accept this book. Some editors responded out of ignorance; could there actually be enough science fiction stories by women to fill a book? Others were skeptical or hostile, no doubt trying to protect the tribe from contamination. Still others thought it was a fine idea, but did not want to be the first to accept the morsels I offered.

My anthology, *Women of Wonder*, eventually did see print, along with two successive collections of science fiction by women, and now the trails those writers made have become clearly defined paths. I had done no more than gather the food to which those writers had guided me, and lead others to their tracks; but working on those books gave me more faith in my own writing. I like to think of *Women of Wonder* as a book that the frightened teenager clutching her copy of *The Stars My Destination* would have enjoyed reading.

It may be that a lot of my own writing, in some way, is for that girl as well. Much of my work, and not just the books ostensibly published for young adults, is filled with people in their teens, many of whom are outsiders or outcasts from their tribes, who often *want* to be like everyone else and feel that their inability to fit in is a defect. In *Watchstar*, my protagonist, Daiya, is a girl preparing for her ''ordeal'', the rite of passage all young people in her telepathic village must endure, in which they are cut off from their community entirely and must confront their fears – fears that are given form and substance by the mental powers these people possess. In this society, people must conform, since even their thoughts can harm someone else. Daiya, with her questions and doubts, cannot fit in, and fails her ordeal; she becomes an outcast, yet cannot give up the ties she feels with her people.

My characters often wander quite a bit. In *Earthseed*, my first novel for young adults, my teenaged characters roam inside a hollowed-out asteroid that is itself a ship wandering through space, looking for a planet where the young people can settle. The cybernetic mind of this ship is the only parent they have ever known, and the only source of information about an Earth they've never seen. But much has been withheld from the ship's mind; gradually, the young people discover that a lot of what they've been told is either misleading or a lie. They are forced to confront their own weaknesses and to overcome them before they can leave their ship.

In my novel *The Shore of Women*, I chose to write about a world where women live in vast, walled cities, while men roam the wilderness outside and follow the life of hunters and gatherers. A nuclear war is in these people's past, and women are determined that men will never again acquire the means to wage such a war; women control all technology and teach the men to worship them as divine beings. My central characters are Birana, a young woman unjustly expelled from her city, and Arvil, a young man and a hunter who helps her to survive. The two begin to seek a refuge where they can be safe, but also have to overcome their most deeply felt beliefs in order to reach out to each other. This story, however, is not theirs alone, but also that of Laissa, a young woman who begins to question her city's ways. Laissa's wandering is through historical records and archives, while the chronicle she eventually writes becomes a blow levelled at her society's assumptions.

No doubt my own experience is reflected in these tales, as well as in others. Yet these apparently recurring themes are not something I care to speculate about too much for fear of scaring off whatever stories my mind might be tracking now. I would not want to limit myself to only certain trails.

All of us who write are nomads and hunters, at least for a while. There are, however, traps for us as well.

We might find a well-travelled trail and decide to keep to it, instead of looking for new grounds. Some of us are tempted to settle near a likely grazing ground and to hunt the same herd over and over, preferring the safety of the familiar to the risks of new territory. Some of us domesticate our game, or stay in one place, tilling the soil and harvesting the same plants until the ground we work can yield no more. A lot of us see that even if we pursue the hunt, it's less frightening to join a band or tribe led by one explorer, and to share his game instead of seeking our own.

Too many of us fall into such traps, and there are plenty of people preparing them for us – readers who want us to stay in familiar lands without finding anything new there; editors who want to appease both their tribal chieftains and the rest of the tribe; critics who believe we belong in a particular territory and nowhere else; and writers who cling to the security of being among a like-minded clan or group instead of realizing that companionship can come only after a hunt that must be made alone. This desire for security and the settled life seems contrary to what working in science fiction and fantasy can offer us – new ideas, a different and illuminating perspective, a means to depict imaginatively the changes that may alter what we are or underline the truths about our nature, a method of heightening the familiar and making it seem very strange indeed.

Even when a writer explores new territory, without familiar trails, there are other risks. You might expend more energy in the hunt than the game can possibly yield. You may find nothing you can use. You may bring back your capture and see the tribe refuse it. If you write for a living, as I do, you learn that you have to roam over a greater area in order to avoid the traps, and cannot afford the luxury of pursuing only one kind of prey. You learn when to wait, when to strike, when to abandon one story when a more likely prospect suddenly presents itself, and how to find your way back to the story you had to leave. Small wonder that so many writers, after taking the trouble of laying down a path to new lands, decide they'd rather keep to it instead of moving on.

The need for hunting and gathering is an integral part of us; that is the life we led for most of our history. It's a life that, barring any future catastrophe, we are unlikely to regain. But we can hunt and gather among the arts, sciences, history, and human minds our society has formed.

Science fiction and fantasy at their best recognize this need, giving us a way to wander to new lands and then to return and share what we have found before we have to go hunting once more. At their worst, they provide a bare subsistence, hunt the same herds until they are decimated, or offer the tribe a drug to keep it tranquil. Such writing dulls the tribe, leaving it without nourishment, illumination, or hope – much like the earlier version of myself I mentioned before, the one for whom I try to write now.

Writing the kind of work many choose to label as science fiction or fantasy has given me the chance to roam and to find mental sustenance. Publishing it has enabled me to share what I've found with others. This is territory I may leave at some point – labels are another way of fencing ourselves in – but one that remains so vast that I'm likely to return to it.

Lately, I have been on the trail of those fascinating nomads, the Mongols, who, in their search for unity and order among themselves, safety from enemies, and more food and pasture land, ended up conquering most of the known world; this search is yielding some game in the form of a novel. I can't say where my writing will lead me in the future, only that I have to follow wherever the tracks I find lead me.

10

Thank you for the Music

Michael Coney

"There is nothing quite so terrifying," my mother once said to me, "as a mad sheep."

This was probably the most influential remark she made during my childhood. It gave me a healthy respect for the unknown, a glimpse into the strange private world of the insane, a dislike of paradoxes, a distaste for mutton, and the beginnings of cynicism. But above all it introduced me to the wonders of language. My mother's precise wording still left room for my personal ultimate fear: a nest of lobsters in my bed. A mad sheep was the worst, with a unique terror all of its own, and for years I gave those woolly, deceptive horrors a wide berth; but lobsters were *almost* as bad.

My mother was an extremely clever and able woman and my late father was no slouch either. It is due to their influence, genetic and otherwise, that I can do the things I do, including writing. But I have not been kind to them. As a child I saw them through perceptive and critical eyes, so I saw the worst. As an adult I wrote about them in a thinly-disguised autobiographical novel called *Hello Summer, Goodbye*. This is what I wrote about my mother.

My mother is short and I am tall for my age, so that it is impossible for us to keep in step as we walk. She trots along beside me, legs going like pistons, and insists that she puts her arm through mine, so the pair of us reel along the street like drunks. Added to which she talks incessantly, looking up at me all the time and smiling fondly, and generally giving the impression that a very peculiar relationship obtains between us. I find myself praying that people think she is an old prostitute I have picked up; and to emphasize this effect I try to assume a shamefaced look – which is not difficult, under the circumstances.

And about my father, with whom I'd had many a bitter quarrel during that period when I was challenging him for leadership of the herd:

Father's intelligence was waning, he was older and set in his ways, he was used to leaning on the dignity of his position; in short, he had lost the power of reasoned argument.

Ten years have passed since *Hello Summer, Goodbye* and it is time to look at the other side of the coin. These two bright and complex people gave me their genes and their ideas, which is a far more important contribution than any learning and travelling I have done since. I am them, and my stories are their doing, and my interests spring from their influence; and if I sometimes opposed this influence instead of accepting it – well, that must be credited to them too, because they taught me to make up my own mind, to resist pressure, and to fight. And even though I didn't believe all their pronouncements, they had the knack of opening interesting avenues of thought.

"French Canadians, as everyone knows," said my mother one day, "are very unreliable people." A bigot would have nodded assent to such a remark, and a knee-jerk liberal would have turned blue with rage. But to me the truth or otherwise of such a remark was immaterial. It was the possibilities that mattered. I like to think that my interest in anthropology and genetics was born from such speculation, and has flowered in practically every story I've written.

And once again, her wording was elegant and persuasive, much more so than my father's somewhat crude "All Welshmen are bloody thieves." All credit to my father, though, for being the more expert at developing his theme, as when he followed this remark with, "All Cornish are bloody thieves too. They come of the same stock." My mother was Cornish, incidentally.

The French Canadian in question was living with a close relative of ours. He got her with child and then left her, demonstrating the depth of my mother's insight. My mother wrote to me, cataloguing the misfortunes of this relative, whose baby was sick, who was having problems at work, who was heavily into debt and God knows what else. "And to cap it all," wrote my mother, "her horse died of a heart attack while undergoing castration." My wife read the letter and wept with laughter, which reassured me that there was nothing wrong with my own sense of humour. It was simply that my mother's rare talents needed harnessing and directing. I wrote about my wife in *Hello Summer, Goodbye* too, and I was very nice about her.

Although, speaking of castration, her insistence on having our tomcat neutered bothered me. "He'll be a much happier cat," was her reasoning. Freed, presumably, from those nightmare visions of lust which plague the rest of us men.

My mother is a talented artist as well as an undiscovered writer, and actually sells her work. My father, on the other hand, was a craftsman. He'd played representative rugby and water-polo, and had trophies for swimming and boxing. He devoured knowledge voraciously, and in his spare time he built model sailboats and aircraft, steam-powered miniature warships, and a magnificent series of miniature steam locomotives. The last of these was the finest: a Royal Scot built from his own drawings, from his own wheel and cylinder castings and endless brass parts which he'd turned on his lathe. I used to drive it up and down the track at Cadbury's in Bourneville, pulling up to twenty people on trucks. I've loved trains ever since.

There was a time in those ancient days of steam when we were all train spotters. We cycled to lonely spots and watched the trains go by, all day, never tiring of the sport, speculating in the way boys do, philosophizing, or just sitting alone awaiting the beauty of the next locomotive. We loved them all: the hurrying Scots, the stately Kings, the knightly, old-fashioned Bulldogs, even the effete Gresley Pacifics. Best of all we loved the Duchesses with their lines of brutal power, their vast boilers and muscular cylinders.

We enjoyed a simple male bonding: the trains, my friends and myself. The locomotives were undeniably masculine and only a fool would refer to one as "she". Girls didn't like locomotives; the pistons frightened them. And yet technically the steam engine is a female thing; the power resides in the cylinder and the piston is merely the cylinder's tool.

Train watching was a perfect opportunity for introspection and I used to make the most of it; weaving fantastic dreams of power between one train and the next; inventing death rays and perpetual-motion machines, splitting the atom and exploring the Amazon basin, shaking the hand of Winston Churchill ("If there were more young fellows like you around, Coney, I'd feel a little

more confident about the future of the Free World . . ."), diving
headlong to nod in the winning goal ("Coney sparks the Villa to
sensational victory in the last minute . . ."), and accepting the
Nobel Prize for my seven-page mystery novel, *The Murder at
Tamworth Station*.

Wonderful days which I relived in a story called "Those Good
Old Days of Liquid Fuel"; but I had to base the story around
spaceships instead of steam engines otherwise *F&SF* wouldn't
have understood it. It was fun to recapture the mindless joy: "No
doubt we were sublimating our adolescent urges in those days, but
in our innocence we thought we were watching the spaceships."

More recently came *The Celestial Steam Locomotive*, which
straddled the dimensions of Space and Time known (to the characters at any rate) as the Greataway. "Her fingers traced the brass
beading around one curved splasher. The warm metal was vibrant
and alive. 'The Locomotive is the most beautiful thing in the
world. It's the distillation of everyone's idea of what a machine
should look like. It's composed of a million smallwishes, a million
dreams of beauty.'" And sustained only by the imagination of its
passengers. A pity that Houghton Mifflin's cover shows an American engine with cowcatcher and headlamp, instead of the Great
Western "Castle" which I'd envisaged.

The trains influenced *Cat Karina* too. The coastal sailways of
Karina's world combined twin obsessions: sailing and railways.
Sometimes I wonder how mainstream writers can keep writing,
with nothing exciting to invent. Perhaps they're all basically hacks.

Some memories are more vivid than others. I recall a chilly
morning at Birmingham (Snow Hill) station, and a slow beat of
exhaust from somewhere in the fog. An unseen locomotive was
struggling to bring a freight train up the gradient into the north
end of the station. Occasionally the beat became muffled thunder
as the engine lost its footing and slipped back a few yards. Eventually it broke into view, headlamps staring and boiler bulging with
effort, a Class 8 2–8–0 of Stanier design oozing steam at every pore,
striving to lift its load over the lip of the hill – and failing. With a
baffled roar and sparks spurting from the spinning wheels it slid
back into the fog, down to the bottom of the hill to try again.

The GWR had built this locomotive as a wartime standardization
measure, but basically it was an LMS engine and out of its element
here. Every so often it would reappear, smoke fountaining into the
cold morning air, then it would fall back again, beaten. I felt sorry

for it. So many tries, so many failures. At last the authorities dispatched the station pilot, *Lady of the Lake*, to assist. Encouraged, the Class 8 made a mighty effort and with quickening exhaust the two of them brought an endless train of freight wagons into the station. *Lady of the Lake* uncoupled, and in triumph the Class 8 departed on level ground, wagons rattling behind.

I like to think I learned something from all that. I like to think of myself as Robert Bruce but with something more spectacular than a spider to draw inspiration from. The Class 8, in a strange land, with the elements against it and battling intolerable odds, had won through like the true champion its creator, William Stanier, knew it to be. I like to think the incident taught me the value of quality, of persistence, of courage in the face of adversity.

More likely, however, it taught me that if you make a big enough ass of yourself someone will take pity on you, usually a woman. And that, perhaps, is an even more valuable lesson.

I feel sorry for those people who never knew the glory of steam; they missed so much. Once my daughter Sally took the train from Esquimalt to Courtenay, British Columbia. It's not a steam train but it does rattle through mountains among steepling douglas firs, over frightening timber trestle viaducts, and along a coastline renowned for its beauty. It's not really a train either; just a railcar. But it runs on *rails*, and it has that indefinable railway *atmosphere*, and when she returned I asked Sally, then fifteen years old, how she'd enjoyed it.

"Not bad," she said with mild enthusiasm. "Saw a dead horse."

I said I don't like paradoxes, and I don't like this one. As a child, many of the things I was taught as facts later proved to be wrong, but the things I found out for my innocent self were usually right.

They taught me there was one God and I believed them, and despised the ancient Greeks who attached gods like trade-marks to every conceivable object. "God is an old man with a beard, sitting on a horse cloud," Dad Ose told Manuel in *The Celestial Steam Locomotive*, and the events in that book were in some way a revenge on the way Society had taken me for a sucker, when I was a kid.

I also believed that tortoises hibernated, and that mushrooms sucked back into the ground during the heat of a summer's day. The gnomes in my novel-in-progress, *Marazion*, believe that about mushrooms too. As for the tortoise, I put mine in a shoebox in late autumn, and packed him with straw against the winter cold. He struggled for a while, but soon accepted his lot. I closed the lid and stowed him away in a corner of the disused stable at the bottom of the garden.

In the spring I remembered him, and how the thoughts of food and sunshine would be jostling each other in his slow brain. I visualized him darting across the lawn like a runaway tank, frisking like a lead-footed lamb. I opened the box and took him out, but he showed no sign of emerging from his shell.

In fact he seemed to have deserted his shell altogether. It was empty. I held it up to the light and looked through it. There was a hole at the back for his tail, and there were two holes on either side for his legs. The inside of the shell was spotlessly clean. Of the living, loving part of him, there was nothing. His time had come, and God had spirited him gently from his shell and up to heaven. I buried the shell with proper reverence and returned to the house feeling cleansed.

It was unfortunate that I subsequently overheard an Orwellian remark by my father to my mother.

"The rats got that bloody tortoise of Mike's. Christ, they'll be after the dog next. We'll have to put some poison down. With luck we'll get that bloody cat from next door, too. Kill two birds with one stone."

If the tortoise reaffirmed my childish belief in One God, the dog, whose name was Chips, taught me about madness and death. There was something Poe-like in the manner of Chip's passing. I'd never liked the dog, which had been very old all his life, and which had a habit of standing stock-still with trembling haunches, staring at aliens. And I'll swear that my mother once used his food dish to bake a treacle tart. I refused a slice at dinner and they never knew why; but my suspicions had been aroused by the exact shape and size of the tart. Of course my mother had taken it out of the dish by then; in fact the dish was on the floor filled with some abominable stew which Chips was presently staring at; but I was not to be fooled.

Then one morning there were strange pounding noises coming from the kitchen. My mother and I met at the top of the stairs, exchanged glances of mutual fear, crept downstairs and opened the door.

Chips lay on the floor, foaming at the mouth and banging his head against the table leg. I could tell at a glance that he was certifiably insane. Madness had always terrified me. Whimpering with dread I scurried from the room, leaving my mother alone with that unpredictable monster whose strength and ferocity, I was convinced, could be compared to a choleric crocodile.

I used to read the humorous sea-stories of W.W. Jacobs. I loved them; the bizarre situations, the drunken sailors, the accommodating widows and shrewish wives. But in the middle of one volume was a story called, I think, "The Three Sisters". Those sisters were mad. They scared the hell out of me. I was frightened to pick up that book in case the pages fell open at "The Three Sisters", and my eyes alighted on the fearsome words. Finally, one bright summer day, I picked up book and glue, found the awful place where one sister ran screaming into the night, blanked out that part of my brain which controls reading ability, and stuck the pages together . . .

My father set a large wooden box on the lawn, upside down. Then he carried the thrashing, foaming figure of Chips out, dumped him on the grass and put the box on him to form a dark asylum. Next he brought a stinking potion from his surgery – he was a dentist – and put it under the box with Chips. My father said it would put Chips to sleep, but I knew it was a death gas.

Chips uttered a doleful "Woof!"

"He's better," I said. I wanted this dog I disliked to live and be normal. I wanted everything to be the way it was, and I'd gladly have eaten a slice of treacle tart.

I've always wanted to write a book where nobody dies, but I haven't done it yet. The best I can do is to try to make death *mean* something, and to step right inside my own character's minds when they react to it, so that my reaction is theirs – and sometimes all too obviously, as when poor El Tigre saw the bloody results of his rebellion in *Cat Karina*, and knew he hadn't really won at all. That was a good example of the character taking over the author.

Chips barked for a long time while I wandered around the garden trying not to listen.

Then the canopy moved, and he could see the joints and segments. And his mind snapped into focus, and he realized that Shenshi stood directly beneath a monstrous spider. Fluid was dripping from the creature's jaws as it began to stoop toward him.

Bawling with horror, he flung himself to the ground. He drew his knees up to his body and covered his head with his arms, and felt another drop of moisture fall onto the back of his hand. It began to eat at his flesh, corrosively. *(Gods of the Greataway)*

When I was a child we didn't have a refrigerator, so the milk would sometimes go bad and clot up inside the neck of the bottle. The lower half would thin out, and the whole would turn greenish. My mother would utter a croak of disgust and take it away.

One day a muslim bag appeared in the cellar of our big old house. It hung from a hook, full of something pulpy to my prodding finger, and soon it began to drip moisture into a jar. This liquid was crystal clear, yet terrifying. I became obsessed with the fear that I would sleepwalk into the cellar one night and drink it. When I write of a corrosive fluid drooling from the jaws of a monster, *that* is the fluid I'm thinking of.

Aeons later my mother took the bag down and carried it into the kitchen. She opened it up on the table and inside was a *brain*, white and slippery. Or was it a brain?

It certainly looked like a brain, although it was too small to be human. I knew that, because there was a human skull in the cellar and the brain cavity was quite large. The skull was the property of some long-gone medical student, so my mother said, although I always suspected it to be the remains of a deformed half-brother of my father.

It could have been a chimp brain, but commonsense told me my mother had no reason to keep a chimp brain in a muslin bag. It looked a little sloppy around the edges; and I knew that, whoever its late owner was, he couldn't have been too bright.

Then suddenly, with appalling certainty, I knew what it was.

It was the brain of Chips!

Just about then my father grunted, leaned forward with a knife, cut a slice from the brain, spread it on a Carr's Water Biscuit and began to eat it.

I went down to the bottom of the garden where the old stable was, and looked at the mound under the crab apple tree. The soil was undisturbed. The vision of Chips' skull, empty as a tortoise shell, faded. The child is a resilient life-form.

The sun came out and I climbed the tree and surveyed my world; the roofs and the railway and the neighbour's cat on the compost heap asleep, or maybe poisoned; and everything was wonderful again.

The world is still wonderful, and often I sit between that world and my typewriter, trying to build a straight and perfect road from one to the other. Unfortunately that road must pass through my brain on the way, and on too many days my brain resembles one of my mother's creations: having the appearance of intelligence – the convoluted cellular structure, the pale wetness – yet inert, and possessed of an inner rot.

Those are the days when I work hard at writing, pounding sentences together as though with rivets. On those days I wonder if it is worth the effort; but I persevere, and after a page or so the words begin to flow a little more easily. Whether the sentences combine to make a useful contribution to science fiction is another matter.

And then on the brighter side, there was the music. My parents both played the piano; my mother's head nodded from side to side and my father's long fingers rustled over the keys like dead leaves so that sometimes I'd find myself listing to the fingers instead of the music. They favoured the classics, and were critical of my liking for Richard Rodgers, Cole Porter, Gershwin. "There's never been a good musical written since the days of Gilbert and Sullivan," said my father.

"What about *Oklahoma*?" I would ask.

"Bloody American junk."

However, my mother once said to me in private, "Your father only ever went to one Gilbert and Sullivan thing – I forget what it was called. He walked out half-way through. He said he couldn't take another minute of this tumty tumty music."

It was a cerebral thing, my liking for American music. I admired the craftsmanship of a good song, but it didn't often touch the heart. Those were barren days before Bill Haley, days of mass-production melodies to an AABA formula.

Except for three minutes every Saturday night. Ten o'clock would find me home and in bed, headphones clamped on, fiddling with a temperamental radio which a stranger might have mistaken for an orange box (built by my father, of course), tuning in to Edmundo Ros.

For an hour I would listen to catchy sambas, hard-driving mambos which presaged the early rock, and, once in each programme, a magical, lilting beguine. Now *this* touched my heart. The unison of melody and rhythm possessed me in a way no other music did. For three minutes every week, I was a boy fulfilled.

"You know he's actually an Englishman," my mother told me. "His name's Edmund Ross with two esses. The photographs are of a different man altogether." This was before TV, so I had no way of disproving her. Years later I met Edmundo's brother, Hugo Ross, at a party in Antigua, and found him satisfyingly black. Through all those years my love affair with Latin music continued, and was consummated with the coming of the bossa nova. With its complex rhythm, jazz improvisations, and haunting minor key melodies by such as Luiz Bonfa and Antonio Carlos Jobim, it provided the perfect counterpoint to writing science fiction.

I can't say why. I don't know why it helps to build a scene in a novel around a piece of music. Music, being totally abstract, certainly helps to clear the mind. Maybe it also creates the mood, putting the writer in the appropriate frame of mind, so that he doesn't have to start cold. Sometimes it helps with the background, fleshing it out, humming away like a tangible part of the book – as happened with *Cat Karina, The Celestial Steam Locomotive* and its sequel, which may be called *Gods of the Greataway*, unfortunately. Sometimes it intrudes right into the storyline.

"And the girl was tanned and straight with hair the colour of a fair sunset, and she stepped delicately over the pebbles although her feet were now becoming accustomed to the rough ground . . . She didn't glance at him yet." So walks a Girl from Ipanema, in *Gods of the Greataway*.

Sometimes the connection is not unconscious. Jobim wrote a strange song called "The Waters of March", and I was listening to it one day. The disconnected words and rolling melody held a million possibilities, and I was in a plotting mood. I was also stuck for a good strong human interest theme for *Locomotive*, which so far was all ideas and no heart.

What were the Waters of March? What was the meaning of the line: "And the riverbank talks of the waters of March?" As I pondered this, the gentle rhythm flowed, and the words began to come.

". . . The river flowed brown for most of the year, having picked up silt and broken vegetation during its journey through the rain forest. But once a year it flowed clear and green, and carried to the delta . . ."

What did it carry to the delta? This is Brazil of the future; a lot of things have changed in 91,000 years. So what's the most unlikely thing? Think of something; go on, *think* . . .

". . . and carried to the delta a flotilla of tiny boats carved from balsa: model galleons, frigates and dhows . . ."

And? Listen to the music . . .

". . . and in each boat lay a human baby, crying and waving tiny fists at the sky."

That's the inspiration. That's the basic idea, caught in a time span of three minutes and fifty-five seconds, according to the album *Jobim*. Not much to build on, but intriguing. Next came the work; the hows and the whys, the plotting, the explanations and the denouement. That's the fun of science fiction. You don't get it in the mainstream. I'm lucky to be writing it. I think it was an accident of birth.

11

The Profession of Science Fiction

Gene Wolfe

To begin, it is no profession. If the truth were known, there are only two real professions: law and medicine. In a profession (I am told) one sits in one's offices behind a brass plate, waiting for someone to insult one with money. Sherlock Holmes, perhaps, began as a professional, but even he soon found he had to go out into the streets and work, though he advertised himself as the world's one and only consulting detective. I have been most of the other things that are sometimes said – mostly by their practitioners – to be professions. I have been a soldier ("the profession of arms"). I have been a teacher and an engineer and a journalist. All these are jobs.

Being a science fictionist is not even that; it is an affliction, like being a horse player or a bag lady. One weeps when no one else so much as wipes away the furtive tear, and one laughs when no one else smiles, and in the end it affects the brain.

I sold my first sf story to Frederik Pohl, who was then editor of a now-defunct magazine called *Worlds of If*. Mr Pohl was also the editor of *Galaxy*, but I, knowing nothing about the science fiction "world", did not know that. I sent *Galaxy* a story I called "The Mountains are Mice", and when *Galaxy* sent it back with a form of rejection, I doggedly mailed it out again – to *Worlds of If*.

On that submission I got a cheque and a letter, and the letter said something like "I'm glad you let me see this again. I feel the rewrite has improved it quite a bit."

If I had been an honest man, I would have sent back the cheque, but as it was I took it to the bank (it was fairly small and needed somebody to go along with it) and came home glorying, and I have had a soft spot in my heart for Fred Pohl ever since. He changed the title to "Mountains Like Mice", and I wrote him to say that I understood they enjoyed them fried but could take them or leave them alone boiled, but I retained the soft spot. He never bought another word from me; I still retained the soft spot.

Now, however, I am forced to tell the truth: I have a soft spot in my heart for Fred, but Fred has a soft spot in his head. That worries me, because Fred is a science fiction writer and I am a science fiction writer, and we have enjoyed remarkably similar careers except that Fred has been successful and has a great many friends. (No doubt *you* knew about Fred's soft spot as soon as you read that bit about "Mountains Like Mice"; I am not quite so sharp.)

I wasn't really aware of Fred's weakness until I got to the middle of his remarkably readable autobiography *The Way The Future Was*. Somewhere around the centre of the book Fred says that he knows just how oppressed minorities feel because he was in the US Army. Then he details his military experiences: quartered in a Miami Beach hotel while he was being trained as a weatherman; sent to Oklahoma, where he palled around with Jack Williamson; sent to Italy to serve in what must have been the original *Catch-22* outfit; marrying a WAC and being given a honeymoon in Paris by the Army, during which Fred and his bride ate at a mess supposedly reserved for generals.

Right, Fred. Tow that barge. Tote that bale.

Frederik Pohl is obviously sick, and I believe I know what it was that made him sick, and so do you. It was science fiction. Sooner or later (mostly later) one discovers that everything one's parents told one is true. (Theodore Sturgeon made a fine short story out of that.) When I was a child, my parents let me know that reading sf and fantasy would destroy my mind, and I wish I had found out they were wrong.

Fred does, of course, know how it feels to be a member of an oppressed minority, and in fact he may very well know how it feels to be a member of any number of oppressed minorities that do not exist. (He probably does not know how it feels to be a black or a Jew, but that is another matter.) Because he has this knowledge, he subconsciously attributes it to the Army.

No doubt all eight of you reading this are waiting with breathless interest for me to get on to my favourite subject. But before I drop poor Fred, I want to talk – however briefly – about the following quote from a later chapter of *The Way The Future Was*. The author is talking about the type of stories Harlan Ellison sought for *Dangerous Visions*.

It is an article of faith with some writers that such stories exist, kept from an eager audience by the poltroon editors. It is an article of faith with *me* that this is hogwash. Some editors do hesitate to publish off-track stories, but if the story is any good, some other editor, sooner or later, will snap it up.

Now half a minute's reflection will show almost anyone – certainly anyone one tenth as intelligent as Frederik Pohl – that the last sentence is arrant nonsense. It is a restatement of a bit of boilerplate that editors and publishers have used for at least fifty years, and Fred (for reasons I hope eventually to demonstrate) has absorbed it without examination. What does *sooner or later* mean in that last sentence? Within a year? Certainly not. Within a decade? I could pretty readily quote cases to show that even a decade is too short a time. Within fifty years, then. Fifty years is a large limbo; it will hold a lot of stories.

It will not, however, preserve them in dry ice. "Ball of Fat" is outdated now by a century, yet because we know something of conditions in France during the Franco–Prussian war it has not gone rancid. But what about a *good* science fiction story written in 1930 and laid in the then-fifty-years-off world of 1980? For that matter, what about such a story laid in 2000? Suppose this story was written as well as Sherwood Anderson himself could have written it – in 1930 – and it predicted such things as computers, flame throwers, hand-held calculators, atomic bombs, the rise of the Arab states, and the civil rights movement. What would be chance of its being published if it were not published before, say, the year 1940?

But forget all that. For a story to be published, it must be marketed. If a hundred writers write a hundred good-but-off-track stories, and all these stories are rejected forty times, isn't it at least possible that *some* of those writers will have lost faith in them by that time? (Forty rejections might easily take ten years; the manuscript would have to be retyped *at least* three times to have any chance at all.)

A typical publisher or editor would say, of course, that *Dangerous Visions* itself proved him correct; after all, the stories printed in *Dangerous Visions were* printed – in *Dangerous Visions*.

Once upon a time three men were walking beside a river when they saw a beautiful woman drowning. The first man cast his eyes toward heaven, folded his hands, and said, "Lord, I know you would never permit this lovely creature to perish."

"Amen, brother." said the second man.

The third man leaped into the river and after nearly drowning himself, pulled out the woman. Whereupon, naturally, the first and second men said, "I told you so."

But does anyone seriously suppose that *Dangerous Visions* got *all* the off-track stories that were in existence at that time? Harlan almost immediately put together *Again, Dangerous Visions* containing as many more. And he has since assembled a third book (many of us call it *Dangerous Revisions*) rumoured to be larger than the first and second books combined.

I am not saying all this to glorify Harlan Ellison; he needs no help from me in that. I merely wish to show that the idea that all good writing finds a publisher eventually is absurd – or to be a little more precise, meaningless.

Now I would like to change the subject from writing to crime. Please bear with me. I am going to tell you how crime statistics – and at least some criminals – are created. Every word, every detail, no matter how fantastic it may sound, is true to the best of my knowledge.

It was the afternoon of our wedding anniversary, and I had taken the day off. When the telephone rang, we were about to drive to a shopper centre for lunch. My wife answered it. I heard her say "Hello, where are you?" and knew she was talking to one of our children. Soon her voice changed; she was talking to an adult, and she sounded frightened. When she hung up she said, "Matthew threatened some other boys with a knife. The police have him." As we were getting into the car to go to the police station, she added, "I'll bet it was those boys from the theatre."

Matt is our youngest, a quiet boy of twelve whose chief passion is fishing. About four months earlier, he had broken a neighbour's friendship light with a slingshot – accidentally, he said. That was the most serious disciplinary problem we had ever had with him.

The previous night we had let Matt go to the movies with a schoolmate. My wife said that when she had driven to the theatre to get him, he had been surrounded by four or five shouting boys. When he was in the car she had asked if they were his friends, and he had told her they were "mad" at him. He and his schoolmate had been sitting near the front of the theater, and these boys, several rows behind, had thrown mints at them. (We live, it would seem, in an age so rich that children willingly use candies for missiles.) Matt's schoolmate had called them " a bad name", and the boys had waited outside the theatre.

Over an intercom in the police station, my wife and I could hear the arresting officer telling a woman clerk to give him some warning when we arrived, while she tried to explain that we were already there. Apparently her microphone was defective or she did not know how to use it; eventually he got the message and began to do whatever it was he felt he had to before talking to us – perhaps settle with his partner what they would tell us.

A few minutes later he came out to greet us and lead us to a conference room. He was young and good looking, and might easily have served as the model policeman on some public affairs broadcast. As it happened, I had met him once before – he was the son of a deceased co-worker. Matt was nowhere in sight.

"Apparently, your son pulled a switchblade knife on some other boys," the arresting officer told us. I said I found that hard to believe. "That's what the boys say, and he admits it. He's never been in trouble before, has he?"

My wife recounted the friendship light episode, which the arresting officer seemed to shrug aside, and asked if the boys involved were the ones from the theatre. He said they were (we later discovered that only one of the boys from the theatre had been in the group that had found Matt the next day, but he had been the leader, three years older than any of the others), and seemed somewhat surprised to find we were aware of the incident. "Your son appears to have threatened these boys with his knife in the theatre last night as well."

My wife said that when she had driven to the theatre to pick Matt up she had seen no knife – only Matt surrounded by larger and older boys.

"Well, they say he did."

My wife named several neighborhood boys who she felt might dislike Matt and asked if any of them were involved.

"No, these boys are all from — ." The arresting officer named a town about ten miles from the one we live in.

We thought at first that we had misunderstood him. When he repeated what he had said before, we asked what these boys were doing in our town.

"They said they were going to the high school – one of them has a brother in our school. Do you have any idea where your son could have got the knife?"

We did not. I mentioned what the arresting officer, as a policeman, must surely have known: that switchblades had been outlawed in the US for many years.

"They said it had a pushbutton, but it might just have been the kind of knife that locks open. Do you have any such knife around the house?"

My wife said, "Could it have been your brown-handled knife?" and I explained that the knife she was referring to was a pruning knife I used in the garden. This knife has a hooked blade about three and a half inches long and a brass spring that must be pushed aside to close the blade.

"Your son's knife appears to have been more like a hunting knife," the arresting officer said. "Where is your knife now?"

I told him that as far as I knew it was in my dresser drawer at home. From this time forward his attitude toward me changed radically. I owned a dangerous knife, and was thus a potential criminal. I had left this knife where it might have fallen into Matt's hands. It did not occur to me at the time to point out that our kitchen, like every other kitchen, contains half a dozen knives more suitable for use as weapons.

"Does your knife have a chromed or highly polished blade?"

I shook my head. I have used that knife to cut roses and dig out dandelions for years. I told the arresting officer that if he would only let me see the knife, I would tell him at once if it was mine.

"We don't have it," he said. "They threw it away."

"*They* threw it away?"

"They had taken it from him. The funny thing is that he was the one who called us." (This was also untrue – a clerk in a store where Matt had taken refuge had actually made the call – but the arresting officer seemed to believe what he said, and because we had taught Matt that the police would help him, we believe it too.) "Maybe we ought to have him in now."

The arresting officer's partner led Matt in. His face was tear-stained, but he was no longer crying. He told us he had been dismissed from school and had been walking to a friend's house to play. Four boys, led by one of the boys who had pushed him around outside the theatre, had come up behind him on bicycles. Two of these boys were eleven, one, a younger brother of the leader, was ten. The leader was fourteen, but the arresting officer's partner insisted he was no larger physically than Matt. At twelve, Matt is smaller than many of his classmates; the leader must have been quite diminutive for his age, if this were true.

They had struck Matt and kicked him. He had run from them – across a busy Federal highway and eventually into an apartment complex. There he had entered one of the buildings and pounded on the door of one of the apartments. No one had come, and the four boys had driven him out of the building again. In the parking lot, Matt had taken out his pocket knife and tried to hold off his attackers.

The arresting officer interrupted, his voice as humourless as the slam of a cell door. "That is aggravated assault."

Matt said he had found the knife in the street in front of our house about two weeks before. I am not certain this is true. Such knives are for sale in many stores for a dollar or two, Matt sometimes earns money by cutting grass or raking leaves for the neighbours, and it is possible that at this point he was afraid to admit he had bought the knife. He had not told my wife or me about it, although he had shown it to his older brother.

I asked him how the other boys had taken it from him.

"They said if I would let them see it, they would stop beating me up. Only they took it and beat me up some more."

They had chased him several blocks farther until he took refuge in a skiing store, halfway across town from the point where he had initially been attacked. A clerk had called the police to drive away the gang of four boys waiting outside, Matt had told the policeman that they had taken his knife, and he had been arrested. The arresting officer's partner had stopped the four boys, then released them. He said he had searched them – there on the street – for the knife, and that they had said they had thrown it away. He had searched the area where they had told him they had thrown it, but he had been unable to find it.

"In my day," the arresting officer said, "in yours too, I'm sure," (it seemed to be an attempt to return to the old friendly footing that had prevailed before I admitted to owning a pruning knife) "we knew how to defend ourselves without knives."

My wife said we would try to enroll Matt in a boxing or karate class. Then came the most incredible part of the entire interview. I find it difficult to write because I feel know it will not be believed, but it is true. The arresting officer solemnly warned us that if we enrolled Matt in such a class, the police might choose to consider his hands dangerous weapons.

In the end Matt was released. We were told that the police have "started a card" on him, and that he is classified as a potentially violent juvenile. In the eyes of the law, he is a criminal guilty of aggravated assault. Aggravated assault, it seems, is the legal term for a tearful little boy futilely attempting to hold a gang at bay with a pocket knife.

All this may seem to have nothing to do with the Affliction of Science Fiction, but I am convinced that it does. There are two principal forms of human thought; if I were even a little bit Chinese I would call them *The Path of the Beast* and *The Road of the Angel*, or something of the kind. The first consists of reacting to simple cues, the second of reasoning from more or less consciously formulated premises. Most people do the former; science fiction, the strumpet step-daughter of the hard sciences, tends to teach us to do the latter.

I felt persecuted, bullied, by the policeman, who was reacting to the word *knife* (the actual knife itself had done nothing, and he had never even seen it) as mindlessly as my trash compactor does to the touch of a button. Fred Pohl, doubtless, found the Army reacting to cues of various kinds in the same wholly automatic fashion, and thus was moved to resent it, though it had furnished him with a glorious, years-long adventure.

But although the Path of the Beast and the Road of the Angel are wholly separate, the neurons of each human brain trace both; mention "off-track" stories to Fred, and you evolve the pro-grammed, unthought response.

Once one has followed the Road of the Angel even a little way, however, a great many things become obvious. It is obvious, for example, that we should devise some planet-wide substitute for war, and that it would be to everyone's advantage to do so. It is obvious that society should repress those who act aggressively, and not those who attempt to defend themselves from that ag-gression. Yet people who have understood these things, and the hundred more like them that could be rattled off, must continue to live where they are. They are by definition maladjusted, just as a pig who had somehow understood that the end of pigness was porkness, and wept or tried to climb out of the sty, could truthfully be said to be maladjusted.

That, of course, is not real "mind rot"; but real decay of the intelligence is not only possible but common. The person who takes the Road of the Angel soon perceives that he is on the road and not yet at his destination, which he will perhaps reach only after death; and that the road winds through a looking-glass land where reason is murdered by words and he is ill adapted to survive. Having lost the instincts of the beasts he seeks to substitute for them a contrived and habitual lunacy, and becomes, like little Alice, a bewildered pawn. He is afflicted. I am so afflicted, as my parents warned me I would be. Matt will no doubt soon be so afflicted if he is not already. Fred is so afflicted, and so, I think, are you.

12

The Profession of Fiction

M. John Harrison

1. BEST LAID PLANS: SOME OVERLAPPING HINDSIGHTS

Dreams are empty. They are an emptiness which needs itself, a need which in fulfilling itself empties itself out. Dreams are the undercutting action of desire. They undercut themselves infinitely to spin off new dreams in an endless slippage of desire. Look at any new advertisement. Read any new manifesto –

1966–69: *The Committed Men*. Identify the illusions central to the genre. The clearest illusions we have are to do with "meaning" and "choice", with self-determination, problem-solving. Sf draws illusions of this nature across our fears: of death, of the ordinariness of our lives, of the consequences of our actions. A fantasy-world is precisely one in which action has no consequences.

1968–78: *The Pastel City, The Centauri Device, The Machine in Shaft Ten, A Storm of Wings*. Subvert these illusions, not for the sake of it, or for political or literary reasons, but because to do so might be to reveal – for a fraction of a second, to yourself as much as the reader – the world the fictional illusion denies. Clearly, stories of immortality reveal death at the heart of themselves, stories of communication inarticulacy, stories of vast space and interstellar flight oppression and earthboundness, and so on.

1976–88: "Egnaro", *Climbers*. Recognise (all too slowly) that these two poles of the dialectic – the writing of fantasy/the subversion of fantasy – make a discourse. This is in itself a form of escape. A discourse can be solved. It is like a chess problem. The world cannot be solved, nor can any non-self-reflexive problem with a "leak to the world".

1985 onwards: *The Course of the Heart*. Paradox reigns. We can never escape the world. We cannot stop trying to escape the world.

We begin by trying out illusions. Once we accept that illusions "blind but do not hold",[1] that we have at our disposal finally only the worldness of the world, then we find some way of "escaping" into that. We learn to love what we longed to run from. We learn to run away from fantasy and into the world, write fantasies at the heart of which by some twist lies the very thing we fantasise-against.

This hurts.

2.   FAILURES OF ARTICULACY

1958. Ill in bed, I read a thriller by an imitator of Mickey Spillane. Its hero was called "Johnny Fedora". Johnny Fedora, appallingly ready with a Colt .45, nevertheless had thin delicate fingers; he played the piano when he got the chance. That was enough for me. I was thirteen years old. I signed up without a thought. My first novel, written shortly afterwards and now sadly lost, featured Johnny's pale shadow: and Johnny was still playing to packed houses in my head when, twenty years later, I recognised him as "Lord Galen Hornwrack" in *A Storm of Wings* and, embarrassed, finished him off forever.

It hadn't taken me twenty years to recognise that humanity is a virtue: only to learn that pulp fiction won't let you speak about it. Johnny's thin fingers and moonlit sonatas did not humanise his Colt. They were only the pulp-writer's device for hiding it – for obscuring consequences.

For the romantics among us – between, say, 1965 and 1975 – a kind of earnest irony, a turning of the common turns of fantasy and sf, was the goal. We would not get tainted. We would bend the genre – we would bend popular fiction in general – back against itself and to our will. We would make the genre speak to order. It was time. It looked possible. In fact it looked easy.

But in the end the subject-matter of popular fiction has an inertia, a doggedness, we could never have predicted. The interstellar drive "says" only itself. The only emotional charge the sword carries is its swordness. These stock units overbear the metaphors you try to make with them, so that when for instance Gene Wolfe speaks of swords and torture he does not twist the genre against itself at all – though he may think, or even for all I know hope and pray, that he has – he only speaks of swords and torture and how you can become King by eating the brains of your predecessor (which not only dooms you to repeat his barbarism, but is also only what sword-and-sorcery has been advocating since Robert Howard).

Thus *The Pastel City* is the site of a murder. It is the optimum arena for the very bullfight it condemns.

A writer is the victim of the illusion of untaintability only for as long as he is unaware of it. After that if he carries on, he has chosen the illusion, and passed on the role of victim to his reader.

Perhaps more importantly, the techniques of popular fiction have an inertia, too. When the god leaves you, presumably to breathe into the next little boy or girl (thirteen years old, prone to illness – especially vertigo – and daydreams, reads widely and is uncertain with other children), it leaves you for a time with nothing. You are as naked and incompetent as the day you started. If you have learned how to write:

> Mor flung back his head and howled like a beast.
> He lunged blindly.
> Cromis whirled, tangled his cloak about hand and baan. As the blade cut free, he crouched, rolled, changed direction, rolled again, so that his body became a blur of motion on the stone-flagged floor. The nameless sword slid from its sheath: and he was tegeus-Cromis the Northkiller once again . . .[2]

Or even its parodical double, as in:

> This was too much for Hornwrack, who, eyeing the apparition superstitiously, got out the sword of tegeus-Cromis and followed it about, making lethal cuts in the air. "Back to your sewer!" he shouted. "Back to your madhouse!" while Cellur in an attempt to restrain him plucked feebly at his cloak and the apparition evaded them both, chuckling . . .[3]

You can simply find no way of saying:

> I was embarrassed by Elizabeth's passion for things, in the way you often are by the enthusiasms of people you have looked up to as a child. She had no objectivity. She filled the house with runny-eyed tomcats she had coaxed in from the dustbins. She re-papered the walls bright yellow, with window blinds the

colour of Carnation milk. She wouldn't throw the weediest geranium cutting away. It was contained, like the black kitten juggling madly with a bit of lamb-bone in the hall, in the intense sympathy she had for everything in the world. To temper this she overcharged me so savagely for the two furnished rooms I had at the top of her house that I had to work three days a week at a bookshop in the town to eke out my income . . .[4]

Clearly, the techniques don't cross over. If you want to speak directly about – or to – what is human in people, it's no good learning sword-talk.

3.   ACCENTED MOMENT SIGNS[5]

Modernism isn't a question of describing objects, events, situations or emotions which we recognise and which make us exclaim, "Yes, that's exactly how it is!" Nor is it a matter of communicating someone else's "moment of being". What modernism can give you is a surprising sense of what it's like to be inside your own life. For a second you are encouraged to reinhabit yourself. You stand at a window, looking at the flowers – thick, yellow, a yellow solid enough to touch – of a pot-marigold. Suddenly everything extends out from you and back through you – the room behind, the flower in front, your past, your present, your future – you are contained within everything that is contained within you. There is nothing mystical about this frisson. It is only the state we live in, the constant rediscovery that we are alive.

I was born in Warwickshire, which is a beautiful country if a dull one. One of my earliest memories is of sitting hypnotised by the sound and weight of a river, by its strange, powerful, yeasty smell as it poured over a weir. It was a hot July morning. Sunlight spilled and foamed off the broken water.

All the objects of my childhood, the rooks, the buttercups, the clumps of nettles in the grass at the base of a wall, the pike hanging like a spent torpedo in the shallows of the mill pond at five in the morning, were transfigured and intensified in the same way. In a childhood like that, perception is a drug. In a kind of excited fatigue you watch your own hand come closer and closer to the dry grey wood of an old gate at the edge of a field, and find yourself unable for a second to context one by the other, or find a single context – unless it is something as huge as "the world" – which will accept them both. In the end you are able to comprehend (in the sense of intuit) only the intense existence, the photographic actuality of such objects; of yourself and your encounters with them. In that kind of childhood everything is fused into the light like the flowers fused into a glass paperweight.

Later I tried to identify this light as "self awareness", "awareness of time", perhaps "the sexual trances of early adolescence". Later still I saw that the child is contrived wholly of the things he has already watched: a web in the grass, water going by; the curve of a bridge, the sound of a jet, the flare of light off the windscreen of a polished car. These elements are reassembled as a way of looking at other things. It was this continual fusing and liquefying of accumulated experience which I had analogised as a light bathing the landscape.

A book – its meaning – is not what the light discovers. What is interesting in any book, or picture, or film, is the light itself. Cast now by the adult artist on new objects, the objects of his work, it is valuable for the very act of illumination.

This act is central to *Jacob's Room* or *Dubliners*. It is why we find ourselves drawn again and again to Turgenev or Flaubert. We value *The Sacrifice* or *Stalker* not for the conclusions Tarkovsky draws, but for the way he chooses then irradiates the objects of his concern. We value McMullen's *Zina* not because of the "truth" Cronstadt the psychologist fails to divine from Trotsky's daughter, but for the search for truth itself. Cronstadt is himself the casting of a light.

This light, though experiential, serves paradoxically to defamiliarise the objects it falls on. The moment in which it falls is the moment of being.

4.   THE COVENANTS OF EXPERIENCE

H.E. Bates says of the modern short story that from the 1920s onwards it "described less, but implied and suggested more; it stopped short, it rendered life obliquely, or it was merely episodic; so that the reader, if the value of the story was to be fully realised at all, *had to supply the confirmation of his own experience* . . ."[6]

The italics are mine.

As a readership, the fantasy and sf audience has three distinct – I almost wrote "strict" – limitations. The first two – that it is narrowly read, and that it is inept at retrieving content from sophisti-cated structures and surfaces – were confronted by writers in the mid-1960s. It is received wisdom now to claim that the confron-tation was successful, and that these things are no longer true (that indeed f&sf readers are able and willing to deal with *more* complex surfaces and structures than many "mainstream" readers). Even if this is not an evasion – powered by a fairly deliberate muddling of the "main stream" (which I take to be an evolving modern canon) with "popular general fiction" (which I take to be Barbara Taylor Bradford) – there is unfinished business, and in the 1990s we might try confronting the third limitation, which is that the readership is often too young to supply experiential confirmation of subject matter, and by its very reading maintains that state of innocence.

Many readers of *Interzone* greeted my short story "The New Rays" with a child-like disgust at the details of the central charac-ter's plight, the metonyms of sickness and death; but otherwise with a freezing lack of affect. One generic reviewer, otherwise acute, applauded it as a portrait of a pervert enjoying her own degradation. Not one of them had any sympathy for the poor girl at all. Why? Ordinary readers – particularly, I found, mature women whose reading was most often selected from the Popular General Fiction shelf – were able to handle the details of the story without panic, and also to experience considerable concern on behalf of its central character.

Neither did they have difficulty with a subsequent story, "Old Women", though it revealed the equally "degraded" mechanisms of a relationship much closer to home.

"It's the way we are," one of them said to me. "I'm not sure I like it, but it's the way we are, isn't it?" Then again, after a moment, in a voice so speculative it made you wonder what part of her own life she was reviewing: "It's the way we are."

Pure gold, from someone able to read your subject matter per-haps better than you can yourself!

In *Angel*, her novel based on the lives of Marie Corelli and Ouida, Elizabeth Taylor puts the case clearly. Of Angel, the bud-ding romantic fantasist, she says: " . . . at sixteen, experience was an unnecessary and usually baffling obstacle to her imagination." Children are – and this seems to be a cultural if not a biological necessity – terrorised by the adult experience of life, which, glimpsing it obliquely, at times of stress, and in fragments which makes no sense, they try to ignore. Many fantasy and sf readers are living out a prolonged childhood in which they retain that terror and erect – in collusion with professional writers who themselves often began as teenage daydreamers – powerful defences against it.

Thus they prefer fiction which, like "hard" sf, ignores adult experience or ropes it off in a reductivist way; or which, like fantasy and horror fiction, diffuses and defuses it through fairy-tale and myth; or – perhaps most characteristically since the New Wave, "inner space" and the soft sciences – which generalises and politicises it. (Post New Wave readers, especially those who consider themselves most adult and intelligent in their use of the genre, seem not to fear experience so much as individual experience. They are not frightened of life so much as life's particularity. The trap is circular. The less you engage your own adult experience, the less you value it, and the more you tend to rely on systematic ideological validations of it. This is no better than the school playground, with its establishmentally validated experiences and sociative norms, you believe you have left behind.)

It is this fear of experience – this essential lack of self-esteem – which, paradoxically, enables readers to confront without fear novels like *The Book of the New Sun*. Gene Wolfe, they are quite willing to be persuaded, is not writing about individual acts of murder and torture, done to individual human beings by other individual human beings. He is writing "parabolically" about an idea. The world of murder retreats to a comfortable distance again, to the sound of "Johnny Fedora" playing popular classics . . .

5.   INTO THE FIRE

In the early-to-mid 1980s I found myself claiming in a letter to a friend:

> My journal is a machine for understanding what to write, built in the two years since my previous models of writing – largely inherited from the New Wave – failed me; an argument with myself I can't really begin to express to anyone else. So much discarded and so much taken up. It's not that I won't be the same writer again, but that I won't be the same person. That I am able to admit this at all demonstrates an increase in confidence. When I led my first Extreme rock-climb I found myself

tottering about at the top, blasted and made drunk by a gale of adrenalin, thinking, "Being able to do this frees me." I was wrong. Before I could by anywhere near being free I had to be able to stand at the top of a piece of writing and say that.[7]

I had been ready to give it up. If there's nothing like adrenalin, "the Pan within", the fall into experience and the vertigo that precedes it, why write anything at all? Because meaning is an act. And because every time you look up from reading or writing, something is new in the landscape:

The high walls of the station at Kilburn High Road are covered with the most beautiful graffiti. They are not scrawls whose content – "LUFC wankers die tomorrow", "No brains rule" – and context are their only significance, but explosions of red purple and green done with great deliberation and technique, shapes like fireworks going off, shapes that bulge like damp tropical fruit, with an effect of glistening surfaces. They are names – "Eddie", "Daggo", "Mince" – but names which have been transformed from sign or label into illustration: pictures of names. After them, everything else along the lines seems so dull, the walls of the cuttings like nothing so much as the walls of some great windowless linear prison. The kids who do this call it "bombing"; they bomb their Weltinnenraum on to the walls of the prison.[8]

Even so, why write fiction, especially fantasy or sf? Why continue to interpose between reader and subject a mediating metaphor no longer technically necessary or philosophically desirable? Clearly, "M. John Harrison", the author implied by "A Young Man's Journey to Viriconium" or "The Gift", is contradicting himself.

There are two exits from this scandal, one by way of content, the other formal, linguistic (or perhaps felt, tenuous, beloved; or perhaps both at once). Neither should be viewed as an escape clause. (It should already have become apparent that I welcome both the self-contradiction and its centrality in the work. It is an engine, like all scandals, a source of power.) Neither is exclusive of the other.

Firstly, then, I still write fantasies so that I can write about fantasy.

Reviewing *The Ice Monkey* in *Foundation*, Roz Kaveney pointed out,

> . . . (In) "Egnaro" . . . Harrison makes some effective editorial remarks about the habit of fantasy . . . There is in Harrison a profound commitment to the fantastic mode and a deep dread of what fantasy might make you, where it might lead you.[9]

Not to mention where it has already led you. Unstated but implicit, especially in the short stories written since "Running Down", has been not so much the warning, "If you do fantasy this is what you could become," as the assessment, "If you do fantasy this is perhaps what you have already become." Lucas is shown as a willing and self-corrupted victim of the parasitic idea or structure Egnaro. I make no apologies for this. Under political and economic ("Running Down", "Egnaro", *Climbers*), social ("A Young Man's Journey to Viriconium", "Old Women") and above all emotional ("The Incalling", "The Quarry") pressures, we all retreat and deform. I hope I have shown this with compassion. But escape should not become escapism – the habitual daydream which rejects direct adult experience of the world, or the cynically engineered extension of this daydream offered by market-driven publishing houses and exemplified by, say, *The Dragonbone Chair*.

A permanent escape, a feeling that you have given life the slip, is pathological, or anyway very sad. Frankly, the rewards of confronting your circumstances are greater. I shouldn't be taken to mean this literalistically. Even a game with a leak to reality can be an escape, indeed it often makes the best one. *Climbers* and "The Ice Monkey" illustrate how obsessive commitment to an activity, the circumstances of which are often painfully not to say fatally "real", is used by climbers as an escape from emotional and social demands; a retreat from life. In this sense the walls of the Verdon Gorge are as much a fantasy-world as Middle Earth; the wreckage of Sheffield is the landscape of a political fairy-tale.

Fantasy has become the subject matter of my work in another, quite different, way. The relationship, through language, of the world (as lived) to the written (as recording) is fraught from the beginning. Every act of writing is already a fantasy – if not a wishfulfilment – if only because the word is not the thing. Neither is there, within the category of the written, any hierarchy of "truth"; if writing is *never* the world, one can claim, then there really isn't anything to choose between the deliberate fictions of Bruno Schulz in *The Street of Crocodiles* and the accidental ones of the "science writer". Schulz has identified something corrupt and lovely at the heart of the rose; Paul Davies, stumbling amateurishly along the interface between science and rhetoric, hasn't yet realised that all analogies are bad analogies. I have tried to act out this divorce of label and referent (often messy, always bad for the children) in stories like "The Lamia & Lord Cromis".

If this seems to lead only deeper into the fire, we had better try the second exit, which may be described as linguistic or metaphysical, as you wish.

6. IN BREACH OF THE FAMILIAR

The whole direction of human effort is towards the relief of anxiety. This leads to the steady domestication of all new experience. Because of this, Shklovsky says, "Art exists to help us recover the sensation of life; it exists to make us feel things, to make the stone stony. The end of art is to give a sensation of the object as seen, not as recognised. The technique of art is to make things 'unfamiliar' . . . The act of perception in art is an end in itself."[10]

The tradition of f&sf is to provide a cheap relaxing substitute for the excitement that has gone out of life through usage. But this is quite the opposite to the achievements of writers like Iain Banks, Tanith Lee, Geoff Ryman or Scott Bradfield, who, in books like *The Wasp Factory, Forests of the Night, The Unconquered Country* and *The Secret Life of Houses*, have redeemed and reinvigorated some aspect of the world. Writers as good as these offer neither a substitute nor a didactic panacea, but flare the real thing into existence for a moment.

One of the rhetorical figures used by writers to defamiliarise objects, situations or circumstances (or at least to light them briefly in a new way so that they stand out from the background they have sunk into) is metaphor. I use the word in its capacious modern sense, which sucks in all kinds of comparisons, similes, metonymies, analogies, homologies, acts of allegory or symbolism and so on.[11] In this sense a metaphor is any twinning in which there is a leak or pivot of significance between the two poles of the figure – although only one of them needs to be visibly present, as in a Symbolist story. The word "paralysis", they used to say, never appears once in "Araby", "The Kiss", or "The Daughters of the Late Colonel", nevertheless informs every page.

On this basis anyone might take a stab at the vitalising metaphor of "The Great God Pan", for instance, which is less about dark arts than emotional incompetence. A whole generation wounds itself in its ideology, goes to ground, and is haunted by its own crippledom.

In "Running Down", my first successful piece of fiction, the environmental disorder that haunts Lyall is equated directly with the affective disorders we discover knotted round his core of insecurity and self-concern.[12] Increasing "entropy" models or mimics his increasing solipsism. Britain declines by metonymy: geological catastrophe as lack of care.

This attempt to make entropy a metaphor for political ill-health continued with the Low City plague of *In Viriconium*, then ended: by 1981, nobody in Rotherham or Huddersfield needed metaphors – with their lives in the grip of a political fantasist more determined than me, they could look out of any window at the foam of perilous seas and fairy lands forlorn.[13]

(Thatcherland is not England. Just as there is no "English" landscape – only a palimpsest of agricultural and industrial usage, history fossilised into fields and moors – so there are no "good and sound historical reasons" for "English values". There is only a whisper of dreams, some strong, some fading, all powered by the needs and greeds of the moment. The moment passes, and ageing dreams topple off it. The moment passes and drops new dreams like sacs of amino acid, new programmes, new genetic messages. They die as they fall, they shift into something else even as they gel into their final form . . . The only "political" question worth considering, the only question of "cultural history" worth considering, is who, at any given moment, is dreaming hardest and most powerfully; and whose dream is whose nightmare.)

The sites of nightmare in our domesticated age are never so much geographical as rhetorical. "John Wayne's brave fight," they say, "against cancer." "She lost her brave fight against the disease." "The story of so-and-so's brave fight." I wanted to defamiliarise the treatment sheds where to help you in that brave fight they destroy your psychological stamina, violate your dignity, and scab your spirit during your last days. "The New Rays", sleeting down impartially on nurse and patient alike, gave me my metaphor. "The Incalling" had already suggested, in the relationship between Clerk and his tormentors, a model for that medical rhetoric which claims "We can help you live", without explaining what life will be like after the chemotherapy and the radio-implants – or how long it will last.

7. THAT WAS THE RIVER, THIS IS THE SEA

Gérard Genette[14] describes how in 1730 Cesar Dumarsais' treatise *Des Tropes* "turned rhetoric into . . . a turnstile of the figurative defined as the other of the literal, and of the literal defined as the other of the figurative", enclosing it thereafter "in this meticulous vertigo". The writer, in a burst of pure adrenalin, locates himself exactly at the spindle of the "turn" stile. About him in rhetorical space all he can see is the irresolvable flicker of precedence, as it is passed back and forth between the poles of the figure:

> All you can remember about the city you're in is a display of popular wedding stationery – 20 per cent off – which, as you walked past it, seemed for a moment to merge indistinguishably with the cigarette ends, chip papers and supermarket receipts on the pavement – so that for a moment everything became illegible for you, because the floor of the display window and the street, the outside and inside, were only extensions of each other.[15]

Wedding stationery stands by metonymy for weddings, by metaphor for hope, new starts, the possible. We know what used chip-bags suggest, especially in Bradford. Where do we look for the fourth term of this homology? Evidently in the "meaning" of the story from which the image is taken: story and image complete each other endlessly – or, as Charles Newman (*The Post Modern Aura*) would have it of antinomies, they "reciprocally evoke" one another.

But this matters less than the massive gesture of make-believe at the grammatical pivot of the comparison: "seemed to merge indistinguishably with". Attempting to breach the familiar, the writer finds – and celebrates – an act of fantasy at the heart of his method. Out of that weird and plastic zone at the crux of metaphor, energy pours in two directions. We need the world to make fiction. Could it be that we need fiction to make the world?

Peckham High Street, January 1987. Just up from the railway station and on the same side, there is a rental place called "Apollo

Video". In its window a television runs constantly. On the screen tonight a Japanese boy watches as a sword is beaten into existence out of the sparks of the anvil. In the context of the film he is only a cliché. (He will grow up to be a Ninja fighter. His eyes are huge now as he contemplates this future in the steel.) But look away from the screen and you can see the sparks fly out of it and down the High Street, where amid dancing snowflakes – from which they are for a moment indistinguishable – they light up something else altogether: an old black man staring into a shopfront full of winter woollens.

Language is a scandal because – by an abuse of its own basic assumption, which is that it has some honest marriage with the real – it can make connections like these. Words pass the experienced world back and forth between them as a metaphor of a metaphor, the sign of a sign, until it is worn out. Only then – always too late, always in time – do we realise that meaning is an act, by the performance of which, instant to instant, we repossess our lives.

Notes

1. John Clute, 1989.
2. *The Pastel City*, 1971.
3. *A Storm of Wings*, 1978.
4. "Old Women", 1983. *Woman's Journal*, March 1984.
5. Jacob von Uexkull measured the visual moment of animals in the late 1800s, and argued from there to the way human beings perceive time. From then on Umwelt was a fact, and words like Weltanschauung began to have the possibility of some quantifiable meaning. Someone cheekier than me might date literary modernism from that discovery; especially if he or she had read *Moments of Being* recently . . .
6. H.E. Bates, *The Modern Short Story*, 1941, Nelson.
7. The present piece is only an extension of this letter, a kind of thinking-out-loud rather than a conclusion. Conclusions would in any case be offered not prescriptively but as an attempt to share a personal experience of what it is like to be a writer. As are all the conclusions (I take it) published under the umbrella "The Profession of SF". Further developments of the same argument – not to say some of the same material – are offered in the short stories "The Gift" and "The Horse of Iron and How Can We Know It and Be Changed by It Forever".
8. "The Horse of Iron, etc." *Tarot Tales*, ed. Pollack & Thomas, Century, 1989.
9. *Foundation* 29, November 1983.

10. Victor Shklovsky, "Art as Technique". Quoted by David Lodge, *The Modes of Modern Writing* (1977), himself quoting from *Structuralism in Literature* (1974) by Robert Scholes.

11. This admission of cold-blooded deliberateness means that no one need write to remind me I'm "abusing" the word (or any other). Language is an invitation to meaning, not a set of proscriptions. People have always done the most impressive linguistic feats, without any safety net at all, out of a conception of language as plastic to their will to speak. This has been its salvation in the face of head-teacher linguistics.

12. It is not Lyall and his wife who make up the antithetical pair to what Durrell calls "the king and queen of the affect" (*Quinx*, 1987), but *Lyall and his narrator*.

13. Gregory Benford has pointed out that "Running Down" and *In Viriconium* aren't much of an "illustration" of the scientific principles of entropy. Quite so, since they weren't supposed to be one. While this would be plain to a writer, it wasn't perhaps quite so plain to a physicist.

14. *Figures of Literary Discourse*, 1972. Basil Blackwell.

15. "The Gift", *Other Edens 2*, ed. Evans and Holdstock, 1988.

13

Confessions of a Bradbury Eater

Garry Kilworth

This coming July I shall be 42, which may be the answer to life, the universe and everything – or it could be, as Dudley Moore said in the opening lines to *10*, a betrayal. Certainly it snuck up on me suddenly, just after my twenty-seventh birthday, and caught me with my pants down. I had intended to achieve one of two goals before my forty-second birthday: I wanted to be either rich or famous (or both).

I have several confessions to make. First of all, I failed the eleven plus, which is why I am doing a BA in English at an age when most men are falling over their feet to get to the armchair. Education began by correspondence course at the age of 22, completed at 33, with a degree in Business Studies. I also began writing science fiction seriously (which means with a view to publication) at the same time I completed my degree. Previous to that one or two half-hearted attempts had been hopefully winged to *New Worlds*: there are several letters from Mike Moorcock to prove their inadequacy. (Where *did* he find the time to encourage newcomers? Whilst editing a poetry magazine I didn't have time to write to my own mother.) I've never quite managed to completely throw off that early dismal failure at primary school, which is probably why I'm still into Education. It's rather nice being a very mature student. Other students are always mistaking me for a tutor and sometimes call me "sir".

My childhood, mostly spent in Arabia since my father was in the Air Force, was somewhat Huckleberry Finnish. I played truant a lot which gave me time to read all those pulp magazines of the Golden Age. I was always an avid reader of fiction of any kind – torch under the sheets at midnight stuff – and later, following gosling-like in daddy's footprints, was sent to places like Gan

Island where the only thing to do besides swim was read and write. The motives of the individual who joins one of the services seldom coincide with those of the organisation. Potential pilots will join because it is the only way to learn to fly high-speed jet aircraft, not because they enjoy dropping napalm on Asiatic villages. The rude awakening comes later. I had a taste for travel which even now remains unsated and my personal contribution was encoding and deciphering messages in dark holes underground. In 1961 I joined the CND marchers which, incongruous as it may sound, was no uncommon thing among young servicemen in the early sixties, and resulted in a posting from Air Ministry London to a remote airfield in Norfolk.

My lust for travel and exotic lands was quenched by long periods in Singapore, the Maldive Islands, Kenya, Germany, Bahrain, Aden, Malta, Cyprus and Masirah in the Persian Gulf. If you're wondering why I bother to list them, it's because I loved them all and like a book collector refuse to omit any prestigious title. As I travelled I wrote, mostly poetry and sf, my "sensawonder" having been primed by Wells and Wyndham, Ron Goulart and Brian Aldiss. If I could have touched the hem of Brian's garment at the age of 20, I would have been fulfilled. (Or would have risen from the dead, or cured of leprosy, or *something*.)

My father, an ordinary airman, came from farm labouring stock and my mother from a trawler fishing family. The dreamy kid they had spawned, who was forever bunking school and getting caught with a fishing line in his hand, was a bit of an enigma to them. When my first story appeared in the *Sunday Times*, my mother regarded me with a kind of suspicious awe, as if I'd done something faintly illicit.

That first story, "Let's go to Golgotha", the shared winner of the Gollancz/*Sunday Times* sf competition of 1974, was the biggest kick I ever got from writing. After that the hard work began, just at the point when I sincerely believed it was over. I wrote something like six stories after "Golgotha" which failed to find a publisher. However, I had discovered there was an institution called "fandom" of which I had not previously been aware. One day, while drowning slowly in a quicksand of rejection slips, a letter arrived from a guy who signed himself Robert Holdstock. "I have one or two stories under my belt," he said modestly, "and so do you. I'm getting together an anthology called *Time in Hand* and I'd like to include something by you. No gratuitous sex or violence though," which just goes to show how perverse human nature is. I met Rob in London and a long and firm friendship developed. He introduced me to a workshop group called "Pieria" and contact with the sf writing world was firmly established.

My first Pierian story was "A Warrior Falls", which sub-sequently appeared in the appallingly unsuccessful Penguin Anthology *Pulsar Two*. It was not a good story and I almost threw up with nervous tension reading it out to a group of strangers but it did put some confidence back into my pen. One or two of the group actually liked a couple of phrases I'd used, though I was (and still am) accused of wandering prose. My philosophy on that aspect of writing has always been firm. I believe I am an intuitive writer and spontaneity I regard as a strength. This doesn't mean I throw craftsmanship by the board, but that, for my particular style of writing, overpolishing often destroys the original intention. I write longhand and each sentence is carefully considered before application and occasionally a little purple creeps in: if the voices in my head aren't too loud, it stays. Three drafts of a novel is my maximum and if the cuts haven't come by then, they never will.

In the early days my worst critics were within the sf field, though not as a complete body or I would have jumped from Westminster Bridge with a copy of *Dhalgren* tied round my neck. A particular comment, which always had me mystified, was that I did not develop this or that idea fully enough. My answer would have been, had I been *allowed* to answer, that the particular idea did not interest me enough to develop it beyond a certain point, otherwise I would have done so. A novel has a course to run and I go into enough backwaters as it is, without following a completely different river from the one on which I first began the journey. Paul Kincaid gave one of my novels a single syllable review. We have since met and appraised each other with a more sympathetic eye but still retain the right to disagree as much in science fiction – not just my novels and his reviews.

The observations of critics, whom Fielding described rather unkindly as clerks usurping the judge's bench, do affect a new writer to the field, either serving to entrench certain ideas or to alter them. Sure, the whole business is subjective and at least critics do *read* the books (don't they?) and even adverse comment is public notice. They make one pause to consider exactly what one *is* trying to say. Even a favourable review might evoke a passionate response in the wrong direction. Another able reviewer once wrote that while I did not *appear* to be a sexist (note the vague inference that I had yet to prove my innocence), I did sometimes describe women *by* the size of their breasts. What? I reread the passages in the novels and found that I had indeed included in my description of two women, through the viewpoint of one of my male characters, a reference to the fact that their breasts were small, medium or large, as I had mentioned that they had angular jaws and/or Greek noses. I had also described one of the men as having wiry arms, balding head and small testicles. The personalities and intelligence of both sexes were also plumbed to the advantage and disadvantage of both, depending on the characters, but obviously I had entered a sacrosanct area. Let me state here and now that *I* believe in the equality of the sexes, whatever my protagonists might, in the ignorance of their times and situations, portray as their views on the subject. As a writer and a house-husband, I need to retain this belief in equality in order to overcome my inferiority complex, as I vacuum the home and make the beds before my female partner returns from a hard day at the office, to beat me at a game of Scrabble. Having successfully raised a daughter in the belief that she can compete with men in the world of engineering, and a son in the knowledge that it is not effeminate to want to be a chef, this kind of inferred criticism deeply wounds. I am aware that if one puts a baby amongst wolves, it will grow up to be a wolf in all but physical appearance. Environmental indoctrination is, after all, the main theme in my novel *In Solitary*. My best friends will tell you I am about as macho as a mixture of Woody Allen and Bambi.

The energy level I have as a writer is directly proportionate to my enthusiasm for the subject matter. Sf gives me a lot of drive because its imaginative scope excites me. During the first six years of writing (seriously) I held down a full-time job during the day, commuting two hours each way to London from a remote corner of Essex. If I was writing a novel I would plan the evening's work on the journey to and from London, and commit those plans to paper in the hours from eight to twelve at night. My first three novels, two thrillers and an sf book, failed to find a publisher. This can be pretty dispiriting when it takes nine months to complete a single novel. I am not trying to call on the violins at this point – I'm just trying to say that it's all been worth it. That first published novel could have cancelled out five manuscripts collecting dust in the drawer. On rereading the rejects, of course, one gives a hearty sigh of relief that they never were published – all except one, which had a Jerry Cornelius character for its hero, but was a thriller and apparently he was not sympathetic enough for readers in that genre. Since I gave up my bread-and-butter job to write full time, I find I am producing less. There's some sort of equation here that escapes my unmathematical brain but it has something to do with the fact that when you squeeze an apple into a tomato skin you get a nice tight fit.

The approach to writing short stories is obviously completely different to that of a novel. I compose almost all the first draft of a short story in my head and on committing it to paper can maintain that high pitch of enthusiasm for the idea throughout. I like to write a short story from beginning to end without putting down my pen. Of course this is not always possible but I am usually more satisfied with the result when it is.

It is fashionable in some quarters to remark that no good sf has been written since 1960 (or 1940 or 1950) and in the literature world, opinions often masquerade as facts. I do not believe that "real" sf stopped at a precise time of day in May any more than I believe good art ceased with Raphael. There are just as many good sf stories now as there were when Kingsley Amis was young, and just as much trash reached the shelves then as it does now. The Spartans' attitude of "everything is perfect, let's stop progress" only reflects on those that employ such rigid and blinkered view-points. If examples of "good" stories since 1960 *are* required, then I'll quote some particular favourites: Wolfe's "The Death of Doctor Island"; most of Tiptree's stories; and Holdstock's "Mythago Wood". We all feel nostalgic for the pre-1960 years in sf, me included, but for heavens' sakes let's not turn an emotion into a basis for a philosophy. (This dismal attitude towards current sf is particularly galling when it comes from the pen of those who do not write any publishable fiction themselves.) J.G. Ballard has stated that he believes sf to be the authentic literature of the twentieth century (not just the three decades following the war), and said in a television interview that there are some exciting stories and novels being written *right now*. He is right, of course. There is *always* some exciting literature being written *right now*.

It is inevitable that writers should be fashionable or unfashion-able at certain points in their careers. Asimov, Heinlein and Brad-bury have recently run the gauntlet of adverse criticism, in this country at least. Like many authors they do not produce their best in later years, though there are exceptions (Frederik Pohl being one of them). I was raised on a diet of Bradbury stories which to me were as intoxicating as opium and I will never renounce them. Jack Finney, too, I swallowed avidly, and believe him to be a much under-rated writer. *Invasion of the Body Snatchers* is not his only work and was out of the run of his normal medium. His "Galesburg" stories evoked an atmosphere which went to my head faster than champagne. Enjoyment of a story, for me, does depend a great deal on its atmosphere, which is one reason I like science fiction. A tale that is as dry and stale as a bar room at eight o'clock in the morning does not arouse my enthusiasm, however original and clever the plot. Originality *is* important but its absence does not concern me if the plot is approached from a new angle and a definite mood is developed. Perhaps a little anecdote will serve to illustrate this. I was once standing at a bus stop next to a couple of West Indian youngsters who were discussing a pop concert they had been to. "Man," said one, "that music was real trash, y'know. Nuthin' new. All old, old, old." "What do you expect, man?" said his buddy, "they's only few basic notes to use." The first speaker waved his arms in the general direction of the street. "See those people. They all got two arms, legs an' a head, yet they's all *different*. That's the way the music should be." And the same holds true for sf stories. There *are* only a few basic plots: it's the way they're put together that counts. Investigation of an alien culture, whether invented or borrowed from this world, is as fascinating to me as the exploration of an aspect of physics is to others. I do not consider the "science" in science fiction to be the predominant factor governing the quality of the work.

What I do consider important, or rather what is important to *me*, is that the "imagination" should be allowed unchecked flow. This may seem like a rather puerile statement but I find it worrying that critics within the sf field, as well as out of it, seem more concerned at drawing parallels with mainstream fiction, or wishing to regress to earlier decades, than looking for stories which develop the world of the imagination. Science fiction is a genre and it is expected that people who do not read it have no real grasp of the fundamental concepts that lie behind its works. One of those concepts is the exploration of the imagination, whether it is in the direction of inner or outer space. As soon as one begins to lay down restrictions and draw boundaries, the literary form becomes static and eventually stagnates. However, one does expect that *within* the genre, appreciation will be given to brave ventures at extending the boundaries of imagination, instead of complaining that themes have become too exotic, or that the stories in sf magazines are not as well written as those in mainstream anthologies. (Judged by whose standards?) In reaching for new worlds, there must be experimentation, and experiments, by definition, attempt discovery without being confident of the results.

Thus we must expect to find ordinary mortals in sf magazines, as well as the occasional giant. The giants should be allowed to carry the lesser beings unless one wishes to abandon the search for fantastic creatures altogether. The mainstream produces well-written, unusual stories but it works within its own confines and these restrictions harness "imagination" in the widest sense of the word. Wordsworth wrote many beautiful poems but because of the restrictions he placed upon himself he never produced a poem that plumbed the depths of imagination. Coleridge wrote many mediocre poems but he also produced the unrivalled "Khubla Khan". Surely we have enough *heart* to support our own literature and its adventurous spirit.

In mainstream fiction, authors and readers have in recent years begun moving towards a factual element as a basis for enjoyment of the work. They like the familiarity of real events interlocked with fictional drama. *The Day of the Jackal* and *The Eagle has Landed* are two examples in point. The books seem to vie for percentages of truth. "Twenty per cent of this story is known fact." I would like, one day, to attempt to capture some of this readership, to have the courage, audacity and pretension to state that "Ninety per cent of this sf novel is true. It just hasn't happened yet." Prefacing the same novel I should also like to have the cheek to dedicate the work to earlier influences on my career as a reader. It would say something like, "To the lost gardens of Enid Blyton, Lucy Atwell, Beatrix Potter and the rest of the lads of the 32nd Parachute Regiment."

14

A Shaman's View

David Brin

How to tell others about the "Profession of Science Fiction"? It isn't exactly one of those careers your guidance counsellor ever described to you, nor is it the sort of thing you are likely to encounter during an afternoon at the Job Mart. It would seem to be, in fact, one of the *least* describable fields of endeavour around.

For one thing, I've never met an associated group of individuals with fewer common characteristics. The sf authors I know range from Stalinists to right-wingers to protoanarchists, from sweet old ladies to former Green Berets, from temperamental geniuses to hard-nosed realists.

Oh, a few commonalities can be listed. Most of my peers are flaming individualists, for instance. Many seem to suspect that "consensus" is a dirty word, one that is symptomatic of a group badly in need of stirring-up. The majority would rather have an amiable argument than a dinner at a four-star restaurant, but like best of all to combine the two. Also, they all seem to love to mix and match metaphors and bizarre notions, to pun, to play devil's advocate.

Still, no two writers seem to *write* in exactly the same way. Some keep their current projects absolutely secret, lest some mystic energy leak away if they tell anything before it's all safely down on paper. Others take the attitude of the "tribal story-teller", and find their enthusiasm only stoked ever higher the more often they describe the tale they plan to tell.

So, how do I describe the Profession of Science Fiction? Obviously, this must be a personal account, so I'll eschew academese (I can speak it, I have my union card) in favour of an earthier tone. One coming from *me*.

Shall I be biographical? Philosophical? Evocative?

Why not combine all of these. Since I claim it's what we do best, let's talk in terms of *metaphors*.

AN ODD COMPARISON

Here's our first one. Let's start by looking at *scientists* – today's caretakers of knowledge who are the era's accepted interpreters of the world. This has caused no end of bitterness among those who once wore that mantle, and yet the comparison cannot be denied. Scientists certainly can be called today's "high priests".

Some metaphor. And certainly it can be observed that the Scientific cloister attracts many of the same types that once flocked to the Catholic orders, or to the Rabbinate or, for that matter, to the temples of Ra. Only nowadays the miracles they learn how to deliver are palpable – both more rewarding and more dangerous than ever before.

Oh, there are a few ways in which the new clergy violate priestly tradition. For instance, they seem to be much less prey to the age-old clerical fetish for obscurantism and keeping secrets. Rather, scientists sometimes appear positively obsessed with sharing their lore (e.g. getting a grant to do a BBC series on their favourite topic).

Nevertheless, the analogy holds. Science even has its heretics – UFOlogists and psychic researchers – and it has its own "orders". Physicists may be likened to Jesuits or Brahmins, interpreting the Grand Design. And mathematicians are the equivalent of Kabbalists, who delve into mysteries that one supposes might drive other men mad.

An interesting comparison, but what does all of this have to do with the "Profession of Science Fiction"?

Well, first off, it is clear that science fiction takes part in the values promulgated in our culture by modern science. Even when sf turns a critical, scathing eye toward a certain type of technical advancement, or warns of dire consequences, it nevertheless remains part of that culture, operating from within its overall web of assumptions.

Unlike most prior world-views, which harken back to some ancient, lamented Golden Age, science preaches a "look-forward" attitude toward wisdom – holding that next year's version of "truth" will be better than this year's, and so on into the future. Science fiction actively participates in proselytizing this theme of guarded progress and acceptance of change. Even when it deals in warning messages, sf nevertheless conveys the fundamental assumption that the future is ours to shape, for well or ill. To past priesthoods this would have been anathema. But to the modern clerics – the scientists – this is accepted dogma, only more reinforcement of their own treasured beliefs. It is not surprising, then, that so many of them read sf.

Still, I have a much more personal reason for working in this analogy-metaphor. As one invited to tell his own story – how I took up the profession of science fiction – I feel that I must first confess that it was not my first love. And it never will be.

THE AUTOBIOGRAPHICAL BIT

You see, at an early age I was one of those spoken of earlier, a young man apparently doomed to be attracted to the priesthood. In other days I suppose I would have striven to become a rabbi, or a pastor, or perhaps a temple theoretician. It's a condition easy to diagnose in a youth. The symptoms include a tendency to take long walks and stare at stars while mumbling to oneself. There is also a moody intensity over metaphors nobody else seems to be much worried about, and an eagerness to find out "what's going on".

As a youngster I met men and women from many walks of life. It was clear even then that my greatest gift was with words. Everyone spoke of how much money I'd make if I entered Law.

I *hated* the lawyers I met! They struck me as a money-grubbing, unscrupulous lot. Pfeh! They didn't even seem to enjoy their profession. (The true test of that, I figured, was whether they would do exactly the same thing, day in and day out, if they were independently wealthy and had to *pay* to do it! All the lawyers I knew would simply take the money and skip off to Bimini.)

I met quite a few scientists, as well. (My father took me to watch Einstein play the violin, when I was five.) *They* seemed to be having fun. Here was a bunch of guys who would – if necessary – bribe somebody to let them do what they loved doing: science.

Oh, over the years since then I've met scientists who were twits, jerks, bad husbands and fathers, cheats, liars – you name it. But it did seem a larger *fraction* of them were stable, decent people who were having a good time. Their lives weren't just devoted to their work, either. The better ones seemed to fill their homes with music and loved to read or talk about anything under the sun. That was how I decided I wanted to live.

Anyway, as I grew older, I came to see that these were the guys who were talking to God in the language He used to make the Universe. That was an idea that appealed to my romantic soul.

Yeah, I was better with words. But somehow I managed to scrape together enough talent at maths to squint at the equations, to blink in myopic wonder at the beauty of them, at their symmetry and fantastic clarity. It was like hearing Bach and viewing Van Gogh all at once. Wow.

Then came the day when I realized I'd never, ever be a Jesuit.

Now mind you, one can draw out a metaphor too far. But I figure it was something like the way a young monk must have felt when the Abbot called him in to tell him he wasn't being sent to Rome, but to a tiny village ten days' ass-ride south of Rheims, there to teach school.

Oh, even a Franciscan or a Dominican can do good work, if he applies himself hard enough. Eventually I got my "union card", my PhD. Sweat can partly make up for lack of brilliance; it was a good dissertation. All along, though, I'd been puttering at this hobby of scribbling stories. It helped ease the pressure of studies, it amused my friends, and there finally came a day when it began paying the bills.

Hell, that's downplaying it *too* far. I loved writing! It was a passion that called beckoningly, drawing me ever away from my chosen profession. When it started paying – not just in cash but in respect, attention, kudos – I found it ever easier to put science on the back burner.

It's hard to be regretful, nowadays. So few people get to do what they *really* want to do, or even their third or fourth choices. I am lucky, indeed. My profession allows me to sleep late, to take trips at a moment's notice, to give television interviews and get invited to dinner by congressmen and MPs, all in the line of duty.

And yet, once a priest . . .?

There are times when I feel I'd trade a million-book best-seller for just *one* paper in grand unified field theory that would make Alan Guth or Stephen Hawking cry out "I wish *I'd* thought of that!"

Tsk. Life isn't perfect. I'm not complaining.

WITCH DOCTORS

So, if not a member of the priesthood, what then *is* a science fiction writer? Well, knowing full well that we must never really believe our metaphors, I offer another one for you to try on.

Always at the fringes of the temple grounds there have also been *shamans*, freelance agents who have danced and chanted and fed their patients strange herbs to give them vivid dreams. Often the afflicted were cured by the power of suggestions alone. And if not, well, at least they were distracted from their misery for a while.

I suggest that this is a good analogy for the role of sf authors. We leap and dance, we hop and gyre. And, most wonderfully of all, we chant. Oh, do we chant! And our incantations certainly do create images in the minds of our clientele. Vivid, startling hallucinations of vast star clusters or rolling storms on faraway worlds – of voyages to times and places past or times and places that never were and never *could* be – chilling images of individual terror and even of apotheosis for our posterity. You name it. They come to us, pass over a little silver, and we take them for a ride.

So, in a sense we are shamans. Is this a worthy role?

Yes, I think so. At the very least we do distract our patients from their troubles for a while. And I believe the mythic values I've seen purveyed from the mortars of science fiction – like assorted healing herbs – are for the most part wholesome medicine.

At our best, we new shamans can even inspire. We sometimes bring about that wonder of all wonders – a *new thought* in some mind out there which might otherwise have remained dead, dead, dead. That I see as miracle working of a high order.

But there is a danger. The danger is to the magician himself. To the witch herself. The professional hazard of being a shaman is that we always seem to be on the verge of falling into the trap of worshipping our own incantations! Like an actor who believes his own press flacks, we tumble into a pit whenever we start taking ourselves too seriously.

Ego is a death trip. Some quite gifted shamans (and many critics, as well) seem to forget one of the most basic rules of magic – that there is no place an incantation works better than in the brain of its author!

"Oh! What a great paragraph!" (I muse, having just typed it.) "What a (chilling, moving, insightful) passage!" (I think, after just re-reading it.) "Nobody else could have done it better!" (I cry out, forgetting that in nobody else will the words resonate exactly the same way. To no one else will the images mean quite as much.)

Again, pfeh. Those who travel down that road all too often ruin their work, as well as their good names. The rewards simply aren't worth it.

RESOURCE WASTERS

Another metaphor I really like was raised by Lee Montgomerie in *Interzone*, some while back.

"Sometimes I think time is running out for sf, locked in a desperate energy crisis. So much of its conceptual fuel has already been burned up, exhausted, reprocessed . . . Sometimes I think sf is already dead . . . endlessly and pointlessly revisiting its old haunts, saying nothing."

Actually, Montgomerie incanted quite a number of metaphors, and gloomy ones at that, reminiscent of the theme Spider Robinson raised in his Hugo Award winning short story, "Melancholy Elephants".

Are sf authors, then, little more than greedy exploiters of a limited resource? The resource of relevant, usable ideas? It is a point I raised some year's back, at the Eaton Conference on Hard SF. (Proceedings published under the title *Hard Science Fiction*.) In that essay I suggested that the best authors tend to avoid any concept which has already been explored well, and prefer instead to go off in search of even newer ideas. We tend to admire this fetish for originality, but it may very well be that in doing so authors "mine out" conceptual territory that may not be limitless after all!

Chris Evans has put it another way. "In a sense, every sf writer in the world is labouring in the shadow of H.G. Wells. None has achieved his mastery of form, his originality and invention. Of course, Wells had the advantage when he was writing that practically the whole field was there for the making . . ."

Do I seriously believe this model of my profession, as rapacious exploiters of a limited resource, as *eco-criminals*, in a sense?

Well, we can be so sanctimonious at times, so bloody self-righteous, that maybe I find it interesting to see us in a black hat, for a change. Hmm.

A PAUSE TO GET SERIOUS

Leaving aside metaphors for a moment, science fiction is really a wonderful profession, one that can be remunerative, can force one to endure a little flattery, and often delivers some pretty good times, all for doing what one would have been willing to *pay* to do anyway. As I said, that was one of the benchmarks I long ago set for a worthwhile profession. So even though it means I must be a witch doctor, rather than a priest, I suppose I can live with my plight.

Now this, of course sets me up for disdain from a certain type of critic – the sort who will inevitably say, "He's having fun. Therefore he can't be a true artist." Fortunately, it is easy to laugh at the sheer impudence of such a remark. Anyway, Lawrence Kubie demolished that logic in his epochal book, *The Neurotic Distortion of the Creation Process*, in which he demonstrated conclusively that genius and pain aren't such great partners, after all.

It's nothing more than a Hollywood myth that the artist is born to suffer. And artistic types have been the first to help foster this fable. It plays well, especially with the girls, and people will put up with your most outrageous behaviour, excusing it as "artistic temperament". Oh, what a lovely scam!

Certainly, some creative geniuses *have* suffered. But I am tempted to suggest that they prevailed in spite of the handicap of misery, rather than in partnership with it. The sculptor, Bruce Beasley, is just one of many counterexamples of men whose brilliance dazzles nearly as brightly as their joy with life.

An artist (including the sf author) is best served by leaving it to posterity to judge his work. Any need to see oneself as some sort of genius probably arises out of ego roar anyway, and is totally disconnected from the truth of the matter, whatever it may be. Believing such nonsense only delivers one into the hands of those critics whose cycles of "discovery" and "re-evaluation" can be so mean-minded and so sadly predictable.

I continue to do as I always have – to circulate my manuscripts among those I respect, dropping those pre-readers who heap on praise and retaining those whose complaints show me where I am becoming self-indulgent or still have much to learn. Where some castigate "readable" authors as "panderers" to the common tastes, I maintain as my role model Mark Twain, who wrote sensational, ground-breaking literature which, nevertheless, could be read with joy and profit by teenagers a century later. To those who admire opacity in writing I say, enjoy, *bonne chance*, have it your way, and I will do it mine. To those who cry out about "eternal human verities", who maintain that literature must always reflect some supposed perpetual human obduracy or stupidity, who insist it dwell on our incapability of improvement or ever learning from our parents' mistakes, to all such I offer what pity I can.

As I see it, we are living in the most exciting time in the history of the human race. I give one in three odds that we'll fry ourselves, in which case our generation will certainly have had it best of all. On the other hand, two-to-one I predict – *within our lifetime* – a civilization so dazzling as to make us all blink in wonder at our incredible good fortune.

Wherefore those "eternal verities", then, if we are bound for Conflagration or the Dawn? Literature which grinds over the same old territory *ad nauseam* does nothing to prepare us for either eventuality. I also find it incredibly boring.

Maybe *that* is what the profession of science fiction is all about. We are the ones who toy with new myths, with the images and ideas our culture may need as it rushes headlong toward a future that may glow or may burn but in any event will certainly feature profound change.

IS HE SERIOUS?

So here we are, at the conclusion of an idiosyncratic treatise on his profession by one of science fiction's so-called "apostles of optimism". I've heaped on the metaphors . . . An sf author is a tribal story-teller. No, he's a genius. No, he is a priest. No, he's a shaman. No, he is a rapacious exploiter. No, he's a humble craftsman. No, he's a daring explorer of unknown territory.

Are we actually expected to accept these metaphors at face value? Is Brin being serious?

I'll give you one last hint about that.

There is an illness which strikes creative people particularly hard. This disease has ruined countless writers, artists and scholars throughout time. It is called *ego roar*. And against this plague you have only one surefire defense . . . a willingness to laugh at yourself, to work hard and remain fiercely devoted to your craft, yes, but also *never* to take yourself too seriously.

Buddha say*, "Before enlightenment, chop wood, draw water.

"After enlightenment, draw water, chop wood."

Hmm.

---

* Wow, man. Heavy. Now that Buddha fellow, *he's* a guy who shoulda won an award!

15

Riddles in the Dark

Gwyneth Jones

Before we start I'd like to make a disclaimer. I think I'm not really ready for this Guest of Honour speech business. I haven't made a great study of the phenomenon but I do remember a little, and I know you're supposed to start, first thing, by being modest about your achievements – a few throw away lines about the awards and the film rights 'n all that. Well, I don't happen to have a great deal to be modest about, in a genre to which I've contributed one published story and two books, only one of which anyone has read. So although as a good socialist I thoroughly approve – it's like one of those Utopian stories where everybody has to take their turn at being President, for half an hour or so a year – I don't think you ought to expect too much. In the circumstances it's going to be a bit difficult for me to spend forty-five minutes discussing my hoover (that's oeuvre. It's an American expression meaning all of your writing that you'll own to in public) and dwelling lovingly on the highspots in my career . . . my nights with the famous 'n all that. But I'll do my best. What I'm going to be talking about mainly is a relationship – because I'm a girl and that's what girls are into isn't it, relationships, not rocketships – my relationship, tangential or antagonistic or whatever, with science fiction.

So let's talk about science fiction. That seems to make sense because I spent the whole of the space alloted to me in the convention programme notes talking about fantasy, and saying how I really didn't consider myself a science fiction writer at all. But as everyone knows these days, or you certainly ought to, opposites don't so much attract as imply and contain one another – or maybe, as I also said in the programme notes, I have a highly selective memory. Anyway, when I was a little girl growing up in Blackley, Manchester, I used to read a lot of science fiction – mainly for the exotic travel and the knowledge. The exotic travel was a very important feature – I remember vividly my response to a Gene

Wolfe story which I now know as "The Fifth Head of Cerberus", but which I thought at the time was called Mr Million. I had no idea whatsoever that it was to do with clones. I had no idea what was going on at all. It was the city that struck me: the kind of all-purpose corrupt-oriental milieu which Gene Wolfe borrows and intensifies so well. But I didn't know about the borrowing. I'd never seen or heard of anything like this place, in my wide experience, so I assumed, quite naturally, that it didn't exist. In fact this is one of the serious disappointments of my life as an sf writer. When I was a little kid I thought those alien cultures and strange landscapes were imaginary, I mean completely made up out of nothing, in a way that I knew my own fantasies were not. I thought if I kept on I might be able to do like that one day, I might be able to invent places that were *like nothing on earth*. Alas, I know better now. This is the trouble with becoming an initiate in the hermetic rites. You have to learn all these disillusioning little details; you find out about the sordid airline ticket stubs or the British Army service record; you find out that it takes gold to make gold.

But though the travel was fun, the knowledge was the real gear. In those days, it was all topology. You know the way nowadays it is all private health scheme prosthetics; in those days when I was starting out it was all doughnuts. That's donuts, for the Americans here today. I used to read this stuff about the universe being like unto a rubber sheet, and oh, some Larry Niven story or other about two boy scouts scrambling about inside a giant donut, and I would be walking round in a daze meditating on the wonders. A few nights ago I saw an interview with Richard Feynman, one of the tribute repeats, and he was chatting away making lots of disclaimers about how it could have happened to anyone and he hated all the silly fuss and Nobel prizes and so on – just like me up here. Then he tried to explain what *was* in it for him – and he ended up sitting there with a big cheesy smashed-looking grin on his face saying "I know what it means to know something". Well, I would not go that far. But I do believe I knew what it meant to *think, for a while*, that I knew something: not by fallible circumstantial means but by logic, by the irreducible necessities. Unlike Feynman, I never did anything earn the privilege. I did go on to study something like a philosophy of science course, and I've always been interested in the science of fiction: but I did not find my way to the *scientific experience* – the joy – through anything like hard graft in a lab. It was a free gift that science fiction gave to me, and I am enduringly grateful.

But then we have a gap of years in which I did some really serious dropping out, I mean, I went all the way. I became a Civil Servant. Well, I know some of you puritans will want to leave the hall now, and I quite understand that. Yes, it's true. I have worked in a job centre. I have done lunchtimes on the SS counter. I was a pensions clerk. I've been right down to the bowels of civilisation. I know what it means to weed the dead. But I fought with my unnatural craving. I told myself, there *are* people who manage their weekly or their monthly fix, ecch, and I'm glad to be able to tell you all now that I came out the other side, whereupon I was met by an angelic figure who took me by the hand and led me through the wonders of my first science fiction convention. You're all familiar no doubt with the Chinese dictum that says anyone who saves a person's life is responsible for that life forever after? Well, if you have any complaints I'd like to refer you to Lisa Tuttle. As far as my born-again career in science fiction goes, she's the one. Lisa is to blame for everything.

It's curious the way people always expect you to *explain* your interest in science fiction. I suppose this doesn't apply to the proverbial fourteen-year-old male, but anyone outside that group is likely to get challenged. If you tell them you like reading *What Car*, or doctor and nurse romances, or Trollope's Barchester novels it's oh yeah, and on to the next subject, unless by any chance you've hit on a shared passion. But if you say *sf* then at once it's *Oh Really? Why do you do that?* As a child, I never had to worry about this. I can't remember ever having the sense that other people conjure up from their adolescence that I was one of a weird and subversive band of outcasts, no more than I remember any contact with the phenomenon of sf fandom. But when I came back to sf, or fantasy and sf, things had changed. The change was feminism. I am a feminist, and I'd written a book, *Divine Endurance*, which I was happy to have described as feminist science fiction, and therefore, thereby, I'd walked into a – well, let's call it a vigorous dialogue – that continues and seems likely to run and run, between the dear undead genre and the wild women. So I had to start formulating new answers to that stupid question, besides the foreign travel and the hope of learning a trade.

I mean, not in real life. In real life when people ask me why I'm wasting my time and energy on this pathetic Droids and

Transformers back-of-the-cereal-packet ashpit of popular literature. In real life you just say *because I like it* or *You see, I'm into
subatomic bondage.*

But in the context of this relationship of mine . . .

I'm not going to go in to the debating points in great detail here.
Plenty of people, including myself, have explained elsewhere
exactly how the rules of the sf game (in so far as they can be
discovered) are ideal for the kind of mental experiment feminism
required. When the people say – isn't sf all about male-dominated
areas, high tech and computers?. . . I can clasp my hands and say
(clasp hands) – oh, no no no, science fiction doesn't have to be like
that. It can also be about things which are true and beautiful and
womanly like sociology and town planning. I can also respond,
just as cheerfully: damn right those are male-dominated areas.
And this is something that has to change, so why not start with the
fiction?

However, I will now reveal that I'm not convinced about the
second one. I'm really quite interested in seeing women move in
on those male-dominated areas of high tech and computers – but
I'm not sure how much sf has to do with achieving this end. People
sometimes talk as if they imagine that hard science fiction is like a
sort of extra-removed think tank for the disciplines it observes –
something like, the plot device of today's Greg Bear novel will be
getting someone a Nobel prize in five years' time. That's nonsense.
Today's hard science fiction is built on yesterday's "cutting edge".
It can't be otherwise; you can't be hot-from-the-machine-shop-
floor accurate and be ahead of the game. Sf isn't a thinktank. It's
more like – mm, the green lung of the city of science. Trying to use
it as a route to get more women into science and technology is like
trying to move in on the fancy neighbourhood by setting up home
there on a park bench. It's a doomed attempt really, though in a
way sort of romantic . . . the idea that someone like me, or one of
my literary descendants, might do for others what Larry Niven
and Asimov did for me.

But would that make more scientists, or more science fiction
writers? On the whole I believe – I think I read this somewhere –
that it is hard to underestimate the effect science fictional development has on real life.

(Aside) Anyway most sf doesn't run on "hard science" at all,
and this goes for "most of" any individual text, whether its overt
agenda involves the fifth force or sociology or psychic dragons.

Most of any sf runs on imaginary innovation, which straight away disarms the whole question of who owns the computers. You don't have to be a woman or a man to be good at that, you only have to be a poet.

When I come to think of it, I don't think much of the first option either. I dislike intensely anything that smells of gender reification. Many male sf writers are very keen on the sociology and town planning of the future: the fact that they're generally not very good at *describing* new kinds of human relationships doesn't mean they're not interested. And that brings me to a point I'd like to make. There seems to be a story going about at the moment, to the effect that feminist sf isn't real science fiction at all – it is a *raid* on the genre. These ruthless female bandits, post-holocaust amazons no doubt (many of them without so much as a single degree in astrophysics). They've never written sf before and they come along, smash open the science fiction shop front, and run off with all the high tech gear. They chuck away most of it after they've tried to eat it, found you can't use circuit boards as sanitary towels and so on. They keep a few of the little bitty glass bead things to wear in their nipple rings. And this is something which comes from both women and men, this interpretation. Now, I'm a very impressionable sort of person – no, very reactive: a real air-sign profile – so when I hear this story either I apologise . . . oh um, sorry, yes, it's awful isn't it; me, I don't write that girly stuff, I only write *real* sf . . . or, equally, I start cheering the bandits on. Down with the male-dominated structure 'n all that. But it seems to me on reflection that I don't like either reaction. If you like you can call f & sf a special interest group within the broad church, like trekkies, but I don't see anyway you can declare it illegal or invalid: even if the whole book is devoted to loving descriptions of how we run the creche rota on the subsistence farming cooperative. (Don't tell me it's boring and there aren't enough shoot 'em-ups – have you ever read any Olaf Stapledon?) It's like this. If you have a doctor and nurse romance in which the sexy surgeon is a woman and the wistful nurseling is a boy, that's a liberating subversion of the genre, on one level at least. But science fiction is different. From its very beginnings it has been as much about sociology as it is about rocket ships. It has always been a vehicle for meditations on the future of the race, warning visions, attempts to invent the ideal rules of human conduct. And feminism just now, both in the genre and the world beyond, is not simply about the wild women.

It is a portmanteau term that covers social relativism of all kinds: the whole what if and why not and let's take this to its logical conclusion of human interaction – the imaginary cutting edge of this particular area of knowledge. In other words "feminism" is the current state of psychohistory. And that's got to be science fiction of the purest kind. Olaf Stapledon, H.G. Wells, Asimov, for heaven's sake, they'd all tell you: oh, those rocket ships are just a joke, it's never going to be that way. But the psychohistory – now that is serious.

But let's get back to my relationship. Because curiously enough, although I started writing just in time and with all the right preoccupations to take advantage of that particular new wave, feminism was not my route into the genre: far from it. You see, I'd been three years in Singapore, I was back in England and my writing career was in trouble. Macmillan had dumped me because my children's books weren't making any money. I was still writing fantasy for children, I also had a teenage sf novel in which nobody was interested, and I had *Divine Endurance* lurking under the bed, gathering dust. I was beginning to feel the difference between not making any money, and not being *published*, when Rayner Unwin decided to take on a children's book and asked for another. This was in the days when Allen & Unwin had a fantasy list which consisted of Tolkien, Tolkien, the calendars and related merchandizing; and one or two nice little kiddies books. Whatever you do, said my agent, *don't* tell him about that thing you keep under the bed. He thinks you're a nice girl. So I promised. Well – I told him. It just happened one day, when we were having tea together in his office, like Lucy and the Faun in Narnia, I always used to think. I lost control and it just slipped out. To my amazement he got quite excited. His eyes lit up. "You're sure none of the characters are children?" Now those of you versed in Tolkien lore will remember that when he was eight years old this same Rayner Unwin advised his Daddy to buy a funny sort of kiddies book with no children in it, called *The Hobbit*. Not one, I said. Scouts' honour. Well, two of the main characters are actually toys, but that's not what he asked me, and by the time he realised what a strange monster he'd taken on he was well hooked; we both were.

Oh, that was an epic struggle. Rayner must have realised quite soon that he did not have the twenty-first century *Lord of the Rings* in his hands, but he stood by me like a gentleman. He did the kind of job on *Divine Endurance* that editors just do not do anymore . . .

um, maybe like the fantasy equivalent of being edited by Leonard Woolf or T.S. Eliot. He had an opinion about every comma, every adverb. He didn't like the feminism, he didn't understand why I wouldn't give up my little socialist enclave in Ranganar, he thought my refusal to have long exciting battle scenes was priggish and hypocritical. "You're writing about a war, aren't you?" he would say. "No one forced you to choose that scenario." Oh, there's nothing like a long drawn-out struggle with a fair minded enemy, when you're trying to find your voice as a writer: I wouldn't say there's nothing *better*. No, it wasn't like Lucy and the Faun. It was exactly like Bilbo Baggins and Gollum having their riddle contest under the mountain. Because strangely enough this respectable pillar-of-the-establishment gentle-hobbit and the weird gibbering little monster turned out to have a great deal in common. They knew the same riddles, which is very telling.

I want to come back to those riddles in the dark, but just for the moment I'll skip to the time when *Divine Endurance* was coming out, and they wanted to put "A Fantasy Novel" on the cover. Now I don't usually care about covers. I have trained myself not to care: it is useless grief. I simply make a note of the injuries I suffer, and one day when I have the time and the money I'm going to track the perpetrators down and ruin their lives: but that's by the way. On this occasion I dug my heels in and put my foot down. I was not going to have that word on the front of my book. Why not? Because fantasy means massive sub-Tolkien wallpaper epics? Because fantasy is girly sf and I wasn't going to be stuck down among the women?

Because if you say something's a fantasy, you mean it isn't real.

Whereas if you say something is science fiction, you might mean absolutely anything. Now is that true? It's a notorious problem, anyway. I've talked about definitions of the genre already, without saying so, and I only managed to come up with negatives: the feeling some people have that fictional social experiments are only sf as long as they're not feminist, my own sense that the relationship between "proper" hard science fiction and the working disciplines known as "the sciences" is not what it seems. There is also the theory (Christopher Priest et al.) which says that anything anyone wants to call sf, thereby becomes sf. But that is not as cunning or as complete an answer as it sounds: it merely displaces the process of recognition into the minds of these people who find various things and want to call them sf. What kind of thing, then?

Certainly not only books; or even only entertainment. A hearth brush? A spider? Na – probably not. A leaked political document? A bus timetable? Mmm. . . . this gets interesting. You can hear the people saying, as the last taxi in the world weaves by and disappears, leaving them stranded at 10pm in the middle of Becton. (Becton, in case you are wondering, is a kind of giant open-air underground car park in that part of upwardly-mobile London dockland which used to be called Essex.) There they stand, in this eerie desolation, studying the bus timetable – and they're not fans by the way – but still they cry, with great conviction Oh! This is pure science fiction!

What I'm getting at is this: people do know what they're talking about when they say "science fiction". In the system of differences that is language, there is a cut-out *that* shape, and though any particular case may find opponents as well as supporters still this only confirms the existence of a theoretical consensus, an imaginary diagram from which all possible examples in some way deviate. What makes that bus stop in Becton science fiction rather than fantasy? Well, if fantasy is the unreal and sf is things that are real but don't actually exist, maybe it's the bus. Or if sf is about the concrete and fantasy about the abstract, there's plenty of concrete in Becton. I'll tell you what I think. There's been a lot of talk at this convention about peripheries and centres, about the greatest possible expansion of any given term. It seems to me that what people mean when they say "science fiction" at its greatest possible expansion, is anything that involves an attempt to make sense of something alien – which includes the supernatural realm and the design for a twenty-first century toaster. In the end it includes all that's outside ourselves.

And here's where science (our attempt to make sense of the outside) and fiction (our attempt to make sense of the inside) intersect at this moment in time. We have two ways of making models of reality: one is by means of words, the other is by means of words. (And if you think you can think without them even in mathematical logic, just try it and see.) That is always so – but sometimes there are periods of confusion during which the human investigators forget their absolute limitations and start talking about a *real world out there* to which mathematical physicists have access, and the rest of us don't. We are coming out of one of those periods now. There is no possible way a human being can experience a subatomic particle directly. The various constituents of that crazy alphabet soup *are* the observed traces of their own passage. Whatever they get up to on the other side of the veil, they can have no other existence in our universe. In the circumstances it is very very interesting indeed – much more interesting than a space shuttle named after the starship Enterprise – that the name of the basic, fundamental fiction of science is taken from the bizarrest-most cutting edge of our alternative encoding. Like the man said – electrons are not things. Quarks are not things. They are words. They are, oh most precisely: science fiction.

But that wasn't what I'd decided when I'd finished *Divine Endurance*. At that time, quite honestly, I was simply worried about the girly smear.

Revenons à nos moutons. A funny thing happened to me when I'd written *Divine Endurance*. I suddenly found that I had burst upon the science fiction scene from nowhere, amazing everyone with my outrageous naïvety. So that now I sit here like Charlotte Brontë, brought down to London to meet Thackeray and the lads, and being quite overcome . . . well, I disagree with this interpretation. *Divine Endurance* did not come from nowhere. It comes like most sf, from other science fiction: in fact by the time I'd finished with it I would say Intertextuality (the word glows) was the whole point of the exercise. In the first place Cho is obedient throughout to Asimov's Laws of Robotics . . . indeed the whole story is an expansion of one of those late, logic-chopping Robot stories. And then there's the scene where Cho is unmasked as a product of the Tumbling Dice Toy Factory: where the Ruler reads the truth in the tiny shining message engraved in her eyes . . . *I cannot read the fiery letters, squeaked Frodo* . . . that's what you're supposed to recall at that point, dear reader. I meant, quite deliberately, to say "Cho is the Ring": and part of what *Divine Endurance* is about is to protest, in reply to Tolkien, that *the machines are innocent*. Then again, there was the Arthur C. Clarke pronouncement about advanced technology being indistinguishable from magic. Throughout the book but especially in the interaction between Divine Endurance and Cho I was trying to find a diction for the *constituents* of that transparently, "magically" malleable environment, instead of the usual gosh-wow bemusement of the "ordinary humans" who collide with it.

Did you notice that Cho is a *geisha* – an "art person"?

Did you notice that the "only word" by which the veiled ladies run their country is *submit* – Islam?

Like a lot of other hardened sf writers, I can never resist a pun.

But anyway, to return to the relationship. If *Divine Endurance* had become "genre fantasy" while I was writing it, along with *Lord of Light* and *The Dying Earth* and other old friends of mine, well then I was going to be sure and write science fiction this time. So that was how *Escape Plans* was defined. And like *DE* it is riddled with intertextualities, caves of steel, obscure prison planets, endless puns and all kinds of silly stuff. But there is also something else going on. I didn't like the way *Divine Endurance* had ended, with that classic *eucatastrophe*, as Tolkien calls it. I became obsessed – or realised I had always been obsessed – with the problem of Utopia. Why is Utopia so boring? Why is it that nobody can write a book or a story that goes beyond the eucatastrophe, without either having it sound like messages from Doris Stokes (everything is very beautiful here, tinkle tinkle, there are lovely flowers . . .) or else somehow sneaking the bad old world in by a back door (war on the frontier, invaders from the past). Heaven, as Mr Byrne puts it, is a place where nothing ever happens, which doesn't exactly make for good fiction. Yes, I know the effect is an obvious consequence of the way things are, and simply commonsense. But *why*?

So, anyway, in *Escape Plans* I started to map the boundary between earth and heaven. I invented a world that was the Aristotolean earth, a black hole in the middle of the universe (if universes have middles); and sent in a redeemer from the unimaginable outside. I removed the gender debate from my experimental set up. This wasn't to be a story about how beautiful life would be if we had sexual equality: and therefore in ALIC's world they *have* sexual equality (just like we do here). I removed just about everything I could think of, and finally got ALIC up against the wall. What kind of heaven could I posit for her that was undebunkable, made of pure necessity? I need a place, a state, of eternal life and eternal happiness. Well, nothing, they say, is beyond the dreams of avarice. But precisely what kind of "nothing" did ALIC glimpse for a moment there? Nothingness happening and happening forever, the creative void, event without duration, where earth and time do not exist, where no process is irreversible so no "harm" can ever be done. I got up to that wall, in my mental experiment, and with ALIC I glimpsed what lay on the other side. When I say that the place where story refuses to take us bears a startling resemblance to the world of the bubble chamber, to quantum reality, then I got the spine-tingling adrenalin hit I look for, Feynman's cheesy grin, the joy. I felt as if I knew something.

So there I was, here I am, knocking on heaven's door, trying to explain exactly why and how we are shut out, how we got here from there, to coin a phrase. The (re)working of myth, that's what I'm doing. But is that fantasy, or is it science fiction? Actually, this question got a thorough going over at a panel at the last Mexicon, which I had the honour to moderate (I mean, attempted to control). I had an extremely lively line up on my hands, with Geoff Ryman giving a spirited (and I use the term advisedly) defense of Tolkien, and Mike Harrison – um – agreeing to differ, and Colin Greenland in between being wonderfully scathing about the whole concept of the happy ending. Anyway, all three of these gentlemen did for the old school-of-Tolkien, U.K. Le Guin-type epics pretty thoroughly. Dragons and princes and general futurish-mediaevalish gorgeousness was declared illegal. (Wow, I thought. I'm jolly glad I never wrote anything like that). Rockets are our dragons now, Mordor is in the high-rise estate: and the Ring is, well, you name it. We are not exactly short of deadly dangerous desirables, are we? We finished that panel by reclaiming the territory. Fantasy is living myth, we said. It is not myth reconstructed or deconstructed, it is not a theme-park exhibit: it works. It does what myth does for the world that produces it.

Now this brings me back to Bilbo Baggins and Gollum: me and Rayner Unwin and the riddles in the dark. Because, as I said earlier, we did have a background in common. All the time I was reading sf when I was young, I was also reading the English metaphysical fiction of Tolkien, C.S. Lewis, Charles Williams, David Lindsay, Robert Hugh Benson, George MacDonald. I took that stuff on board very, very thoroughly. I have the mythopoeic interpretation of the universe well sussed out. (All except for the pronunciation. I always wonder are you supposed to sound the "e" or is it just put there to fool yer)? I respond to it instantly – like the epigram from Vaughan Williams that Holdstock uses at the start of *Mythago Wood*, I was born with that music in my blood: love and loss, sacrifice and redemption, renunciation and promise. But eventually you grow out of those English dreamers. A more earthily inclined unacknowledged legislator might complain where's the drugs and sex and rock and roll? Where's the shit? I began to ask – where's the politics? And even, so naïve as I am, where are all the women? If myth is "people trying to explain things", if it is a natural consequence of human existence, then we can't be managing with just the high-minded part. Where's the rest of it?

What I need here is a unified field theory.

The trouble is, what people don't notice is that what they recognise as myth – the fall from heaven, the Soul's search for Love, the Corn King and the Spring Queen, and all the interesting exotic variations plundered by genre buccaneers – these actually represent the philosophy of myth, the ivory-tower state-of-the-art esoteric research department. Most of it is not like that at all.

So you want to know what live myth is like? It goes like this: (clasp hands) a myth I collected myself from a primitive tribe which no longer exists, "How Death Came Into The World". Once upon a time, before anything was or anything had been decided, jaguar's grandmother said to her, I want to go to the market and get some oranges and bananas. So then jaguar laid an enormous turd, which she stirred into mud with a penis stolen from the tapir, and she used the mud to dam the river so her grandmother could get to market. . . . Well, wait a moment? Didn't you just say this was "before anything else was"? Where did these bananas come from? . . . Myth doesn't take any notice of little contradictions of that kind. Because primitive storytellers were, or are, too stupid to remember what they said in their last sentence? No – because this is a story about the outer edge of human experience, a thinking mind up against one of the big not-alloweds. This storyteller is the very reverse of unsophisticated. She or he is well aware that when we talk about such things as death, or contrariwise about creation, our concern is not governed by the forward arrow of time any more than those matters themselves. Where are we coming from now? why do we die now? are questions that are just as mysterious and interesting as the question "how did death start?" – in fact, except on the most superficial level, the two inquiries are indistinguishable.

Bizarre subject matter, denial of the rules of time, preoccupation with knowledge. . . . Aha, I think I'm there. However weird the stuff about jaguar's grandmother may sound, at some point it had rules and the rules made sense. Stop me if you've heard this one. (I don't claim to word for word accuracy.) Lévi-Strauss reports a myth of the north-western American seaboard, which is about why a particular people could fish with good hope of getting a catch in alternate seasons, but not for the other half of the year. And the story goes, these people had an argument with East Wind, who was refusing to let them fish, and they enlisted a series of allies to help them to come to terms. Finally they asked the Skate: and at last Skate managed to come up with a deal. Why the Skate? The story gives it no special qualities, no benign powers. So you either take this as an arbitrary whim, or you think about the Skate. If you try the latter, you may come up with the idea that a Skate, a flat fish, is a binary encoder. Head on, it's a line, sideways it's a sort of diamond shape. A Skate can alternate, like the seasons.

Now that's a tiny example of the kind of thing that goes on. The ramifications are absolutely endless: messy, mutually contradictory, full of sex and jokes and blatantly designed to entertain as well as enlighten: and littered with cultural detritus that has long ago lost its meaning. This is the cookery of myth, the rough surface stuff that actually works as against the abstruse theory. In our country, I think we call it science fiction.

I was going to finish up by saying: at last, the two codes move together: the bubble chamber and the printed page or strip of celluloid, we're on the point of reaching a final intersection of human thought and the physical world. But no, I don't believe so. Ten years from now or five hundred, the quark will be one with phlogiston and the epicycles. But the people, if there are any people, will still be trying to explain the world in just the same way (that threshold does not move, it only shifts around the pole of time): huddled together in our isolated little enclave of consciousness, asking riddles in the dark.

16

Git Along, Little Robot

Richard Grant

Everything I Know About Cowboy Poetry

Last year, somebody published an anthology of cowboy poetry. I have not read it. I have never seen it. No one I know has ever seen it. But the *New York Times Book Review* – on a lark, I suppose – assigned somebody to review the thing. The review was cordial, if slightly bemused. This prompted somebody from the state of South Dakota (as I recall) to write a letter to the editor. "You've got to understand," said the letter-writer, "that cowboy poetry is the most reactionary literary form in existence. Debates among cowboy poets concern such grave questions as whether all stanzas have to have four lines or whether six lines are occasionally justifiable. Reckless experiments like free verse are unheard of."

That's all I know about cowboy poetry.

Some of What I Know About Science Fiction

It is a good thing for science fiction, I guess, that cowboy poetry exists.

What is the Purpose of Science Fiction?

"The purpose of science fiction is to evoke in the reader a sense of wonder."
"The purpose of science fiction is to tell an entertaining story."
"The purpose of science fiction is to challenge our fundamental assumptions about reality."
"The purpose of science fiction is to help us to foresee the problems and possibilities presented by emerging technologies."
"The purpose of science fiction is to reaffirm the materialistic status-quo, reducing human beings to the status of commodities."

"The purpose of science fiction is to subvert the existing order by presenting alternative societal models."
"Science fiction has no purpose."

What is the Purpose of Fiction?

The purpose of fiction is to alter the reader's consciousness.

Pardon Me?

The purpose of fiction is to alter the reader's consciousness. A writer of fiction tries to get inside the reader's mind and produce some definite effect: amusement, horror, excitement, sympathy, sexual arousal, outrage, worry, hope. Or indeed, wonder. The experiences that a work of fiction can evoke are numerous and many of them, probably, are so vague or so strange as to be nameless. That's how it is with matters of consciousness, which is (as we know) at once universal and profoundly private.

One often finds critics trying to describe the way a particular book has made them feel. "Exhilarating!" reads many a book-jacket blurb. "Astonishing!" "Her prose is breathtaking!" "I was spellbound!" "One comes away from this book chastened." "The final scene will haunt the reader for many a night to come." "One experiences *The Lime Twig* as though in a dream." "*John Dollar* is so good that the reader will want to devour it at a single gulp." (I'm not making these up, folks).

What the critic is trying to convey, in such cases, is not what the book is about, but what it *feels* like. This is a difficult undertaking, and of course there is no way to be sure that every reader will feel the way the critic does. Still, the effort is often worthwhile, and it may be the only meaningful approach to certain works. *The Magus*, by John Fowles, was once recommended to me as follows: "It will really scramble your brains." As I was seventeen years old at the time, the notion of having my brains scrambled was much more appealing than would have been a meticulous recitation of the plot or, heaven forfend, the underlying ideas of the book – those staples of criticism in the science fiction field – which was precisely what the other person intended. I went forth and read *The Magus* right away, and though my brains were not adequately scrambled, I could see what the guy was getting at.

Let's think more about altering consciousness, though.

What it Feels Like

Life feels differently in different places. Each of the places I have lived – a small town; a suburb near an interstate highway; Cape May, New Jersey; Washington, D.C.; Rockport, Maine – has a distinct character and my life in each of them has has a different quality. What we like or dislike about a place, I think, is not so much its physical attributes, its relative convenience or climate or cost of living, as the effect that the place has upon us, the way being there makes us feel. We value a view of distant mountains, say, not because mountains have any intrinsic significance but because looking at them attenuates our awareness in some fashion – makes us feel expansive, perhaps, or serene, or above the fray.

There are number of components involved in making us feel the way we do. One of them is surely aesthetic (mountains are beautiful) and probably one is emotional (mountains have romantic associations). There may be an intellectual component as well. We may place a high value on mountains because they represent something to us – perhaps some notion of freedom, or of the grandeur of nature. Or, conversely, the sight of them may depress us, as we contemplate the damage to the trees on the windward slope from acid rain. A friend of mine once felt badly after moving from the city of Washington to the suburbs of Virginia because he could not get the pre-Civil War, slave-holding South out of his mind. Maine has a certain appeal to me because I like the environmental policies of the governor. But even to the extent that our feelings about being in a certain place have an intellectual or associative root, it is not the idea itself that is at issue; it is the way that idea cheers or distresses or does whatever it does to us – the way it makes us feel.

We sit on our porch, we sip our drink, we feel the breeze in our hair, we listen to whatever noises there are to be listened to, we cast our eyes upon the mountains or the great oak trees or the dying hemlocks or the interstate highway or the neighbour's chain-link fence, and we occupy ourselves with whatever thoughts drift into our awareness. All these things (and more, of course – the complications ramify) have their effects on us. They influence, even if they do not absolutely determine, our state of mind.

State of mind. I'm in a New York *state* of mind, the singer croons. Down the street at the local boat-building apprenticeshop they sell a T-shirt depicting an old hippie in nautical garb above the slogan: State of Maine/state of mind. These cultural artifacts make more or less exactly the point I'm getting at, and they make it in a niftier, more immediate fashion. That's art, for you. Art is the telefax of awareness.

The point is, our state of mind – or if you will, our state of consciousness – is constantly and endlessly variable. It is context-sensitive. It responds right away to any change in our mental landscape, to any stimulus that arises either from without or from within. We can get ourselves into a state-of-Maine state of mind the way Thoreau did, by plunging into the north woods and letting civilization fall behind us, camping at the edge of a pristine lake, watching the eagles soar in the blue sky above. That is the outside-in approach. Or we can do it the other way; we can stay right where we are and *think* about pristine lakes, deep spruce woods, eagles in the sky.

There is a third way, too, and it presents an especially interesting case, a kind of synthesis of the other two: partly outside-in and partly inside-out. We can read Thoreau's *The Maine Woods*. We can enter the book as we would enter an objective, physical place, and let the descriptions of Maine, and the sensory impressions they convey, have their effect on us. Of course the lakes and trees and eagles in the book are not physical things. They are words; they are words linked in sentences, braided in patterns of meaning. We read the words and their meaning unfolds within us. The book changes our state of mind.

The Maine Woods is, of course, only a record of a particular journey; a long-winded essay. The tools available to an essayist are quite restrictive compared to those available to a writer of fiction. An essay may, indeed, bring about a change in our awareness. But a work of fiction can do more. It can not only carry us to a distant place but it can make us feel horror, excitement, outrage (and so forth) while we are there. And the world where it takes us need not be a real place like nineteenth-century Maine. It can be a vast and visionary landscape like Gene Wolfe's "Urth", or nightmarishly constricted like the fictional worlds of Samuel Beckett, or familiar and transmogrified at once, like Steve Erickson's Los Angeles. A work of fiction can really scramble your mind.

The Head is the Best Part

Consciousness is a wiggly concept. One can make much of it or little. A paragon of the no-big-deal school of thought is Hans Moravec's book *Mind Children*, in which it is blithely stated, and not elaborated upon, that consciousness will be "emergent in complex systems". Computers, that is. This is more or less in keeping with the approach taken by Douglas Hofstadter (*Gödel, Escher, Bach, etc.*) who seems to regard consciousness as a sort of metamathematical phenomenon. If we keep looping around and jumping to the next higher category, these authors seem to imply, eventually we will leap to the highest category of all, genuine self-awareness. Mr Hofstadter's work, in fact, can be read as an ongoing Grail-quest whose object is the Ultimate Self-Referential Sentence – a semantic loop so transcendentally clever that it will spiral right off the page and look the reader in the eye.

There are other approaches. Baba Ram Dass, né Richard Alpert, came back from India to write a neat little tome called *Remember: Be Here Now*, which is a sort of psychedelic workbook, filled with thought-experiments designed to turn the reader's consciousness in upon itself. This special kind of self-consciousness is akin to what Mr Hofstadter and company are aiming for, but in this case the orientation is mystical rather than mathematic. A state of mind which is characterized by consciousness having only itself as an object is a well known way-station on the road to enlightenment. But let's not get into all that. The idea that Mr Dass and the mystical school share with their rational positivist brethren is that it is possible, by writing a book, to cause a reader to become aware of being aware.

Let's say we're already aware of that. I'd like to offer, for the purposes of this essay, a third approach to conceptualizing consciousness, one which is neither mystical nor mechanistic. I suggest that we think of consciousness as a *field*, in the physical sense of the term. We know that all forces and all types of matter have fields associated with them, and that we can define all physical interactions in terms of the properties of these fields. Let us suppose that consciousness is part of the universal picture in this regard. We can attempt to define the phenomena of consciousness – its various states, its countless and ineffable interactions, the way it "feels" to us – in terms of the properties of this unique (and possibly metaphorical) field. And let's call it the "mind-field", a reasonably concise term which conceals an important admonition.

We can think of states of consciousness, in this scheme, by analogy with the states of more elementary fields – the discrete state of energy, for instance, of the field associated with an electron – only in this instance we must assume that the mind-field is considerably more complex. We can associate it with a purely biophysical entity, the brain; or with that other, less clearly defined entity, the mind. In either case, we may regard the field itself as operating in accordance with laws which are, in theory, knowable, and which can, in practice, be acted upon, experimented with, poked and prodded and jiggled in one way or another with varying effect.

And that's where *we* come in: readers and writers. I have asserted that the purpose of fiction is to alter the reader's consciousness. Now perhaps I can state this a bit differently.

Writing a work of fiction entails putting words together in such a way as to interact with the mind-field of the reader. The stronger, the more varied and intense this interaction, the more likely the reader is to be moved or affected by the book, to perceive it as "astonishing" or "gripping" or "hilarious" or whatever descriptive terms may apply. If on the other hand the interaction is weak – if the fiction contains, so to speak, a low level of creative energy – then the reader is more likely to apply such terms as "boring" or "unoriginal" or "too long". (The concept of length in fiction is highly subjective on this account. Most readers sit happily through *Dune*, while few survive the 29 pages of Proust's "Overture".) Efforts like these to describe the reading experience are, of necessity, simplifications, flattened-out summaries of a complex and long-term interaction; or, to squeeze our metaphor a bit, one-dimensional projections of a many-dimensional phenomenon. After all, a story contains hundreds of sentences, a novel thousands. In a particularly well-written work, every one of those sentences may provoke its own distinct, subtle and multi-level reaction. Consider, if you will, this sentence from Sheri S. Tepper's novel *Grass*:

> On this first day of the fall hunt, Diamante bon Damfels, Stavenger's youngest daughter, stood among those slowly gathering on the first surface, all murmurous and sleepy-eyed, as though they had lain wakeful in the night listening for a sound that had not come.

One need only consider the many levels of rhythm: implication, mood and nuance here, in one sentence of a long book – how the inner ear is tickled by graceful sibilance, hums with "murmurous", and trembles in the silence at the end, listening for that unheard sound – to appreciate how intricate an artifact a complete work of fiction really is.

Thus, when we read in a review that a certain novel is, for example, "full of real, flesh-and-blood characters", we must take this remark as a kind of metaphoric shorthand. We must assume that the mind-field of the critic was coloured or contorted in various ways that, in their cumulative effect, resembled the experience of being with real people over a period of time. (Critics of a deconstructionist bent are at pains to inform us that the characters in books are *not* real people, as though we were so obtuse as not to understand that. It is these critics who, by their Hubbardite literal-mindedness, are being obtuse). Encounters with "real, flesh-and-blood characters" – in literature as in life – are almost unbelievably complicated. Human interactions are hard to understand and harder still to convey in writing, as anyone who has attempted to write so much as a single scene can attest.

The experience of *reading* about such interactions is complicated, too. In a finely-crafted scene, the reader's mind-field is acted upon at numerous levels (the visual, the sexual, the intellectual and so forth) and in various ways. Imagine a brief scene in which a small number of characters sit down to dine. They speak of politics, of music, of current affairs. From their words and from other clues – their postures, the movement of their eyes, their manner of eating – we discern that treachery is in the air; that certain of the guests are romantically entwined; that one of them is in danger. Each of these elements – not to mention the physical attributes of the dining room, the background music, the time of day – has, as the scene progresses, its own discrete effect on the reader's state of mind. Then dinner is over and another scene begins; and so on, with escalating complexity, to the final page of the novel.

At this point, the typical science fiction critic closes the book, sighs in relief, strolls over to his computer and bangs out something along the lines of "The society here is not entirely plausible", or "This book is an environmentalist tract". With this, the intricate matrix of interactions mediated by the work collapses to a small subset of observed properties.

Interaction is a two-way street. The design of an experiment governs, and limits, the outcome. A critic who is schooled only in plot and premise is not likely to respond in a lively way to mood and nuance and indirection.

Still, it seems rather unjust.

Having Sex, Smoking Dope, Climbing Mountains, etc.

We are all, in our individual ways, quite familiar with altered states of consciousness. We have to be. The mind-field is generally stable (less so for writers, one gathers, than for most people) but it is never static; it changes all the time. It is continually attenuated by signals coming from within and from without. Every thought we conceive, every place we go, every incident that befalls us causes our mind-field to reconfigure itself to some degree. We awaken to a screaming alarm clock; we decide to quit our job; we dress in the pale morning sun while humming along with the Indigo Girls. The vast majority of our experiences are of negligible magnitude, and the resulting changes in consciousness are correspondingly slight. But some experiences are stronger, and some are truly epochal. We climb a mountain. We smoke a joint. We get laid.

You will have noted, I expect, that I make no distinctions as to the *cause* of a given modification of consciousness. It is immaterial, from our standpoint, whether an altered mental state results from healthy exercise, from infusing the nervous system with tetrahydra-cannabinol, or from scouring a William Burroughs novel for one comprehensible sex scene. (In vain.) It is the *result* of any cause, or any combination of causes, that concerns us. We are taking, so to speak, a top-down approach.

From the top down, sex does not consist of eye contact / small talk / dinner / boring movie / get in car / turn key / drive / radio / more small talk / arrive home / open door / turn on stereo / Nick Cave / mix drinks / nervous chatter / tentative kiss / new drinks / Replacements / intense kiss / breathe hard / contact with genital areas / loosen clothing / note mole in funny place / fall off sofa / laughter / new drinks / Lucia Hwong / bedroom / clothes off / search for condom / forget it / beast with two backs / sweat / embarrassing noises / orgasm / whew / roll over.

No. This does not do justice to the thing at all. We would be better off with "Astonishing!" or "Grant is in top form here!" or "Makes you long for a sequel!"

And yet, as inadequate as the bottom-up (or bottoms-up) approach proves to be in conveying the nature of sex, we are in the habit of looking at works of fiction – which can be comparably subtle and momentous, though perhaps not so dramatic – in a very similar way.

You know how it goes. In a run-of-the-mill book review (I am thinking of the sort of thing that appears every month in most of the genre magazines) you get, first of all, a sort of establishing shot; e.g. "*Nightshade* is the first science fiction novel by Jack Butler, whose previous work has appeared in such places as *The New Yorker.*" There follows a summary of the plot. "Vampire . . . Mars . . . 22nd century . . . rebellion . . . artificial intelligence . . . complications . . . girlfriend gets killed . . . ending somewhat unresolved." Then we get, optionally, a critique of the novel's science-fictional premise – "well thought-out Martian setting . . . society not entirely plausible . . . relations between humans and machine-based intelligences . . . blah blah." Finally we are given a kind of summary judgement. "This book may encourage mainstream readers to take a greater interest in science fiction."

Whew. Roll over. Light cigarette.

But what did it *feel* like? What sort of experience did the book provide? Did the author's prose rattle your eyeglasses? Did you marvel at the deft interweaving of allusion and shadow-play? Did the hipper-than-thou attitude of the narrative voice get under your skin? Was it a real mind-scrambler, or what?

From the information available in a typical review, such questions are impossible to answer. Reviews are not, as a rule, designed to convey the essence of a book. They are designed in such a way as to answer certain questions, which are largely invariant from one book to the next.

* Who is the author? (i.e., what else has this person written?)
* What's the book about?
* Who are the main characters?
* What happens?
* Is it any good?

These questions are perfectly natural. In most cases a reviewer would be remiss in not addressing them. And yet there is something incomplete here, something dangerously limiting. The fact that the standard review template is present, like a checklist, in a critic's mind often seems to exert a restrictive influence on how books get read. The critic reads in order to gain enough information to complete the checklist. It's like a take-home English test, AUTHOR (10 pts.): Has written one non-SF novel. PREMISE (20 pts.): Mars has been colonized in the 22nd Century. CHARACTERS (15 pts.): Vampire; girl; robot. PLOT (40 pts.): Vampire recruited to lead rebellion, wins a couple of tactical victories, the whole thing turns out to be a government plot. CONCLUSIONS (15 pts.): Not bad for a mainstream writer; lots of clever lines. ** EXTRA CREDIT – Comparisons to other writers (2 pts. each): Heinlein, Delany, Nabokov.

The problem here is that the act of reading has occurred within certain narrow parameters, and these have been defined in advance. The fictional work itself is not given a chance to shape the manner in which it is read. This limits the range of possible interactions between the work and the reader's consciousness. Like an experimenter who is looking for a specific set of results and no others, the critic is likely to overlook – or wilfully disregard – any findings which are out-of-bounds.

Ordinary critics do not often like extraordinary books. This is not because the critics are timid or reactionary or ill-read. They are simply not prepared to respond to such books in all their mind-altering, shape-shifting complexity. The prevailing critical paradigm is designed to accommodate the bulge in the middle of the bell-curve. Truly great novels tend to fare worse than they deserve. (It follows, too, that truly awful books fare better; which comes as no surprise to readers accustomed to seeing semi-literate volumes graced with book-jacket benedictions, often along the lines of "A born storyteller!") Fortunately, and ironically, such limited vision afflicts writers and critics who have internalized the standard paradigm more severely than it does ordinary, thoughtful readers, who have not. Most readers *like* to be surprised. They appreciate compliments to their intelligence. For an intelligent reader, the experience of transcending genre definitions is an exhilarating one.

Contra Reductio

Somewhere back in our school days, we acquired the habit of looking at fiction from the bottom up. That's when we were taught something about "the elements of a story" – Character, Plot, Theme, Style & Setting – and got into the habit of breaking wholes down to their component parts. Or maybe we simply breathed this *Weltanschauung* out of the air of the Atomic Age. All things are made up of smaller things, we were taught, and if we can just learn all there is to know about every tiny thing, then BOOM! We've got the world by the short hairs.

We see things somewhat differently now. We think of groups and systems instead of individual components; ecologies instead of isolated species; fields instead of particles; a Unified Field instead of a multiplicity of forces and laws. It seems about time for us to devise a new way of looking at fiction, too. Not science fiction in particular. Perhaps not even the whole of literature, which after all these days tends to flow naturally into other categories, such as screenplays and comic books and rock lyrics and computer games. We have kept ourselves so busy drawing lines, haggling over definitions, discovering new sub-genres and micro-genres and anti-genres, dividing the whole into increasingly tinier parts, that we have all but lost interest in the experience itself, the act of reading. And yet the act of reading, it would seem, ought to be what we readers and writers alike are thinking about.

Let us think, then. From the top down, what does a work of fiction look like? How should a work of fiction be approached by readers and critics? How can we convey the essence of the thing, the experience of reading it? How, if at all, does a work of science fiction differ from any other kind? And how can we decide if the work is any good?

The Unified Field of Art

It's easy to tell when a paradigm is wearing out. Exceptions start popping up everywhere; special cases that do not seem to follow the rules; phenomena that cannot be explained in the language of the reigning orthodoxy. Thoughtful clerics knew their geocentric cosmos was imploding long before Galileo flipped off *Il Papa*. The atomistic wall was starting to crack long before electrons were caught tunnelling through it. Just so, the single most popular sentence in science fiction criticism today, in all its variations, may be "This book is impossible to classify."

It is not stretching the facts very far to assert that the more distinguished a work of fiction is, the less sf critics have to say about it. They may mutter indistinctly into their word processors, as they did with Crowley's *Ægypt*. They may try to squeeze a work into a category where it does not belong, as they did with his long story "In Blue" (which was universally labelled "dystopic"). In cases of truly exceptional merit – especially where writers who need and deserve exposure are concerned – our critics bestow what has become their highest form of recognition: they ignore the work altogether. Thus did the *Locus* short-fiction reviewer honour Elizabeth Hand's intense and unprecedented "The Boy in the

Tree". Thus, too, are such brilliant writers as Steve Erickson and William Vollman and Peter Ackroyd ignored by the genre's establishment (though not by its readers).

Clearly the hour has come for a new model of the fictional universe. Thank heavens I got here in time.

Art, I have aphorized, is the telefax of awareness. By this I mean that art is uniquely capable of interacting with the awareness of its audience in an instantaneous way. But of course art is more than just a medium of communication. It is a laboratory for thought-experiments into the nature of consciousness.

A music-lover who flips on the CD player and listens to, let us say, Brian Eno's *Another Green World* – a title I briefly attempted to slap on my second novel – is immediately drawn into an environment which is distinctive, evocative, and atmospheric. It is also, naturally, difficult to categorize. It is not exactly rock-and-roll, particularly not in the context of the late '70s when it was composed. It was called "a minimalist masterpiece" by a later commentator, but unless we can agree on what is meant by minimalism that remark may be less than illuminating. Unlike most music in popular idioms, which tends to be "hot" in the McLuhanesque sense, leaping out of the medium toward the listener, Eno's music, beginning with this album, has grown increasingly "cool". It tends to lure and to enfold. It has become, as I have indicated, an *environment* – a self-defining realm which has evolved according to its own laws. Eno himself must have sensed this passage, for he shortly coined the term "ambient music" and set about designing musical environments in a more explicit way. His goal has been to bring music into accord with the way we actually listen to it: in various circumstances, at varying levels of attention.

I hope the clear analogy of this endeavour to the practice known as "world-building" (a term that brings bulldozers rather too strongly to mind) is not overlooked. We seek, as readers and writers of science fiction, imaginative realms that will enfold us, that will reshape our thinking along new and unanticipated lines, and that will accord with the way we actually read, not with some arbitrary and outdated critical orthodoxy.

Writing is different from musical composition, but many of us seem to sense an important, and appealing, parallel. We keep giving our works musically evocative titles: *Chamber Music, Late Night Thoughts Listening to Mahler's Ninth Symphony, Saraband of Lost Time*. What we are trying to get at, I think, is that a work of fiction does not consist only of storytelling. It does generally (though not always) contain a story – at least one – and the story gives the work a definite spatial character, a shape. It serves as a map, guiding us through the fictional environment toward some foreseeable destination. In the same way, a melody gives shape to a musical composition. The spatial quality of both elements, story and melody, is implicit in the common terms "melodic line" and "story-line".

But the map is not the territory. A work of fiction is more than its plot. The spatial aspect of fiction implies a temporal aspect as well – it takes time to cover distance – but we all appreciate that reading a book exerts a more or less instantaneous effect upon the reader's mind. It is not necessary to have any sense of a story to be affected in a definite way by Ms Tepper's phrase "murmurous and sleepy-eyed". Or consider the opening lines of M. John Harrison's *A Storm of Wings*:

> In the dark tidal reaches of one of those unnamed rivers which spring from the mountains behind Cladich, on a small domed island in the shallows before the sea, fallen masonry of a great age glows faintly under the eye of an uncomfortable Moon. A tower once stood here in the shadow of the estuarine cliffs, made too long ago for anyone to remember, in a way no one left can understand, from a single obsidian monolith fully two hundred feet in length.

Now clearly we do not know what any of this means; the novel has only begun. There is no story element here at all. And yet this is a marvellous opening, an ominous progression of minor chords. As much as the ideas – "unnamed mountains"; "fallen masonry"; "an uncomfortable Moon" – the rich texture of the prose itself seems to deepen our attention, to draw us in. And it does so immediately. The reader need not wait, as many critics seem to, to determine whether the fictional world is plausible, the characters sympathetic, the plot well-placed. As with the opening bars of a piece of music, the momentary impact of the prose has an overwhelming primacy.

This instantaneous quality of fiction – the quality whereby a sentence or a phrase or a single word can provoke in us a subtle change of mood, an alteration of awareness – suggests that in at least one important way, the act of reading is non-linear. Every part of a well-written work has a certain completeness. We can keep slicing the work up, chapters into paragraphs, sentences into clauses, and still we find that what remains are not indistinguishable pieces but tiny, recognizable wholes. The phrase ". . . in a way no one left can understand . . ." – even taken in isolation – conveys some of the essence of Mr Harrison's novel. Quoting two or three sentences at random out of the book would likely provide a better idea of what the novel is (as opposed to what the novel is *about*) than any facile plot summary. Only by referring to the prose itself, and not by reducing it to its "elements" – Character, Plot, et cetera – can we say what reading *A Storm of Wings* really feels like.

There is something familiar about all this: wholes which are composed not of parts but of smaller wholes, the entire picture being somehow present in every part, instantaneously apprehensible. These are properties of holography, of course. I suggest that the general features of a hologram apply, at least by analogy, to a work of fiction; and I propose that we adopt the term "holotext" to describe this aspect of a work. So I would say that a work of fiction has at least these two distinct attributes:

* It is *linear*, insofar as the experience of reading depends on time or sequence. The reader follows a story-line, is exposed to ideas in deliberate succession, feels tension or suspense as events progress, amasses clues to solve a mystery, is surprised by a plot-twist, and the like.

* It is a *holotextual*, insofar as the experience of reading is whole and complete at every moment. The reader experiences a change of mood, responds to the rhythm and texture of the prose, is moved by a sharp or affecting image, becomes absorbed by a "cool" fictional environment, has a feeling of being transported to a magical or frightening or awe-inspiring realm, feels a "sense of wonder", and experiences other such moment-to-moment changes is awareness.

Embedded in the theory of the work-as-holotext is the notion of an *interference pattern*: a pattern produced by two fields in a state of interaction. That is how holograms are made. This idea fits with satisfying precision into the idea of the mind-field, suggesting that it may be something more than a useful metaphor. The experience of reading is not dependent upon the work alone, as we can see every time a critic fails to respond properly to a superior book. Reading is not an action but an *inter*action, between the mind-field of the reader and what we might call the creative energy-field of the book, which produces an interference pattern. In a hologram, the interference pattern can be perceived visually; it is what we see when we look at what seems to be a three-dimensional picture. In a holotext, the pattern is perceived more directly, by a change in our awareness; it is what we experience when we enter what seems to be the multi-dimensional world of a book. The new literary paradigm should by now be taking shape on the horizon.

In the old paradigm, we spoke of fiction in the language of material objects. Characters were "well-rounded" or "fully-formed". A plot was "crafted". A fictional world was "built". Even discussions of style invoked concepts more appropriate to a construction project. An author's prose was "economical"; her scenes "effective"; her pacing "like a well-oiled machine". This way of speaking implies a vision of the creative process as being akin to manufacturing. The author's "raw material" is transformed into a narrative, which is then "refined" or "polished" (and ultimately, of course, "marketed").

Many readers and writers are instinctively uncomfortable with this. They continue to feel that the very best writing depends upon intuition and artistry, not formulas and computation. These people might find themselves in sympathy with the American composer George Rochberg, who for two decades has argued against the "cultural pathology" of twentieth-century music, in which the actual listening experience has been disregarded in favour of an intellectualized, emotionally inert approach to composition. "Music is not engineering", Rochberg has said, "and I adhere to my conviction that music remains faithful to experience as it *feels* to us, not merely as we *think* of it".

So too with fiction. It is the reader's experience – the way the fictional world *feels* to us – that ought to be paramount, and not merely what a critic of the orthodox school may *think* of that world.

Questions and Answers

Q. From the top down, what does a work of fiction look like?
A. It looks like both the map and the territory. It is an irregularly shaped object of multiple dimensions with a one-dimensional plot – the "story-line" – inscribed on its surface.
Q. How should a work of fiction be approached by readers and critics?
A. On its own terms. The reader should avoid bringing pre-formed

notions or overly specific expectations to a new work; after all, it is the nature of art to disrupt, exceed and otherwise defy our expectations. The critic should try to purge the mental template that defines, and limits, the act of reading.

Q. How can we convey the essence of the thing, the experience of reading it?

A. It is difficult to do this without quoting from the work, or without entering into the spirit of the holotext. An adequate description of a fictional work must give some idea of what the work actually *is*, not just what it is about. Reductionist discussions suffice only for purely mechanical works.

Q. How, if at all, does a work of science fiction differ from any other kind?

A. All works of fiction have a holotextual aspect. Even the most naturalistic writing, such as the novels of Anne Tyler, share this instantaneous or non-linear quality with the most extravagant of other-worldly prose. But since sf aims, from the outset, to give the reader a sense of reality having been altered in some way, it follows that the holotext of a well-written work of fiction might be richer, deeper, more evocative than a work whose setting is contemporary working-class Baltimore. That battle-scarred phrase "sense of wonder" is, after all, an explicit description of a particular change of consciousness which sf is supposed to bring about.

Q. And how can we decide if the work is any good?

A. By how strongly it alters the reader's consciousness. In other words, by the quality and intensity of the interference pattern between the mind-field of the reader and the creative energy-field of the book. A work which does not provide a vivid, moment-to-moment experience of altered consciousness *cannot* be judged successful or accomplished, regardless of how well-thought-out its science fictional premise is, how pleasant its characters, how carefully constructed its plot. Many sf works are roundly praised because they fit the conventional paradigm to a T – good "plot mechanics", et al. – yet their prose is anaemic and the experience of reading them is worthwhile only on a shallow level. They fit some theoretician's notion of what a book ought to be, like those weighty and stultifying books on high-school reading lists, which seem to have been written solely for the purpose of translation into Cliff's Notes. The prevalence of such works in the sf field is the most important

reason that mainstream readers and critics find the genre unap-
proachable. No matter how sympathetic such a reader may be,
the fact remains that most sf titles – including those most
warmly praised by the genre establishment – are mediocre in
absolute terms. They provide only a limited and specialized
reading experience. A work of fiction is good *only* if it is good in
every part – if every smaller division of the whole, every
paragraph and every sentence and every phrase, is charged
with creative energy. Only then will the experience of reading
the work be intense, satisfying, and complete.

What We have Learned About Cowboy Poetry

By ignoring the major artistic currents of the twentieth century,
cowboy poetry has made itself the object of gentle derision in the
pages of *The New York Times Book Review*. While its practitioners
have been quarrelling over the tenets of the faith – four lines per
stanza versus six – the poetic world at large has marched through
"The Waste Land" and beyond it, into the abstruse realms of John
Ashbery, the occult dimensions of James Merrill, the just-plain-
folksy domain of Raymond Carver and the bizarrely familiar
fantasy-land of our own Thomas M. Disch. The cowboy poets
don't know anything about this, of course, and one supposes that
if someone handed them an issue of *Poet Lore* they would faint
dead away.

But that's cowboy poetry, which is probably nonetheless quite
fine for declaiming around the campfire. Science fiction, for its
part, is still pretty neat for reading in your bed by flashlight after
Mom and Dad have gone to sleep. I mean, there's monsters in it
and stuff. There's like, spaceships and computers and, I mean,
things you plug into your *brain*, man. It's really radical.

On second thought, it is not really radical after all. As forward-
looking as the ideas presented in science fiction may occasionally
be (and they seem to be growing less so, unless it is only I that am
becoming jaded) they are contained in a fictional form that is
increasingly retrograde. We have been arguing over the precise
definition of "wetware", the proper bounds in which shameless
lobbying for awards should be conducted, and how one may
politely correct an acquaintance who commits the *faux pas* of saying
"sci-fi" instead of "sf", and meanwhile the literary world at large
has moved on.

Perhaps it is *not* ironic that science fiction – a body of writing which is ostensibly concerned with the future, with new and altered realities, with the power of the mind, with all the phenomena of the natural world – should continue to embrace literary conventions of the past, should be hostile toward all that is artistically new, should be almost universally anti-intellectual, and should be ignorant of, if not actively hostile toward, the goings-on in the world at large. Perhaps it is *not* true that people who write about aliens have, too often, no notion of what it means to be human. Perhaps it is *not* the case that writers who imagine journeying to the stars tend to celebrate the ethic of conquest and domination that continues to despoil the earth. Perhaps the folks who compose dialogue along the lines of "Shall I rout this hive of rogue psybots?' Lod queried" – I am not making this up; it's out in hardcover from Doubleday – are really very fine writers and Anne Tyler could learn much from them.

Until someone convinces me of these things, however, I have the following bit of advice to offer aspiring writers.

Do not go to Clarion. Do not train yourself to be an "sf pro". Attend, if you like, a firstrate university creative writing program, or take workshops at local art centres. Train yourself to write for normal, thoughtful readers and not for "fen". Try to write as well as John Crowley or Sheri S. Tepper or M. John Harrison. Strive to exceed the bounds, not to fit cozily within them. If you do this, and other writers do it too, then maybe someday good fiction and good science fiction will be much the same thing. Maybe science fiction will even be a shade better. That's a mind-altering thought in itself, isn't it?

Index